Second Edition

ASSESSING
IMPACT

To Hayes Mizell, whose vision and passion made this work possible.

Second Edition

ASSESSING IMPACT

Evaluating Staff Development

Joellen Killion
Foreword by Stephanie Hirsh

A Joint Publication

CORWIN PRESS
A SAGE Company
Thousand Oaks, CA 91320

The first edition of this work resulted from a grant, Demonstrating the Impact: Evaluating Staff Development, from the Edna McConnell Clark Foundation, Programs for Student Achievement, Hayes Mizell, Director.

For information:

Corwin Press A SAGE Company 2455 Teller Road Thousand Oaks, California 91320 www.corwinpress.com	SAGE India Pvt. Ltd. B 1/I 1 Mohan Cooperative Industrial Area Mathura Road, New Delhi 110 044 India
SAGE Ltd. 1 Oliver's Yard 55 City Road London EC1Y 1SP United Kingdom	SAGE Asia-Pacific Pte. Ltd. 33 Pekin Street #02–01 Far East Square Singapore 048763

Printed in the United States of America.

Library of Congress Cataloging-in-Publication Data

Killion, Joellen.
Assessing impact : evaluating staff development/Joellen Killion. — 2nd ed.
   p. cm.
"A joint publication with the National Staff Development Council."
Includes bibliographical references and index.
ISBN 978-1-4129-5354-2 (cloth w/cd)
ISBN 978-1-4129-5355-9 (paper w/cd)
   1. Teachers—In-service training. I. National Staff Development Council (U.S.) II. Title.

LB1731.K53 2008
370.71′55—dc22   2007031983

This book is printed on acid-free paper.

09   10   11   10   9   8   7   6   5   4   3   2

Acquisitions Editor:	Dan Alpert
Editorial Assistant:	Tatiana Richards
Production Editor:	Veronica Stapleton
Typesetter:	C&M Digitals (P) Ltd.
Proofreader:	Caryne Brown
Indexer:	Rick Hurd
Cover Designer:	Michael Dubowe
Graphic Designer:	Lisa Miller

Contents

ON THE CD: FACILITATOR'S GUIDE TO THIS BOOK

The Facilitator's Guide to *Assessing Impact: Evaluating Staff Development, Second Edition*, included on the CD-ROM that accompanies this book, outlines how to introduce schools, districts, and other educational organizations to the process of evaluating staff development through a two-day session led by a facilitator.

The CD includes a PowerPoint presentation with notes, session handouts (as PDFs), and an introduction to using these tools.

Foreword

I deally, staff development has an impact on the adults who work in schools. But to what end? In 2007, the National Staff Development Council Board of Trustees sought to answer that question as they adopted a new council purpose: Every educator engages in effective professional learning every day so every student achieves. The purpose defines why NSDC exists. The council's leaders intend to make clear that the primary reason for professional learning is to ensure that students learn.

Along with NSDC's new purpose comes a new strategic plan. The second edition of *Assessing Impact: Evaluating Staff Development* directly supports the second priority in the plan: documenting the evidence. NSDC believes that **leaders will implement professional development that evidence indicates will produce the results they desire.** In learning how to document the impact of professional learning on student learning, educators will be better equipped to design and develop professional learning more likely to produce intended outcomes.

In my view, there are several reasons that this is essential.

- An evaluation requirement attached to each new staff development initiative demonstrates our higher expectations for professional learning. Most educators agree that what gets measured gets done. Stating our intention to evaluate indicates both our belief that the initiative is valuable and our expectation that results will be measurable.
- Because resources for professional learning are finite, they are best allocated toward efforts that will make the biggest difference for educators and students. Individuals can argue about the many benefits associated with different professional development initiatives. Few, however, would argue that the first priority must be student learning.
- The information that ongoing evaluation of professional learning provides is essential if we are to improve our efforts. For both our advocates and our critics, demonstrating the impact of professional learning is invaluable. For educators, the data gathered during evaluation can be used to continually guide improvements in the process of teacher and student learning.

The two-year NSDC project—Evaluating Staff Development: Demonstrating the Impact—began in 1999. Its goal was to provide educators with practical, field-tested evaluation tools that will help them improve their data-driven decision making regarding staff development, and document for a variety of audiences the impact of staff development. M. Hayes Mizell, director of the program for student achievement at the Edna McConnell Clark Foundation (and now Distinguished Senior Fellow at NSDC), funded the project and, on November 19, 1999, opened the first meeting of the National Advisory Board with the following remarks:

> In this era of accountability and emphasis on results, it is remarkable that staff development is so unaccountable and so few people seem to care about its results. There is a widespread assumption among practitioners that beyond assessing how participants in staff development feel about their experiences, it is not possible to assess other results. This project is about disproving and countering this assumption. . . .
>
> There is great potential for the tools and resources produced by this project to elevate the quality of staff development available to practitioners. If these resources cause staff developers to think harder, plan more carefully, and focus more intentionally on results, then the real beneficiaries will be teachers, administrators, and students.

The members of the committee were eager to accept Mizell's challenge. As project director, Joellen Killion had confidence that their combined commitment, knowledge, and experiences would provide the framework for a resource that would advance the field and be incredibly useful to all educators. The effort led to the first edition of this book, which Killion wrote and NSDC published in 2001.

The project's work and subsequent publication spurred important conversations in education. Educational researchers increased efforts to evaluate the impact of professional learning on student learning, and countless staff developers used the text to guide their own improvement efforts. Many of these developers were kind enough to share their learning with Killion. A number of national researchers turned to her and the book in developing their thinking. As the field advanced, so did Killion's knowledge and expertise.

The second edition of *Assessing Impact: Evaluating Staff Development* is the outgrowth of this continued work and demonstrates the clarity that has evolved over the past several years. And though Killion will be the first to admit that there are still unanswered questions, our expectation is that this resource, like its predecessor, will guide improvement efforts, stimulate conversations, and promote meaningful action.

Killion, the recently appointed deputy executive director of NSDC, is recognized and respected for her leadership in several areas, including school-based professional learning and coaching, facilitating the work of learning teams, and evaluating the impact of professional learning. Practitioners call on her because they know she will respond with insight and practical suggestions and tools to assist them in overcoming their challenges. With this book, Killion has created a work that will assist staff developers as they improve the quality of professional learning for countless educators and their students and move the field closer to achieving the council's purpose.

—Stephanie Hirsh
Executive Director
National Staff Development Council

Acknowledgments

Many people have contributed in large and small ways to the creation of this book. Hayes Mizell, NSDC Senior Distinguished Fellow and formerly the director of programs for student achievement at the Edna McConnell Clark Foundation, recognized the need for this book. With his support, the National Staff Development Council received a grant to develop it. Mizell's leadership and zealous focus on the only prize that matters in professional development—student achievement—have provided encouragement and resources to assist schools and districts to dramatically improve the quality and impact of their staff development efforts.

Four groups have helped shape my thinking and understanding of the field of evaluation and how it relates to student achievement. They have served as advisers, resource people, field-testers, data collectors, and supporters. The National Advisory Board, an esteemed group of professionals in staff development and evaluation, helped create this book's purpose, scope, and contents. the Technical Assistance Team, a group of highly experienced and well-respected practitioners in staff development, offered a frequent reality check. A third group is the UFT Teacher Center's Advanced Academy. This group of school-based staff developers in New York City served as a sounding board and critic of my ideas. A fourth group is NSDC's Authentic Task Approach (ATA) Team. During a weeklong summit to apply the Authentic Task Approach, a seven-member team of volunteers generously gave up a week of time to think deeply with me about the evaluation of staff development.

I am indebted to the countless individuals who shared sample evaluation tools with me, provided examples of evaluations they wanted to conduct or were conducting, and expressed their frustrations about evaluating staff development. I also appreciate individual evaluators, both inside and outside the field of education, who discussed their experiences, methodology, research, and insights. I particularly want to acknowledge Mary Jean Taylor, a professional colleague and friend. She was my cheerleader, supporter, and technical assistant throughout this work. With her in-depth understanding of evaluation and years of practical experience as an evaluator, she guided me to consider issues I would have overlooked and helped me narrow the scope of my work and keep the focus on the audience and their needs.

I want to thank my colleagues at NSDC and most of all, my family, Terry, Sara, Greg, and Jeff, who give me endless support and encouragement.

Corwin Press would like to thank the following individuals for their contributions to the work:

Mike Ford
Director of Staff Development
Palmyra-Macedon School District
Palmyra, NY

Joyce S. Kaser
Senior Program Associate
WestEd
Albuquerque, NM

Roger Kaufman
Professor Emeritus
Florida State University
Tallahassee, FL

Elizabeth Lolli
Superintendent
Barberton City Schools
Stow, OH

Susan Mundry
Associate Director
Math, Science & Technology
    Programs
WestEd
Newbury Park, MA

Michael Power
Director of Instruction and
    Assessment
Mercer Island School District
Mercer Island, WA 98040

Teresa Rouse
Assessment & Program Evaluation
    Coordinator
Monterey County Unified School
    District
Carmel Valley, CA

About the Author

 **Joellen Killion** is the deputy executive director of the National Staff Development Council. In her work with NSDC, Killion focuses on improving teaching quality and student learning. She has been director of NSDC's highly acclaimed NSDC Academy and its new Coaches Academy for school-based staff developers. She also has managed numerous other pieces of work, including the council's initiatives in results-based staff development, evaluating staff development, and its Results Skills for School Leaders project.

Killion is coauthor with Cindy Harrison of *Taking the Lead: New Roles for Teachers and School-Based Coaches* (NSDC, 2006). She is the author of the first edition of *Assessing Impact: Evaluating Staff Development* (NSDC, 2002) and NSDC's three-volume results-based *What Works* staff development series. She was featured in the School Improvement Network/VideoJournal programs *Instructional Coaching* and *Designing and Evaluating Professional Development*.

In 1997–2001, her examination of schools that received the U.S. Department of Education's Model Professional Development Awards resulted in the publication of *Teachers Who Learn, Kids Who Achieve: A Look at Model Professional Development* (WestEd, 2000). She is also the author of *E-Learning for Educators: Implementing the Standards* (NSDC & NICI, 2000) and numerous articles published in *JSD*.

Killion is a former school district staff developer, curriculum coordinator, and teacher in the Adams 12 Five Star School District in suburban Denver. She was a member of NSDC's Board of Trustees and served a term as president. She lives in suburban Denver.

Introduction

> "Staff development that improves the learning of all students uses multiple sources of information to guide improvements and demonstrate its impact."
>
> —NSDC, 2001
>
> Principle Three:
> "Staff development leaders continuously improve their work through the ongoing evaluation of staff development's effectiveness in achieving school system and school goals for student learning."
>
> —NSDC's Staff Development Code of Ethics

This second edition of *Assessing Impact: Evaluating Staff Development* focuses on the importance of evaluation as a process for continuous improvement, acknowledges the policy arena that calls for more rigorous evaluation, and encourages schools and districts to adopt evaluation as a routine practice to enhance their data-driven decision-making processes.

Much has changed in the field of accountability since the first edition of this book. Most notable is the federal No Child Left Behind Act signed into law in January 2002 and designated for reauthorization in 2007. That act changed education stakeholders' understanding of the word *accountability*. The act drew the nation's attention to problems in education that had long been neglected, including poor education for the nation's neediest children. The act sets high expectations for (a) schools to educate all children and provide interventions and sanctions when they do not, (b) teachers to be highly qualified, (c) districts to report results and provide alternative educational settings for children whose schools are inadequate, and (d) the field of education to engage in and use more scientific research and evidence-based practices. No Child Left Behind significantly increases the importance of staff development for teachers, principals, and paraprofessionals and states' and districts' responsibility in ensuring the quality of professional development.

Like the first edition, this book acknowledges that evaluation without thoughtful and thorough planning for success in professional development is inexcusable. Consequently, the evaluation process begins with planning powerful professional learning experiences integrated into a coordinated program that will ensure deep understanding of key concepts, skills to implement the understanding, and ongoing opportunities for support, reflection, and refinement, along with continual examination of progress and impact.

The book draws from the field of program evaluation to offer strategies and examples of how evaluation looks within the field of professional development and outlines an eight-step process. The process begins with Assessing Evaluability and ends with another significant step not included in most traditional program evaluation processes: In Evaluating the Evaluation, the evaluation team reflects on its work and on what team members have learned about evaluation, not about the program.

The book is designed to encourage practitioners to evaluate professional learning beyond the surface level, the overused satisfaction measures that serve as the measure of many professional development events. Practitioner-based evaluation differs from high-stakes, external evaluation by encouraging full practitioner involvement in planning and implementation. Such evaluations seek to involve stakeholders in the examination of their practice and its results. The process is designed to cultivate "evaluation think," a phrase that Joy Frechtling, a National Advisory Board member, uses to describe how individuals and teams in schools and districts look critically and analytically at their work to discover what is working and what is not in order to redefine their work and to improve results.

PURPOSE OF THIS GUIDE

The purpose of this resource guide is to assist school and district staff development leaders in understanding

- How planning influences the quality of the evaluation
- How to plan and conduct practitioner-based evaluations that focus on results for students and improve staff development programs
- How to increase the usefulness of evaluations
- How to build the capacity of program stakeholders to adopt "evaluation think"
- How the roles of various stakeholders relate to the evaluation of staff development

WHAT THIS BOOK IS AND ISN'T

This book is a resource guide to assist school- and district-level staff development program leaders and other stakeholders in planning and conducting evaluations of their staff development programs that are designed to improve student achievement. Throughout the chapters, the operating definition for a staff development program is this: planned, coherent, in-depth learning experiences and the organizational support system designed and implemented to develop educators' knowledge, attitudes, skills, aspirations, and behaviors to improve teaching and student learning. As a resource guide, this book will assist those who plan and implement staff development in strengthening the power of their program and assessing its impact.

One premise of this book is that when staff development is clearly conceptualized and carefully planned, both the integrity and evaluability of the program will be stronger. *Evaluability* means (1) that the program can be meaningfully evaluated, (2) that the evaluation can contribute to the program's improvement, and (3) that evaluator and program stakeholders agree on the information to be gathered during the evaluation. When a staff development program has a solid, logical, and thoughtful plan, its potential to produce results increases, as do the usefulness and the value of the evaluation.

A well-conceived staff development plan

- Results in an evaluation with more integrity, greater usefulness, and more value
- Ensures that the program's goals and objectives are clearly defined
- Has a clear, logical theory of change
- Guides the collection of relevant performance data
- Increases the likelihood of producing results for students

One note about definitions: In this book, I frequently use the terms *staff development*, *professional development*, and *professional learning*. *Staff development* and *professional development* are used interchangeably here to describe the process of learning among educators; professional learning is the result of professional development and most often occurs when educators are effectively engaged in professional work, interaction, and development.

This book is not a program evaluation textbook, a manual on data collection and analysis, or a statistical analysis or research manual. The book is not designed for professional evaluators, although they may find it useful. It is designed specifically for staff development leaders, program or project coordinators, curriculum directors, principals, or others who want to evaluate their professional learning programs.

THE VALUE IN CONDUCTING EVALUATION

This resource will assist practitioners to consider the value of conducting evaluations of their work as a means of

- Conducting regular and rigorous evaluations to assess the effectiveness and impact of staff development on student achievement
- Reporting to policy makers about their work
- Examining implementation of staff development programs to strengthen them
- Assisting program directors and stakeholders in designing powerful staff development programs by making their program's theory of change explicit
- Providing *practical* ways to evaluate staff development programs
- Constructing an information base for making decisions about staff development programs

Perhaps Patton (1997) has described best what this work also is intended to do:

> Our aim is modest: reasonable estimations of the likelihood that particular activities have contributed in concrete ways to observed effects—emphasis on the word *reasonable.* Not definitive conclusions. Not absolute proof. Evaluation offers reasonable estimations of probabilities and likelihood, enough to provide useful guidance to an uncertain world (Blalock, 1964). I find that policy makers and program decision makers typically understand and appreciate this. Hard-core academics and scientists don't. (p. 217)

Evaluation as Normative Practice

1

Schools and districts are changing how they approach improving teaching and learning. They are becoming more data-driven and results-focused. Staff development is beginning to take center stage as the leading driver in the reform process. As more research is available about the link between teaching quality and teachers' content knowledge, practice, preparation, and experience, the greater the focus is on how staff development contributes to high-quality teaching and leadership.

As the focus on staff development increases, the need for evaluation grows. Data alone are not useful unless they are placed within the context of a systematic investigation of programs and processes. Evaluation—not just data—is increasingly important for reforming schools. Evaluation provides a way for school and district leaders to answer questions about the impact of their work. Evaluation provides insight into what is working and what is not. Evaluation can provide information for making decisions about policy and practice. The use of data, not data alone, has the potential to transform teaching and learning and systems to support them.

Data conversations in schools are often profound learning experiences. These conversations are a powerful form of staff development and should be labeled as such. In data conversations, teachers and others, who typically have no access or interest in data, pore over test results, mobility rates, data disaggregations, and archival data such as attendance records to make sense of them. Participants talk about the implications and plan improvement efforts. They gain an understanding of the need for change, establish priorities, take responsibility for their actions, and tell each other the truth about their work. Energy, commitment, and focus emerge from these conversations.

Yet two essential things are missing in the data conversations that could lead to significant results. One is the evaluation framework. An evaluation framework creates a rigorous, systematic, and purposeful approach to data gathering, analysis, and interpretation. The evaluation framework begins with posing the questions that stakeholders want to answer. The framework guides their work and focuses attention on the proximal factors, those most directly in the school's control, and keeps attention away from the distal factors, those over which schools have very little control. An evaluation framework focuses the work of data analysis on results, not on process.

The second missing element is an evaluation of selected interventions. Schools and districts are reaching out for any viable program to improve student achievement, yet they fail to evaluate their selected intervention to assess its effectiveness within the unique context of their school or district. Some create their own programs, relying on their internal expertise and history of success. Other schools and districts select from the wide array of programs available. Some programs are well-established, research-based programs. Others are emerging practices that hold great promise. Some are unproven and untested ideas that sound good but have not been evaluated.

In either case, beyond looking at the next year's test results, few schools and districts evaluate the effectiveness of what they choose to do to address identified student achievement needs. Too many staff development efforts are still focused on selecting and implementing interventions rather than achieving specific results. The mental model we hold about our work as staff developers may block us from taking a results-oriented approach. For too long, we have judged our own work by standards such as the number of participants who enjoyed a program or participated, degree of diversity of programs or courses available, or creative uses of time. Regardless of our rhetoric, as long as these are our standards, we have not, in fact, adopted results for students as our highest goal.

Many times data analysis is used to identify needs and select areas for targeting improvement efforts; however, assessing the success of the interventions is not yet normative practice. Because there is no ongoing process for gathering data about staff development interventions, leaders are forced to make decisions based on black-box rather than glass-box evaluation. (See Chapter 3 for an explanation of these evaluation approaches.) Implementing evaluation as a natural component of staff development programs will encourage a systematic assessment of staff development that is based on results for students rather than services to educators.

Table 1.1 (Minnesota Department of Human Services, 1996) outlines a useful template for engaging in client-focused, results-driven program management. The template emphasizes two powerful aspects of moving from a service-focused program management approach to a results- or client-focused approach. A client-focused approach advocates strong participant involvement in all aspects of the program development, implementation, and evaluation process. The table provides clear steps for staff development leaders to follow to establish and sustain a focus on students within a staff development program. With little or no effort, the processes can be translated to fit the context of public schools rather than social services.

The value of the steps outlined in Table 1.1 is that the whole system works together to achieve the identified outcomes for students. The steps raise the stakes for those in leadership roles to elevate the importance of evaluation beyond monitoring to a genuine inquiry or "evaluation think" to improve programs, make management decisions, and be accountable for results.

Leaders of staff development programs can no longer just manage them but must now become leaders of them.

Results-oriented leaders know how to create systems, build coalitions, motivate employees, monitor performance for effectiveness, and be responsible for results. Osborne and Gaebler (1992) remind us that results-oriented leaders live by these principles:

- What gets measured gets done.
- If results are not measured, it will be difficult to distinguish success from failure.
- If success is not visible, it will be difficult to measure it.
- If success can't be rewarded, then failure probably is.
- If success isn't visible, it is difficult to learn from it.
- If failure is not recognized, it is difficult to correct it.
- If results are demonstrated, public support follows.

Measuring and reporting results, identifying success, and recognizing failure require evaluation. Staff development leaders who include ongoing evaluation as a natural part of their work will become results-oriented leaders committed to increasing the success of all students in our schools.

QUESTIONS FOR CONSIDERATION

1. Is my leadership of staff development service- or results-oriented?

2. How do I involve stakeholders in decisions about the development, implementation, and evaluation of staff development?

3. How do I ensure that the staff development interventions we select are based on research?

4. How do I incorporate evaluation into my work as normative practice?

Table 1.1   Stages and Issues in the Transition to Management by Client Outcomes

	1	**2**	**3**	**4**	**5**
Stages	Identify and engage key actors and leaders whose commitment and support will be needed for a transition to management and accountability based on client outcomes.	Key actors and leaders: Commit to establish a client-outcomes approach. Understand principles, purposes, and implications of change.	Conceptualize client outcomes. Select outcome indicators. Set targets.	Design data-collection system. Finalize methods. Pilot established baselines.	Implement data collection. Train staff and managers for data collection and use.
Issues	Who are the key actors and leaders who must buy in? How widespread should initial involvement be?	What level of commitment and understanding is needed? By whom? How will real commitment be distinguished from repeating rhetoric?	What target groups? How many outcomes? What are the really important bottom-line outcomes?	What can be done with existing data? What new data will be needed? How can the system be integrated?	What resources will be available to support data collection? How will validity and reliability be addressed?
Activities	Establish leadership group.	Leadership group makes strategic decision about how best to proceed and whom to involve.	Work team to determine outcomes. Involve advisory groups and key leaders to bring outcomes along.	Work team to make design decisions.	Collect data. Pilot test. Monitor data collection.

6	7	8	9	10	11
Analyze results; compare results to baseline and targets.	Prepare for use: determine management uses; potential actions; decisions, options, parameters, and accountability report format.	Involve key stakeholders in processing the findings.	Judge performance and effectiveness.	Make management decisions. Report results.	Review and evaluate the outcome-based management system.
Who will do the analysis? What additional data are needed to interpret the outcomes/ results (e.g., demographics)?	What are the incentives for managers to participate? How will managers be brought along? trained? rewarded? Who determines accountability reporting approaches?	How do you keep key stakeholders engaged?	How clear are the data to support solid judgments?	What are the links between internal and external uses and audiences?	What should the system accomplish? Who determines success?
Data analysis; graphic presentation	Training and management team sessions based on data use simulations and mock scenarios.	Facilitate meeting of key stakeholders.	Facilitate key stakeholders in judging and interpreting.	Report writing. Data presentation. Facilitation of management decision making.	Assemble a review team of users and key stakeholders.

Source: Minnesota Department of Human Services

Program Evaluation Overview

2

This chapter reviews some basics about program evaluation. It includes discussion about the definition of evaluation, the difference between evaluation and research, the purposes of evaluation, the difference between program and event evaluation, the types of evaluation, and an overview of the evaluation process.

EVALUATION DEFINED

Definitions of evaluation abound. Esteemed scholars in the field offer many definitions. Because they offer a way of thinking about evaluation in general, the following three definitions of evaluation deserve attention.

> Daniel Stufflebeam (2001) asserts that evaluation is "a study designed and conducted to assist some audience to assess an object's merit or worth" (p. 11).

> Thomas Guskey (2000) offers a definition that is short and direct. "Evaluation is the systematic investigation of merit or worth" (p. 41).

> Michael Scriven (1991) says that evaluation is "the process of determining the merit, worth, and value of things, and evaluations are the product of that process" (p. 1).

Other people have offered a more specific definition of program evaluation: "Program evaluation is the systematic collection of information about activities, characteristics, and outcomes of programs to make judgment about the program, improve the program effectiveness and/or inform decisions about future programming," says Michael Quinn Patton (1997). "Utilization-focused program evaluation (as opposed to program evaluation in general) is evaluation done for and with specific, intended primary users for specific, intended uses" (p. 23).

Carol Weiss (1998) suggests that program evaluation is "the systematic assessment of the operation and/or outcomes of a program or policy, compared to a set of explicit or implicit standards, as a means of contributing to the improvement of the program or policy" (p. 4).

Evaluation, then, is a systematic, purposeful process of studying, reviewing, and analyzing data gathered from multiple sources in order to make informed decisions about a program. This definition implies that an evaluation resulting in a reasoned judgment is made by an individual or team, based on analyzed data that offer insights, enlightenment, or guidance to the individual or group for whom the evaluation is conducted. It assumes that a reason exists for the evaluation and decisions will be made as a result of the evaluation. Evaluation calls for rigor in all phases of the work and is guided by a set of standards that, when met, ensure the quality of the process.

Defined this way, evaluation is dynamic rather than static. Information from evaluations influences subsequent decisions. These decisions will also be influenced by (1) the users' experiences, beliefs, and values; (2) decision makers' experiences and understanding of the organization's culture; and (3) individuals affected by the decisions.

KEY COMPONENTS OF EVALUATION DEFINITIONS

The following five words or phrases are the key components of definitions of evaluation. Each of these terms contributes to an operational definition—one that conveys both the integral concepts and the integral actions.

Systematic

The term *systematic* suggests that evaluations are conducted in accordance with standards and guidelines such as those offered by the Joint Committee on Standards for Educational Evaluation (see Appendix A) in accordance with practices established in the social sciences. *Systematic* also implies formality and rigor in the process.

Standards

Most evaluations measure merit, worth, or impact against predetermined criteria. A set of standards, as defined by the program's goals or in some other way, provides the evaluator criteria against which to measure the program's success. Standards may be scaled to reflect various levels of expectations through time. For example, standards may change over the course of full program implementation.

Audience

Audience of the evaluation is a key factor in determining the kind, scope, and use of the evaluation. Who will use the evaluation, as well as their intended purposes, will necessarily influence the design of the evaluation. Audience and intended uses for evaluation results are highly related components. Patton's utilization-focused evaluation and Weiss's acknowledgment of an audience as an important component in the evaluation process suggest that what makes evaluation more useful and valued by stakeholders is the degree to which the evaluation meets some need expressed by an audience.

Intended Uses of the Evaluation

Knowing what the intended purpose of an evaluation is will influence many decisions made during the planning and implementation of an evaluation. Evaluators and program leaders, therefore, need to identify their audiences and make sure they prioritize the most significant uses. For example, if the purpose of evaluating an induction program is to determine whether teacher retention increases as a result of the program, the data needed will be housed in the personnel department and will require a collection of information about longevity in employment. If instead the purpose of an evaluation is to make improvements to the induction program, data other than employment records will be needed. And, if the purpose of the evaluation is to determine whether students of novice teachers who participate in the induction program receive a high-quality education, a far more complex evaluation design is required.

Table 2.1   Difference Between Program Evaluation and Research

	Program Evaluation	*Research*
Purpose	Used to determine whether a particular program has merit, worth, and impact, e.g., did it meet its goals? The focus is usually on improvement or decision making related to the program.	Used to explore the interaction among variables, to add to the general or field-specific knowledge base about a particular phenomenon, to test a theory, and to advance that field of knowledge.
Grounded in	A theory of change and logic model	Theory and literature review
Focus	Focuses on program description, documentation, and results of a particular program within its naturally occurring contexts; variations are studied and noted especially in terms of how those variations impact results.	Looks at results produced by groups in which a particular program is or is not present; program is implemented in carefully controlled contexts to minimize variations between groups beyond the existence of the program.
Use of Findings	Identify how the program can be improved, whether it should continue, be discontinued, expanded, etc., for the same context and population.	Generalize the results to develop theory and inform practice in other contexts and populations.
Dissemination of Findings	Disseminate to decision makers, including policy makers, stakeholders, program managers.	Disseminate to field for critique of design, validity, and reliability.

Evaluation Versus Research

Evaluation and research are frequently confused, primarily because they use many of the same methods, tools, and processes. Yet their purposes are fundamentally different. An examination of the purposes of each can be helpful for those who want to conduct evaluations and increase the rigor of those evaluations.

Program evaluators, like researchers, pose questions and methodologies, collect data-analysis results, and disseminate results. To evaluate staff development, the evaluator or evaluation team clarifies program goals and intended results and explains how the evaluation findings will be used. Doing so can increase the usefulness of the evaluation and eliminate misconceptions or avoid problems later in the process.

PURPOSES OF EVALUATION

Evaluation is done for a variety of purposes, and an evaluation's purpose influences decisions about how the evaluation is designed and implemented. Several scenarios involving evaluation of staff development are described below.

1. A staff development director is making decisions about which of her programs to fully fund and which to revise or eliminate.

2. A school-based staff developer is coordinating a schoolwide or team-focused professional learning program and wants to measure the impact of the program on teaching, school culture, and student learning.

3. Curriculum directors work with districtwide committees to revise the mathematics curriculum and select new instructional materials to implement the revised curriculum. They plan and implement extensive teacher development to ensure that teachers have the knowledge in mathematics and the content-specific instructional processes to deliver the new curriculum. They plan to conduct an impact evaluation of their work on student achievement.

4. A district committee has selected and implemented a new instructional approach to science in the middle school. Teachers have received extensive training and support in using the new instructional strategies. Teachers, principals, parents, and the district science coordinator plan how to determine whether the approach improves student achievement in science.

5. An assistant superintendent proposes a significant increase in budget for the staff development department. He engages the members of the school board in conversation about how they should assess the return on their investment in professional learning.

6. A school improvement team is examining several staff development and curriculum programs aimed at increasing students' active involvement in learning. They want to learn about the kinds of evaluations conducted on various programs they are considering.

7. A superintendent wants to know whether a school's use of staff development resources is the best use of those funds. The teacher leader of the staff development committee decides to clarify the question being asked and determine how to go about answering it.

8. A school board member asks the director of staff development whether the mentoring program is increasing retention of novice teachers. The director decides to design and conduct an evaluation to answer the board member's question.

9. A district or state staff development supervisor is preparing an impact report on the use of Title I and Title II funds.

10. A district wants to ask its school board and community to support changing the teacher workday to include weekly 90-minute blocks for teachers to engage in professional learning. To solidify the rationale, the district committee wants to assess the impact of its current staff development program in differentiation to identify what worked, what didn't, what results occurred, and how those results might change if teacher staff development were embedded into the workday.

Patton (1997) summarizes three overall uses of evaluation findings: forming judgment, facilitating improvements, and generating knowledge. Table 2.2 synthesizes these purposes.

Mixed purposes often complicate and confuse an evaluation design and frustrate all intended users because it is almost impossible to meet all the various demands within a single evaluation design. It is best to agree on the priority of each intended use before an evaluation design plan is adopted. Clarity of purpose in evaluation facilitates decision making during planning and implementation phases.

PROGRAM VERSUS EVENT EVALUATION

One of the major assumptions of this book is that what are being evaluated are programs rather than events. A program implies more than isolated events. A program is a set of purposeful, planned actions and the support system necessary to achieve the identified goals. Effective staff development programs are ongoing, coherent, and linked to student achievement. Programs, however, vary widely in scope.

A workshop on classroom management is not a program. Such a workshop is actually a staff development event or an activity. As with all events and activities, program planners would derive the need for a classroom management workshop from identified student achievement needs, such as insufficient engagement or instructional time. The workshop would optimally be coupled with planned classroom-based support, ongoing coaching and feedback, demonstrations, and visits to other classrooms incorporated into a comprehensive, ongoing plan designed to develop educator knowledge, attitudes, skills, aspirations, and behaviors. Two challenges for those evaluating staff development are, first, determining what level of program to evaluate, and second, determining the elements of the program.

Table 2.2   Intended Uses, Users, and Purposes of Evaluation

Intended Uses of Evaluation	Intended Users	Purposes of Evaluation
Determining merit, worth, and impact	Program directors, policy makers, and decision makers	To determine merit, worth, and impact of a program
		To determine the overall effectiveness of a program and make decisions about its expansion, continuation, or discontinuation
		To compare a program with other programs
Facilitating improvements	Program directors, such as staff development or curriculum coordinators, principals, school-based teams	To make improvements to an existing program
		To determine a program's strengths and weaknesses
		To identify unexpected benefits and barriers
		To determine progress toward the intended results
		To identify and solve unanticipated problems
		To assess participants' progress toward intended results
Generating knowledge	Program developers, such as staff development and curriculum coordinators	To add to the body of knowledge about the program's effectiveness
		To enlighten thinking about staff development
		To identify patterns of best practices or principles of effectiveness across programs
		To shape language and thinking about practices
Providing accountability	Policy makers and decision makers, such as boards of education, superintendents, program managers, principals, program funders	To assess compliance with intended purposes and mandated processes
		To provide evidence of fiscal responsibility
		To provide evidence of public accountability for resources

For example, a district may have a staff development program designed to improve performance of all staff members and students. One component of an overall staff development program in a district might be an induction program designed to address the specific developmental needs of new teachers. A school district's overall staff development program might include other programs developed to meet the needs of other employees or to address other goals. The district might have a program for experienced teachers to increase their ability to differentiate instruction to meet the needs of students. Districts, then, may have several staff development programs operating simultaneously, all within a comprehensive, cohesive staff development program. In these examples, program planners need to determine what is being evaluated—the overall staff development program, the induction program, or the differentiated instruction program.

To conduct an evaluation, the evaluator or evaluation team define the parameters of the program by designating the set of activities that constitutes the staff development program being evaluated. In reality, staff development is ongoing learning that continues without end throughout an educator's professional career. Evaluation of staff development, however, aims to determine whether particular aspects of that ongoing learning are improving the performance of educators and their students within a set time and defined set of actions.

TYPES OF EVALUATION

Summative Evaluations

Evaluations can be done during the planning, implementation, and end phases of a program. Summative evaluations, conducted at the end of a program or project, are perhaps the most familiar. A limitation of summative evaluation is that it provides information only on the outcome or overall impact of a program rather than information that can improve the program during its existence. In general, policy makers may be more interested in summative evaluations ("what are the results?") and less interested in formative or planning evaluations ("how are we getting the results?"). Summative evaluations may have less value or usefulness to program stakeholders, however, who are very interested in understanding how what they have done relates to the results.

Summative evaluations are done at the end of a program or at a particularly important benchmark point. If a program is three years long, a summative evaluation would obviously be conducted at the end of the three years. But if the program continues beyond its three years, ongoing evaluation might be done every three to five years to determine whether the program continues to impact both educator and student learning. Sometimes programs culminate with the end of a funding cycle. When conducted at that point, summative evaluations provide information about the program's success and may or may not serve as a basis for decisions about continuation of the program or justification for future funding. Often, summative evaluations are conducted to meet funders' requirements for an evaluation and have little or no influence on future programs.

An Example: Data Demonstrate Technology's Impact

Three teachers at the high school received a grant to implement a writing lab staffed by trained tutors and students. The lab would provide a physical location in the school where students could drop in and receive assistance with a writing assignment or tutoring on various aspects of written language, such as mechanics, grammar, or usage. The funder, a large computer firm, wanted to know whether the use of computers during the writing task was contributing to the improvement in students' performance on the district and state writing tests. Fortunately, each student who used the writing lab had to bring or produce a benchmark paper as pretest data. Over three years, the director of the lab had collected more than 400 pre- and postlab "help" papers and data about students' computer use in their writing process and the type of help that teachers and tutors provided. He used these pairs of papers to determine whether students' writing had improved, in what areas the greatest gain was shown, and how those areas aligned with the help provided by teachers and tutors. At the end of the three years, armed with a mound of very positive student data, the director was able to demonstrate for the school board the impact that training for teachers and tutors and access and use of the writing lab had had on student achievement in writing. In addition, he was able to justify his request for additional funds to continue the lab with school district funding.

Planning Evaluations

Planning evaluations, those conducted before a program is designed, help identify the social conditions or needs that the program should address. Sometimes when specific needs are not clearly articulated, a program's design may target perceived needs rather than real needs.

An Example: Listening to Teachers' Needs

The staff development committee analyzed student reading performance on the statewide assessment. Tenth graders' scores were consistently well below the state average. Principals and the reading consultant in the district discussed the need to provide training to teachers on reading in the content areas. They envisioned providing eight total hours of training in sessions scheduled throughout one school year. The program would follow a "training of trainers" model. Under the proposed plan, the schools' literacy coordinators would take the lead in training fellow staff members at their schools and then be available to provide follow-up support to interested teachers.

When all the school literacy coordinators were meeting to plan the training, a number of them expressed doubt that teachers would implement the strategies they planned to teach. One even said that teachers were unwilling to incorporate reading strategies into their instructional lessons because they believed that it would take time away from their curriculum. Together with the reading consultant, the literacy coordinators discussed what they perceived to be teachers' apparent lack of interest in improving students' reading performance and their beliefs about student capacity to learn. The group continued to guess about the discontent among teachers until one of the literacy coordinators suggested that they ask some teachers about their feelings. By conducting focus groups at each high school, the reading coordinators discovered that teachers' expectations that students "should be able to read independently" by the time they got to high school were interfering with teachers' willingness to implement strategies for assisting students with reading.

Learning about strategies for reading comprehension was not a prevailing need of teachers; rather they needed to learn about understanding students' reading deficiencies and teachers' roles in addressing them. The design of this program had been based on a perceived need and not a real need. In this case, no amount of training in strategies was likely to change teacher attitudes and improve student reading performance. If the literacy coordinators and the reading consultant had moved ahead with their planned training, they would probably have been surprised and terribly disappointed at the end of the year when their concerted efforts produced few or no results in student achievement in reading. Fortunately, the program planners were able to alter the content of the program to meet teachers' real (rather than perceived) needs before the program was rolled out to the teachers.

Formative Evaluations

While planning evaluations are done at the beginning of a program, formative evaluations are conducted throughout the program. They are designed to give information about how a staff development program is working. This type of evaluation information is essential to improving programs, preventing and managing problems related to implementation, and ensuring that the program is fully functioning. Evaluators can also use formative evaluations to help explain how the program works and how it contributes to the results it achieves. In order to be able to replicate a program and to contribute to the broad conceptual knowledge base of the field of professional development, program planners must understand how the process leads to the results.

An Example: Making Adjustments to Improve Outcomes

The district social studies coordinator had recently begun implementation of a staff development program to develop middle-grade teachers' content knowledge about Asian culture so that they could develop and implement interdisciplinary units in the eighth-grade curriculum. She had focused on helping teachers understand recent economic, religious, and social factors influencing the political agenda in three Asian countries. The curriculum change had been approved by the board of education, and she wanted to help teachers begin to prepare units to use in the following school year with students.

As she visited schools several weeks after the series of courses, which she taught both online and face-to-face, she discovered that several teachers had replaced their existing curriculum with new information that they were learning about Asia. While the coordinator was pleased that social studies teachers had so quickly integrated their new knowledge, she noticed that the planned development of interdisciplinary units was not occurring in any school. Several groups of teachers in a few schools were working together, although the planned development of interdisciplinary units by eighth-grade core teams was not happening in any school.

What the coordinator surmised was that she had not been clear in conveying her expectations and had also not given teachers the information or the time to develop the interdisciplinary units. Her informal, yet important, formative evaluation helped her identify several problems related to her plan. It also gave her the time to revise and adjust without negatively impacting student achievement in the next school year. She was able to act expediently to support teachers before they made too many inappropriate changes. She also was able to use teachers' input about how students responded to the new content as she worked with teams of teachers at each school to develop the interdisciplinary units.

CHOOSING AN APPROPRIATE TYPE OF EVALUATION

Planning, formative, and summative evaluations have distinct purposes. Planning and formative evaluations can provide essential information to program stakeholders and inform ongoing improvements. Although the three types employ many of the same evaluation tools and strategies, their goals are different.

Effective uses of the three types vary from case to case. Using evaluation to improve staff development before, during, and after its design and implementation can sometimes strengthen a program, increase its chances of achieving its intended results, and maintain stakeholders' commitment to engaging in evaluation as they collaborate to make the needed improvements. Staff development directors will sometimes want to conduct all three types of evaluations for one program. In other cases, they will select just one or two types of evaluations to conduct. Table 2.3 is useful for determining the type or types of evaluation needed in a given situation.

Table 2.3   Appropriate Types of Evaluation

Appropriate Type of Evaluation	Appropriate Processes and Action Steps During Phase of Development
Planning Evaluations	Uses participatory (collaborative) and empowerment evaluation processes to • Determine target population • Assess needs • Clarify outcomes • Assess processes • Assess stakeholders' reaction to the intended program
Formative Evaluations	Uses participatory (collaborative) and empowerment evaluation processes to • Assess through input whether the program is working as designed • Give feedback • Collect credible data • Study data in relationship to identified benchmarks to inform revisions, improvements, or minor adjustments to program design
Summative Evaluations	Often uses systematic evaluation processes to • Collect credible data upon which to base judgments about the program's merit and worth • Provide a summary judgment about the program's performance and impact

STEPS IN THE EVALUATION PROCESS

Planning and conducting evaluations is linear work in which the steps are highly interrelated. The success of one step depends on the success of the previous step. While some recursiveness is involved, much of the work is fairly sequential. For example, the evaluator would have difficulty in determining how to collect data unless he or she has already decided what data to collect. The evaluation process outlined in this book has eight steps (see Table 2.4). Each step will be briefly described here. Subsequent chapters contain in-depth discussions of each step.

Getting Ready to Start the Evaluation Process

Until a staff development program is "defined," it cannot be evaluated. If staff development leaders want to commission an evaluation of their program, they should first make sure that their staff development program is sufficiently defined. By "defined" we mean that program leaders have a program that includes goals, planned actions to achieve those goals, and the resources necessary to implement the plan. For more information about defining a staff development program, consult the *NSDC's Standards for Staff Development, Revised* or refer to Assumption 1 in Chapter 3.

Step One: Assess Evaluability

Now the evaluation process can begin. The evaluator will want to thoroughly understand the staff development program. If, for some reason, program leaders have not yet defined their program, the evaluator helps them do so. In some cases, the program exists but has not been clearly defined. Starting from their understanding of the program, the evaluator and program leaders together determine whether the program is "evaluable." This simply means asking "Can this evaluation even take place?"

The evaluator examines the program's design to determine whether it is complete, sufficient, feasible, and logical. This involves examining the program's goals, standards, and indicators of success, theory of change, and logic model, all critical to conducting a successful evaluation. Evaluation planning depends on program planning, and in ideal situations, they are done simultaneously.

Chapter 4 covers assessing evaluability in depth, using program theories of change.

Step Two: Formulate Evaluation Questions

Developing, or "crafting," good evaluation questions depends on first identifying all the intended users of the evaluation and becoming clear about their needs and expectations. Clarifying the purposes of all the potential users is essential. Clear purposes will help to shape decisions about the overall purposes of the evaluation and eventually guide the development of evaluation questions and the selection of an evaluation methodology.

Even though an evaluation may have more than one purpose, just one should be identified as the primary purpose. When an evaluation is to serve more than one purpose, specific aspects of the evaluation will need to be customized and appropriately sequenced to address various needs and interests. The final phases of an evaluation can be "disastrous if it turns out that the evaluation planning process did not resolve in advance the conflicting expectations and/or priorities of different users" (Patton, 1997, p. 65).

Once the users and purposes are clarified, the evaluator formulates the questions the evaluation seeks to answer. These questions will direct the scope and methodology of the evaluation (the framework). Creating a good evaluation question is not easy and may achieve its best result from collaboration among the evaluator, those who commissioned the evaluation, and other stakeholders. With mutually agreed upon evaluation questions, the recipients will perceive the evaluation as valuable. Chapter 5 focuses on crafting authentic evaluation questions.

Step Three: Construct the Framework

Multiple methodologies exist for conducting evaluations. Evaluators of staff development programs tend to adopt either quasi-experimental or descriptive methodologies since most internal evaluations are practitioner-based. Other methodologies might require a higher level of expertise about evaluation than some staff development program directors have or even external technical expertise. The evaluation team will ideally select an evaluation methodology that aligns with the questions to be answered, that is reasonable and feasible, and that will provide the evidence needed to present findings. A thorough discussion of how to construct the framework is presented in Chapter 6.

Step Four: Collect Data

Once the framework for the evaluation has been determined, the evaluator collects data using the collection methods identified within that framework. The data-collection methods selected need to be able to produce the type of data required to answer the evaluation questions. Multiple sources of data can strengthen an evaluation study if they provide multiple perspectives on the same issue. Carefully constructed data-collection tools and well-trained data collectors will facilitate this often labor-intensive process. In this crucial step, the evaluator manages the data-collection process, making sure consistent and careful processes result in accuracy. Chapter 7 presents information about managing data collection and selecting appropriate scoring processes.

Step Five: Organize, Analyze, and Display Data

Organizing, analyzing, and displaying data are the processes of summarizing, collating, synthesizing, displaying, and analyzing data to examine patterns, trends, outliers, and anomalies. Chapter 8 is a more detailed discussion of these processes. Some of the processes are technical and may require the evaluator to use the expertise of someone who is skilled in statistical analysis. Nevertheless, those practitioners skilled in using spreadsheets and computing descriptive statistics will be able to perform a number of valuable data analyses.

Step Six: Interpret Data

Interpreting data is the process of examining the analyzed data and responding to the evaluation questions, based on the strength of the data. The interpretive process, detailed in Chapter 9, requires the evaluator and others who might be included in this phase of the work to form judgments or conclusions that are supported by the data and make recommendations about the program. This phase often uses preestablished criteria against which the findings of the evaluation will be measured to determine the progress or impact of the intervention(s).

Step Seven: Disseminate and Use Findings

Disseminating and using the findings involves preparing both written and oral reports of the findings of the evaluation. The evaluator may prepare multiple reports for dissemination to various audiences to address their specific interests in the evaluation. For some, a very comprehensive technical report is best, while for others a brief executive summary will be appropriate. Using visual displays to share data and to allow the audience to see how the data supported the findings increases readers' ability to understand the report.

Various presentation formats are discussed in Chapter 10. Once the evaluator prepares and disseminates reports, the evaluation process continues as decision makers use the reports to make informed decisions related to the program.

Step Eight: Evaluate the Evaluation

A step not often included in evaluations is meta-evaluation of the evaluation. Both evaluators and stakeholders benefit from having some means of assessing the evaluation's value. This might be done informally or formally. Improving the design of the evaluation, dissemination of findings, or evidence collected are some reasons for evaluating the evaluation. This process benefits both the evaluator, by providing feedback on his or her work, and the stakeholders, by ensuring an opportunity for them to express their views about the usefulness of the evaluation. Both purposes can lead to improved evaluation practices. Chapter 11 lends insight into this last step of the evaluation process and will encourage practitioners to "finish what they start."

Table 2.4   Steps in the Evaluation Process

Planning Phase

- Assess evaluability
- Formulate evaluation questions
- Construct the framework

Conducting Phase

- Collect data
- Organize, analyze, and display data
- Interpret data

Reporting Phase

- Disseminate and use findings
- Evaluate the evaluation

Evaluating Staff Development

3

ASSUMPTIONS ABOUT HIGH-QUALITY STAFF DEVELOPMENT

It is important to consider three assumptions about high-quality staff development and its evaluation. If any of these assumptions is unsupported for the program being considered for evaluation, it may be best to rethink the value of conducting the program or its evaluation until elements of the program are redesigned. If stakeholders opt to continue with evaluation, the evaluator may decide to focus only on formative evaluation to learn about and improve the program's operation before planning a summative evaluation.

Assumption 1: The program is data-driven, research-based, and well-defined

A longitudinal study of Title I concluded that students whose teachers rated their professional development as "high quality" consistently performed better (U.S. Dept. of Education, 1999). Garet, Porter, Desimone, Birman, and Yoon (2001) identified features of effective professional development. These findings support the notion that some staff development programs are more effective than others. Many staff development programs are events rather than programs. Staff development that begins with the end in mind is the first step to ensuring that students will benefit from staff development. That end is more than transmitting information through workshops, but rather attends to the comprehensive approach to professional learning by developing knowledge and skills, addressing dispositions or attitudes, and focusing on integrating new practices into the workplace to produce results for students.

A data-driven, research-based, well-defined professional development program is one that examines data about student learning needs, understands the context in which the program will be implemented, develops goals for improved teaching and learning, assesses educators' learning needs in relationship to those goals, studies research to determine which practices have contributed to achieving similar goals in similar contexts, develops a theory of change that defines the program's planned actions to achieve the goals, ensures appropriate resources to implement the planned actions, monitors progress through formative evaluation, makes revisions as necessary, conducts summative evaluation, and uses the results of the evaluation to make decisions about the program. This definition of a well-defined professional development program is more fully illustrated in *What Works in the Elementary School: Results-Based Staff Development* (Killion, 2002b).

Assumption 2: The school, district, or regional agency has the capacity, including fiscal and human capital, to implement both the program and the evaluation with fidelity to their designs

Both staff development and its evaluation require human and fiscal resources. Some believe evaluation drains resources from the program and deprives participants of services. In reality, evaluation is intended to be useful to program stakeholders because it provides the essential information they need and want for making important decisions about the program. Evaluation can also benefit program stakeholders by identifying what works and what does not work. Typically, the more complex the evaluation design, the more costly the evaluation. But even low-cost evaluations can produce useful information. When decision and policy makers want impact evaluations of programs, they must be ready to provide the human and fiscal resources to support them so that the evaluation is rigorous, valid, and valuable. In an era of accountability, the cost of evaluation must become a requisite part of any fiscal planning.

Typical evaluation costs include (1) the time of stakeholders involved in planning, conducting, and disseminating evaluation results; (2) time of both professional and support staff; (3) staff to coordinate and conduct evaluation activities, including data collection, analysis, interpretation, and report preparation and dissemination; (4) costs from disruption of service that might be incurred if teachers were released from their teaching responsibilities to participate in evaluation activities; (5) costs of direct compensation for participation in evaluation activities, such as paying teachers an hourly stipend to take part in an interview or focus group after the contract day; (6) materials and supplies; (7) technology resources, such as computer time; (8) potential loss of goodwill among stakeholders who feel burdened by the extra workload associated with evaluation; and (9) the time of policy and decision makers who review the evaluation report and make decisions based on it (Wholey, Hatry, & Newcomber, 2004).

Because there are many options for evaluation designs, some of which are more costly than others, it is important to weigh the projected cost against the perceived value of an evaluation. When evaluations are designed to address specific questions of the intended users, the evaluation will have more real value. Involving the users in decisions about the evaluation is critical and is the subject of the next section. When focused on carefully crafted questions, evaluations can become valuable organizational improvement tools.

Assumption 3: Key stakeholders in the school, district, or agencies intend to use the evaluation results to make decisions about the program

Justifying the costs of evaluation requires that the investment be for a worthwhile, utilization-focused evaluation designed for a specific audience (users) and for specific purposes (uses). When evaluations are constructed for identified purposes and for identified stakeholders, the perceived value of the evaluation increases, as do stakeholders' understanding and ownership if they have been actively involved in planning the design of the evaluation and the eventual use of the results (Patton, 1997). The value of evaluations can be determined by three factors: the reliability and validity of the evidence; the credibility of the evaluation to those who commissioned it and who plan to use it; and the usefulness of the information in decision making.

Evaluation is a value-added process. When an evaluation is designed thoughtfully, it can become a part of the intervention itself. For example, when reviewing literature about professional development in order to design an evaluation of a writing program, an evaluator noted the importance of teacher collaboration in learning communities for achieving improved results for students. To build on the research and increase the amount of collaboration among program participants, the evaluator selected data-collection methods that fostered collaboration rather than those that were individually oriented. Instead of asking teachers individually to describe good student writing, the evaluator used focus groups. She also engaged teachers in examining student work, conducting classroom walk-throughs, and using scoring conferences to collect data about the impact of the staff development program.

Not only were these experiences rich opportunities for data collection, they also modeled structures for teachers' collaboration with a focus on student achievement. The evaluation design, in this case, extended the staff development intervention and might have contributed to the impact of the staff development program. As a result of the decisions the evaluator made about the evaluation framework, the evaluation results will be more understandable and useful to all stakeholders, and the strategies employed will add value to the program

Before an evaluation is conducted, staff development leaders should determine the degree to which their program meets the assumptions discussed in this chapter. Through that analysis, they will benefit in two ways:

1. The staff development program is likely to be more focused on goals and is more likely to contribute to student results.

2. The evaluation will be more useful and add value to the staff development program rather than be viewed as an intrusion or supervisory edict.

ANALYZING EVALUATION APPROACHES: UNDERSTANDING "BOXES" AND "GAPS"

A challenge in the evaluation of staff development is the frequent use of a simplistic approach to evaluation. Evaluations that fail to amplify the underlying theory and operations of the staff development program are called "black-box evaluations." Black-box evaluations offer no information about how a program worked to produce results for teachers or students. Glass-box evaluations, in contrast, reveal the transformative process that starts with inputs and arrives at goal achievement.

Black-Box and Glass-Box Approaches

Black-box evaluations focus only on results rather than what occurs in the program or what is presumed to be causing those outcomes and why. In a black-box evaluation, the evaluator is interested only in knowing whether the outcome occurred and not in helping the program stakeholders understand how the program produced its results. They are kept in the dark.

Figure 3A   Black-Box Evaluation

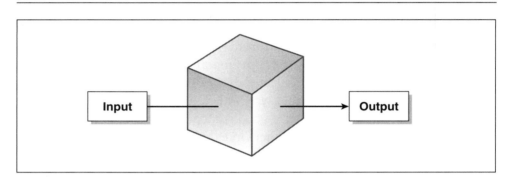

For example, the input: Teachers participate in a 25-hour workshop in reading strategies for underperforming readers. The output: Student scores in reading on a standardized norm-referenced achievement test increase. Because black-box evaluations fail to shed light on how a program's activities and resources interact to produce results, some theorists and practitioners contend that this shortcoming limits evaluators' ability to decisively link staff development with student achievement.

Figure 3B   Sample Black-Box Evaluation

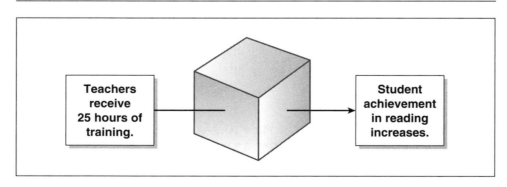

The Effects of Extraneous Factors in Black-Box Evaluations

Another problem associated with black-box evaluations is the potential influence of extraneous factors. Because schools and districts are complex social systems and student learning results from innumerable factors, black-box evaluations are not sensitive to unanticipated contextual or organizational factors that may influence results. Such evaluations are quickly discounted as invalid because there is no attempt to consider how the intervention interacts with its context. And, because necessary conditions that significantly contribute to a program's success may not be clearly analyzed or even known in a black-box evaluation, replicating the program to achieve similar results in the future is left to chance.

Glass-box evaluations, on the other hand, do illuminate how a staff development program's components interact to produce results. They provide critical information to program managers, such as how to improve the program, what aspects are more effective, how discrepancies in implementation impact results, and where problems occur that might interfere with results. When evaluators and stakeholders are able to focus on implementation in an evaluation, they use the information about what is happening in the intervention to make appropriate adjustments and heighten the program's success.

Glass-box evaluation provides information on what occurs and how it occurs within a program. The effectiveness of a staff development program is strengthened when both its implementation and its impact are evaluated. Without some form of process evaluation, a staff development program may begin to erode, deteriorate, or stray from faithful implementation of the elements or principles that serve as the foundation of the program. A glass-box evaluation of staff development provides the information needed for making adjustments and improvements and for increasing the probability of producing the intended results for students. A glass-box evaluation may help program directors understand how the program is being implemented and highlight any inconsistencies, problems, gaps, or redundancies that might interfere with the program's impact.

Figure 3C   Glass-Box Evaluation

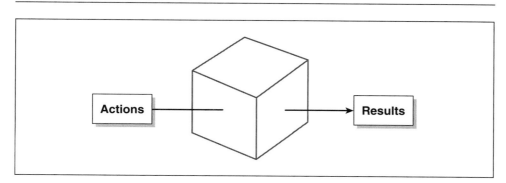

Evaluation data help program stakeholders know what happened and why. They can make educated design modifications rather than respond to squeaky wheels or rely on hunches, biases, guesses, or trial and error. When program developers create and implement innovations, they occasionally must base decisions on their personal intuitions and preferences, but well-designed, comprehensive staff development programs that leave little to chance require solid data for making program changes. Figure 3D illustrates what happens when a staff development program to increase proficiency in reading is conducted in a glass box.

Figure 3D Sample Glass-Box Evaluation

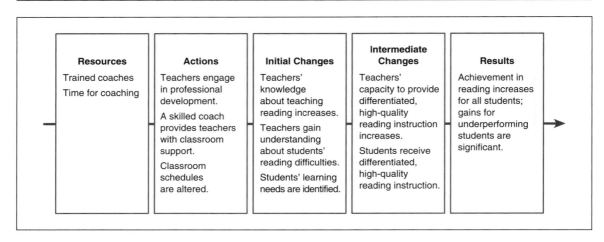

Resources	Actions	Initial Changes	Intermediate Changes	Results
Trained coaches Time for coaching	Teachers engage in professional development. A skilled coach provides teachers with classroom support. Classroom schedules are altered.	Teachers' knowledge about teaching reading increases. Teachers gain understanding about students' reading difficulties. Students' learning needs are identified.	Teachers' capacity to provide differentiated, high-quality reading instruction increases. Students receive differentiated, high-quality reading instruction.	Achievement in reading increases for all students; gains for underperforming students are significant.

A Problematic Distance: The Gap Between Actions and Results

Black-box evaluation studies leave a substantial gap between the actions and results. Because of the gap, questions are unanswered about how, or whether staff development influenced student achievement. From the analysis of content-specific staff development programs for the middle grades, we found that most program evaluations did little to fill in the gap. These evaluations documented staff development activities (such as the length of the staff development activities, number of people who attended, and length of training) and measured only student achievement.

Chen (1990) indicates that black-box evaluations such as these are "characterized by a primary focus on the overall relationship between the inputs and the outputs of a program without concern for the transformation processes in the middle" (p. 18). Chen continues to suggest that such evaluations will offer a "gross assessment of whether or not a program works but fail to identify the underlying causal mechanisms that generate treatment effect, thus failing to pinpoint the deficiencies of the program for future program improvement or development" (p. 18). While summative data (impact data) collected in a black-box process are better than no data at all about a staff development program, they lack credibility with the policy makers who know too well the limitations of black-box studies. Impact data that result from a black-box study cannot help the evaluation leaders decide how to improve either the program results or program efficiency.

Figure 3E   A Problematic Distance: The Gap Between Black-Box Input and Output

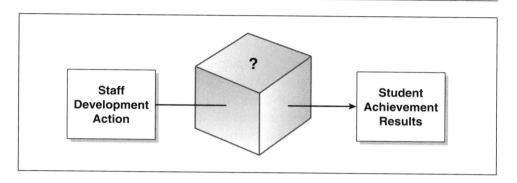

Using Glass Boxes to Illuminate the Transformation Processes

The assertion that "when educators engage in high-quality professional learning, student achievement increases" is increasingly accepted, and yet the research support is still sparse. Examples of individual programs, schools, and districts that have successfully used staff development to improve student achievement are increasing each year. Studies of teacher, school, and student success also contribute to the knowledge base about the link between staff development and student learning (Charles A. Dana Center, 1999; Wenglinsky, 2000; WestEd, 2000).

To consistently produce results for students from all staff development efforts, staff developers will need to have a deep understanding of

- How the components of a comprehensive staff development program interact
- Which are most influential
- Which are essential
- Which are discretionary

With this information, program directors will be able to design and implement successful staff development programs more consistently.

To better understand the relationships between the input, processes, and outcomes, staff development leaders will want to make their theories explicit and test them. Evaluations can help stakeholders surface their program theories. Chen (1990) defines program theories as "a specification of what must be done to achieve the desired goals, what other important impacts may also be anticipated, and how these goals and impacts would be generated" (p. 43). A more complete discussion of program theories is included in Chapter 4.

Both stakeholders and the evaluator will have a deeper understanding of the program and its components when they specify the underlying theory about how staff development is expected to influence student achievement. By testing their theories against what really occurs, program designers can find out whether their theories hold true and, if they do not, will be in a better position to adjust them.

For large numbers of practitioners, these benefits will justify the resources required for ongoing evaluations of both new and well-established staff development initiatives. An evaluation that provides information to strengthen a staff development program's design or implementation is advantageous to program stakeholders and the students in their schools and classrooms.

The distance between educator learning and student learning is not far after all. Designing glass-box evaluations to illuminate the transformation processes affords many benefits and opportunities such as these:

- Provides useful insights for improving the staff development program
- Clarifies the characteristics of the program
- Increases understanding of the conditions necessary for success
- Helps implementers understand context and program limitations
- Prevents program deterioration
- Adds to the knowledge base about programs and effective interventions
- Aids replication and adaptation of successful strategies
- Justifies continuance of financial support for successful programs

DESIGNING USEFUL EVALUATIONS

The quality and value of an evaluation are determined by the usefulness of the results in improving the program's design, efficiency, effectiveness, and results. The challenge for evaluators is to find out with a fair degree of certainty whether a staff development intervention produced the intended results. Isolating the effects of an intervention is not usually important to a practitioner-evaluator who understands that, in schools and districts, many factors interrelate to influence student learning. A school or district can influence some of these factors but not others. For example, through staff development, schools and districts can influence the knowledge, skill, and behavior of educators. They are not able to influence the socioeconomic status of students.

Schools and classrooms are complex environments that do not lend themselves to "pure" scientific research designs. Too many variables related to student learning cannot be controlled. And political and ethical considerations make it difficult to use random assignment of students to treatment and control groups to conduct experimental studies that might allow evaluators to say with some certainty that staff development causes increases in student achievement. What is important for evaluators of staff development to discover and report, whenever change in student achievement occurs, is the context, process, and content of a staff development initiative and how these factors have interacted to produce the desired results.

DATA FROM MEASURES OF STUDENT ACHIEVEMENT

A challenge in the evaluation of staff development is the data available about student achievement. To evaluate a staff development program's impact on student achievement, the measure of achievement must be aligned with all the following: the curriculum content, the pedagogy (instructional practice), the assessment tools, the instructional resources students use in their classrooms, and the content of the educators' staff development program. For convenience, many evaluators choose readily available data sources such as norm-referenced, standardized achievement tests, state criterion-referenced tests, grades, or other extant assessments of student learning. In most cases, measures of student learning are selected for their convenience rather than for their alignment with the focus on the knowledge, skills, or behaviors that educators are learning.

In order to evaluate the impact of a staff development program on student achievement, the evaluation tool, which will measure student achievement, needs to be closely connected to what the educators learned. It is only when they are closely aligned that a relationship can be established to correlate specific educator learning and related practices with student results. When such alignment does not exist, the evaluation might result in invalid conclusions.

Some measures of student achievement may not be sensitive enough to account for differences in student achievement. Norm-referenced, standardized tests, for example, are psychometrically very reliable, yet they are designed to assess a student's acquisition of broad content rather than the specific curriculum adopted by a district or the content aligned with the classroom. For this reason, according to Popham (1999, 2001), inferences related to student academic success or program effectiveness may be invalid. Guskey (2000) adds that, since standardized tests usually include multiple-choice measures, they may not be a good measure of students' application of knowledge.

The case study that follows provides a specific example of the challenge associated with selecting appropriate measures of student achievement.

A *Case Study:* Mathematics Achievement

A school district adopted a reform-based mathematics curriculum with the intent of improving students' achievement in mathematics. To ensure implementation, an extensive staff development program was designed to strengthen teachers' mathematics content knowledge and to expand their mathematics-specific pedagogy. The school board, in approving the resources for the staff development program, requested an evaluation to know whether their investment in staff development and the curriculum would pay off.

The district measured students' math achievement annually on the state criterion-referenced test. The analysis of the test's subskills revealed several problems in using this measure of student achievement to assess the impact of the staff development program:

- Only 40% of the new curriculum was included in the subskills of the criterion-referenced test in the district.
- Language about mathematical processes and concepts differed between the district's instructional materials and the test.

- The presentation of mathematical equations and problems on the test was different from the presentation in the instructional materials.

District officials acknowledged the discrepancy. They recognized that, with the heightened accountability in public schools, they had little choice except to add an additional measure of student achievement that aligned more closely with the program. The district leadership agreed to create their own assessments but took no steps to make that happen.

After two consecutive years of no change in students' performance in mathematics on the state test, a parent group began to question the mathematics curriculum and the investment in teacher professional development. The math coordinator and the math advisory team recognized the contradiction and asked the district to reconsider the implementation of alternative assessments of math performance to have more appropriate measures of student achievement. The expectations for increased student achievement, the newly adopted curriculum and teacher practices, and the measurement tool for assessing student achievement were incompatible.

As a result, a team of local mathematics teachers and experts in mathematics education worked in the spring and summer of the second year to develop and field-test student performance assessments. At the end of the third school year, after analyzing collected data, the district's assessment coordinator reported on the effectiveness of the curriculum and the staff development program.

The state test scores for Grades 3, 5, 8, and 10 indicated a slight decline (in all grades) from Year 2 to Year 3 in the math total battery. The alternative measures of students' performance in mathematics indicated that the students' ability to understand advanced concepts such as statistics and probability, algebraic reasoning, and problem solving improved significantly from fall to spring. Other data collected indicated that (1) teachers had a greater comfort with reform mathematics instructional practices, (2) students reported higher levels of engagement in classroom activities, (3) more female and minority students enrolled in advanced mathematics classes, and (4) more students completed algebra. All findings provided evidence of the success of the curriculum and the staff development program that the state test had not indicated.

Analysis of the Case

This case study raises several issues related to evaluating staff development. Two years of no results had undoubtedly caused alarm and raised legitimate questions about both the curriculum and the quality of the staff development program. In similar circumstances, many school boards and district decision makers might have ended the mathematics reform program rather than look at ways to address the apparent inconsistency between the measure of achievement and the expected results. Instead they exhibited tremendous commitment to the reform and welcomed alternative methods of measuring the effects on student learning.

Planning Phase

- Assess evaluability
- Formulate evaluation questions
- Construct the evaluation framework

Conducting Phase

- Collect data
- Organize, analyze, and display data
- Interpret data

Reporting Phase

- Disseminate and use findings
- Evaluate the evaluation

Assess Evaluability

4

One of the major reasons evaluations are difficult and programs fail to achieve their intended outcomes may rest in the lack of a clear understanding about what the program is. In many cases, especially those related to the evaluation of staff development, the program is insufficient in scope or power to produce the expected results.

When taking this first step in the evaluation process, the evaluator seeks to answer several questions:

1. Is this program conceptually and logically feasible? In other words, does it seem likely that it has the potential to produce the results it intends?

2. Are the goals, objectives, activities, resources, initial or intermediate outcomes, and intended results clearly stated and understood by key stakeholders?

3. Is this evaluation worth doing?

Evaluability is the degree to which a proposed plan for staff development is ready for evaluation because it clearly articulates what will occur, the actions within the plan are sufficient to produce the results expected, and there is a clear understanding of what changes will lead to the intended results. In the following scenario, is the program logically designed? Can it be evaluated? Can appropriate data be collected? Can reasonable activities be completed? Are adequate resources available?

A Case Study

The program at Barron High School is fairly typical of staff development programs and highlights the problems that occur when staff development has design flaws and is not evaluable.

Barron High School wanted (1) to improve students' achievement by helping students understand key concepts that crossed several disciplines, and (2) to build a collaborative culture among staff. The goal was to increase student achievement in language arts, social studies, and science. The planned action was that teachers would design and deliver at least three interdisciplinary units during the school year and that students' understanding of key concepts would increase as teachers emphasized them across all disciplines.

Figure 4A   An Interdisciplinary Staff Development Program at Barron High School

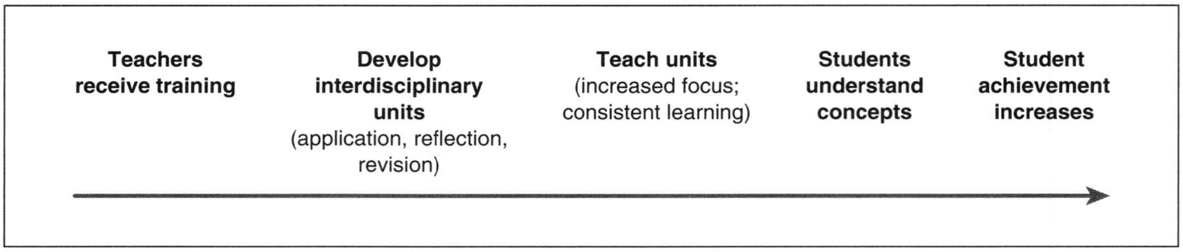

Teachers participated in 20 hours of training designed to develop their knowledge and skills in integrating curriculum and to give them time to work in interdisciplinary teams to design at least one interdisciplinary unit that they would agree to teach within two months after the training. After their implementation of the unit and before their credit was awarded, teachers were asked to revise the unit, write an assessment of the unit, and submit sample student work from the unit. During the two months after the training, the curriculum consultants who taught the class on interdisciplinary instruction offered to assist any team in the development of its unit and to observe as teachers were teaching the unit.

The evaluator, a graduate student in education at a local university, developed a survey to administer to staff to gather data about their units and their views about the degree of collaboration across departments. She administered the survey at a mandatory staff meeting to increase the likelihood of having a high response rate. She also administered a survey to students in their English classes because 85% of the students were currently enrolled in English. Other students were notified that they could complete a survey in the counseling office. The survey asked students for their views about how interdisciplinary instruction had influenced their understanding of one key concept the staff universally agreed to address in at least one unit—the concept of change.

The results of the surveys were as follows. The mean number of interdisciplinary units taught by all teachers in the school was 1. The range was 0–3. Teachers reported limited collaboration with colleagues in other departments. Students indicated very little knowledge about interdisciplinary instruction, and most (more than 60%) were unable to articulate how interdisciplinary instruction influenced their understanding of change. Student performance on the mandatory state test in reading, writing, science, social studies, and math showed slight improvement from the previous year.

There are a number of flaws in this situation in both the design of the program and possibly in the design of the evaluation. We could list many questions about

(1) the design of the student survey, (2) the possible exclusion of a number of students, (3) the selection of change as a focus for the survey questions, and (4) the use of the state test as a measure of student achievement.

What we might more productively challenge than the instruments or sampling is the design of the intervention itself.

- How reasonable is it to expect that interdisciplinary units, no matter how well planned or how many, would increase student achievement in the areas specified?
- What research supported the selection of interdisciplinary curriculum and instruction as the most feasible way to improve student learning?
- Is it reasonable to expect that 20 hours of training accompanied by the expectation to design, teach, and report on one interdisciplinary unit would produce more than an average of one interdisciplinary unit or impact student achievement?
- If the planned activities included having teachers design and teach three interdisciplinary units, where in the plan was there an indication of that?
- Where in the plan was time built in to allow teachers to collaborate, especially across disciplines?
- What systems and supports were put into place to assist teachers?
- What role did the school's principal play in conveying the importance of this intervention?
- How did department chairpersons assist their staff members in meeting the goal?
- What resources did the curriculum consultants provide teachers to facilitate the design of additional units?
- What kind of feedback was provided to teachers about the one unit they submitted for review before they received credit?
- Why did none of the teachers seek assistance from the curriculum consultants?

The point of this case is simply this: We cannot expect results with students from a staff development program that is unlikely to produce them. And we cannot expect an evaluation to produce useful results when the program being evaluated is poorly conceived and constructed. Perhaps Chen (1990) said it best: "Current problems and limitations of program evaluation lie more with lack of adequate conceptual framework of the program than with methodological weakness" (p. 293).

Evaluation of ill-conceived staff development programs wastes limited human and fiscal resources. In these cases, evaluations sanction programs with gaps in their conceptual frameworks by appearing to condone mediocrity. Wasted evaluations rob students and educators of powerful opportunities to learn at high levels. And when evaluations attempt to assess programs with fuzzy goals, faulty conceptual frameworks, or illogical, poorly structured activities, the evaluation may be difficult to design and of questionable integrity. Staff development that is not well planned or focused on what teachers need to learn to help students achieve identified learning goals may impede student achievement.

A major problem in staff development is this: What is taught in staff development may not be learned or applied unless the program incorporates additional activities to support, encourage, and monitor implementation. Staff developers must ask themselves whether their comprehensive staff development program is structured in a way to support and encourage implementation. If implementation support is lacking, then it is fairly safe to assume that only a small portion of learners will use the information regularly to solve problems associated with their practice.

Joyce & Showers (1995), in their seminal research study about the methodologies and outcomes of staff development, found that only 5%–10% of participants used their new learning when there was merely presentation of theory. These numbers increased slightly to 10%–15% when demonstration and low-risk practice were added to the instructional methodology. Only when ongoing support was added in the form of coaching, study groups, and so forth, did the percentage of participants using their new learning increase to 85%–90%. If the design of the professional development program fails to include ongoing support in the form of coaching or study groups, then the results will be few.

CONDUCTING THE EVALUABILITY ASSESSMENT

One way to circumvent the problems associated with evaluating poorly designed staff development programs is to begin with an evaluability assessment. This process assists both the evaluator and the program director in knowing whether the program can be evaluated, has clear goals and activities that are likely to lead to the intended goals, has adequate resources to implement the activities, and has benchmarks to assess progress.

Many staff development programs begin with unclear or fuzzy goals or goals that focus on implementation rather than results. Weiss (1998) suggests that "part of the explanation [for fuzzy goals] probably lies in practitioners' concentration on concrete matters of program functioning and their pragmatic mode of operation. They often have an intuitive rather than an analytical approach to program development. But there is also a sense in which ambiguity serves a useful function; it may mask underlying divergences in intent. Support from many quarters, inside and outside the program agency, is required to get a program off the ground, and the glittering generalities that pass for goal statements are meant to satisfy a variety of interests and perspectives" (p. 52).

Regardless of the reason for them, unclear goals will create gaps in action, sequence, and direction and impede goal attainment. If Chen's statement is accurate—that the problem of evaluation rests largely with the program's conceptual design—then it makes sense that the evaluator and program developers and stakeholders join hands at an early stage to define the program goals with clarity, its resources with completeness, and its activities with logical sequence.

The goals of the evaluability assessment are to ensure that

1. Program goals, objectives, important side effects, and priority information needs are well defined

2. Program goals and objectives are plausible

3. Relevant performance data can be obtained

4. The intended users of the evaluation results have agreed on how they will use the information. (Rossi, Freeman, & Lipsey, 2003)

The four steps of evaluability assessment are as follows: (1) examine the program's goals and objectives, (2) examine the program's theory of change, (3) examine the program's logic model, and (4) adjust the program design on the basis of the assessment. This is an iterative process; depending on the outcome of the first three steps, the fourth step involves making program design adjustments and repeating the first three steps. The remainder of this chapter is intended not only to help evaluators know what to look for in their evaluability assessment but also to help program directors develop these essential program components.

EXAMINE THE PROGRAM'S GOALS, OBJECTIVES, AND STANDARDS FOR SUCCESS

Clarifying the goals of the staff development program is a critical function in designing the program. Goals determine everything. Sometimes the terms *goals* and *objectives* are confusing. A *goal* is a statement of a desired state toward which a program is directed, what the overall purpose of the program is. There are two types of goals, end goals and means goals. End goals define what the outcome of the program is. Means goals define the process through which the end goals will be achieved. Some programs view ends and means as interchangeable outcomes. In staff development, especially the staff development that increases the achievement of all students (NSDC, 2001), this is not the case. Improved student achievement, the end goal, is what matters, not the means goal, or how much staff development is provided. In staff development, end goals rather than means goals are the priority. Means will be integrated into the program design and may be evaluated in the formative evaluation.

Sample Goals and Objectives

End goal: Increase students' ability to understand and solve problems.

Means objective: Use research-based instructional strategies in teaching problem solving.

End goal: third- and fourth-grade students will perform on grade level.

Means objective: Provide coaching to all teachers in Grades 3 and 4.

End goal: Increase student academic performance.

Means objective: Form professional learning communities.

A program *objective* is a specific statement detailing the desired changes a program produces (Rossi, Freeman, & Lipsey, 2003). Objectives are more specific statements that describe the changes the program will bring about and the degree of those changes. Objectives operationalize goals. Evaluators often need to work with program stakeholders and developers to clarify program goals and objectives. Program activities describe actions planned to accomplish the objectives and goals.

Mager (1975) and Tyler (1950) suggest that objectives have four elements:

A = **A**udience: who the target group is

B = what the expected change in **B**ehavior is

C = the **C**onditions under which the behavior will be performed

D = the **D**egree of the change

Rossi and Freeman (1982) recommend four techniques for writing objectives: (1) using strong verbs (e.g., *increase* versus *enhance*), (2) stating only one aim or purpose (per objective), (3) specifying a single-end product or result (per objective), and (4) specifying the expected time for achievement.

Some districts and schools use SMART goals, a combination of goals and objectives. SMART goals identify results as

Specific

Measurable

Achievable

Results-oriented

Time-bound

Sample SMART Goals

By 2010, all eighth-grade students will pass the algebra end-of-course examination at proficiency level or above.

At the end of the school year, all students in Grades 3–8 will read and comprehend grade-appropriate text by scoring at the proficiency level or above on the state reading test.

A Sample Goal and Objective with Activities

Sample Goal

Improve middle-grade students' academic success in mathematical reasoning and problem solving.

SMART GOAL

Five percent increase in academic performance of all students in Grades 5–8 in mathematical problem solving as measured on the state assessment test given at Grade 7 and on school-based performance tasks given at Grades 5–8.

TEACHER OBJECTIVE

Teachers will apply multiple problem-solving approaches across the curriculum.

Sample Activities

- Provide professional learning opportunities for teachers designed to increase their content knowledge and repertoire of content-specific instructional strategies in mathematics.
- Provide classroom support and coaching for teachers in implementing new instructional strategies.
- Develop two interdisciplinary curricular units for each grade that incorporate mathematical reasoning and problem solving.
- Develop and field-test classroom performance tasks for each grade level.
- Create two scoring conferences for teachers on student work in mathematics.

Involving an evaluator in the early stages of program planning will help program directors "begin with the end in mind." A comprehensive plan for a program of professional learning will logically and conceptually connect the identified needs with the desired results. The plan will specify the activities planned to move participants from the need to the intended results (the goals). Evaluators experienced in designing evaluation will be invaluable to developers in the planning stage.

Cases where fuzzy goals are preferable to clear goals are rare. Sometimes program developers may be experimenting with ideas that are on the leading edge of innovation; they understandably might not have clear outcomes or objectives. A district may, for example, be implementing a planning grant. Planning grants are designed to clarify goals and objectives for a future program. A district could, for example, want to focus on clarifying actual needs before specifying goals and planning appropriate activities.

Table 4.1 will help program developers, as well as evaluators who work with program stakeholders, clarify the intended results of the program. Programs may have various intended results. For example, a program can expect changes for students, teachers, principals, central office personnel, parent and community members, or others involved in the educational process. With clear goals, both the program design and evaluation will be much easier. Evaluation of a poorly conceived program with unclear goals not only will be difficult but also will be likely to produce no results for students.

Frameworks for Considering Program Goals

The four levels of evaluation of training originally developed by Kirkpatrick (1974) and expanded by Guskey (2000) and Phillips (1997) offer a useful framework for thinking about the desired program goals during the design stage. The early levels focus on process goals, and the latter stages focus on results for students. In the context of this book, only Levels 5 and possibly 6 address results for students. (See Table 4.2 for an overview of these levels.)

Table 4.1 Types of Changes in Teachers and Students

Type of Change	Teachers	Students
Knowledge Conceptual understanding of information, theories, principles, and research	Teachers understand mathematical concepts they are responsible for teaching.	Students have a deeper understanding of key mathematical concepts measured on criterion-referenced tests.
Attitude Beliefs about the value of particular information or strategies	Teachers believe students' competence in mathematics is important to their success, both within and beyond school.	Students enjoy mathematics.
Skill The ability to use strategies and processes to apply knowledge	Teachers know how to employ a variety of instructional strategies to help students visualize mathematical concepts.	Students demonstrate their understanding of math on classroom performance tasks.
Aspiration Desires, or internal motivation, to engage in a particular practice	Teachers have a genuine desire for their students to understand and perform well in mathematics.	Students want to advance their understanding of mathematics and aspire to advanced work in mathematics.
Behavior Consistent application of knowledge and skills	Teachers consistently employ inquiry-based instructional practices in mathematics to help students acquire a deep understanding of math concepts.	Students regularly apply mathematical reasoning to solving problems in math and other areas of their curriculum

Program developers might set goals at any of the levels in Table 4.2. However, setting goals at Levels 1–4 is setting process outcomes, those that are a means to the end of improving student achievement and not the end goals staff developers seek. Means-focused outcomes, like levels 1–4 in Table 4.2, may be appropriate for formative evaluations about a program's implementation or process. End-focused goals address the intended outcomes for students.

In the case of staff development, the teacher changes are capacities or means to bring about the changes in students. Teacher changes enable student changes to occur. As the Organization Research Service (2004) reminds Annie E. Casey Foundation grantees, "capacities are part of the continuum to achieve comprehensive community change. They are elements that enable influence, leverage, and impact to happen. The line between capacities and influence, leverage, and impact can sometimes be blurry"(p. 11). The capacities are the beginning; they are rarely the end sought.

Table 4.2   Levels of Evaluation of Training

Levels 1–6	Sample Evaluation Questions	Value of Information	Frequency of Use	Difficulty of Assessment
1. Measuring reaction to the learning experience (Guskey, 2000; Kirkpatrick, 1998)	Were participants satisfied with the learning experience?	Least valuable	Frequent	Easy
2. Measuring learning (Guskey, 2000; Kirkpatrick, 1998)	What did participants learn?			
3. Assessing organizational support and change (Guskey, 2000)	How has the culture of the school changed?			
4. Assessing application of learning (Guskey, 2000; Kirkpatrick, 1998)	How often are participants implementing the new practices?			
5. Assessing student learning (Guskey, 2000; Kirkpatrick, 1998)	Has student achievement increased?			
6. Calculating return on investment (Phillips, 1997).	What is the fiscal return on stakeholders' investment?	Most valuable	Infrequent	Difficult

After setting goals and objectives for a staff development program, it is also necessary to set standards, or criteria, against which to determine a program's success. Some evaluators may choose not to do this and to judge the success of the program without explicit criteria. If the goal is to raise student achievement, program stakeholders must determine how high is high enough. If achievement occurs in mathematics and not in science, will that indicate success? These questions are important for program stakeholders to consider in the design of the program and definitely before any conclusions are made about the program's success or impact.

Using past performance as a starting point is one way to begin a conversation about a standard. If student achievement has increased an average of two percentage points for the last three years, and if a new program is being implemented that is targeted to increase achievement, it is reasonable to expect a greater increase. Examining typical growth in other districts might provide other information to consider in creating standards or benchmarks. Identifying multiple indicators is another way to set standards for acceptable performance. Using gain scores for student achievement, coupled with teacher reports about adequacy of their professional knowledge and their efficacy in making instructional decisions, can serve as multiple indicators of the success of a staff development program. Any number of indicators can be the basis for establishing standards for the acceptable performance of a staff development program, as long as at least one indicator addresses students' academic achievement. Program stakeholders and directors sometimes choose to scale expected impact over a number of years. For example, they might expect a modest student achievement gain the first year, increase it the second year, and raise it again the third year. This process acknowledges the well-documented "implementation dip" that occurs with new programs; in the dip during the early implementation stages, scores may fall slightly before they grow dramatically (Fullan, 2001).

Whether to set a standard high rather than low may be a difficult decision. A standard for success that is low may not be compelling to program directors or participants. A standard that is too high may be debilitating. Program directors are hesitant to acknowledge that they failed to meet their goals, yet when those goals are significant, stretch goals, it will be easier to acknowledge falling short.

External standards such as "adequate yearly progress" established in the federal No Child Left Behind Act may also set a standard for success. Such a standard may not, however, be appropriate for all goals. Evaluators will want to determine whether the standard of success for program goals and objectives is reasonable. Involving program stakeholders in establishing standards for acceptable performance is particularly helpful. Such involvement increases their understanding of the program's purpose, may generate increased support for the program, and informs them of the program's expectations.

EXAMINE THE PROGRAM'S THEORY OF CHANGE

Developing a theory of change assists program developers, coordinators, and providers in articulating comprehensively what the staff development program is and how it is expected to produce the intended results. A program's theory of change delineates the causal processes through which change happens as a result of a program's strategies or actions. It links how program developers believe change happens with their choice of actions. The most important component of a theory of change is identifying the underlying assumptions upon which the program is based. These assumptions explain why certain actions or strategies were included. Identifying the assumptions behind the design of a program encourages program designers to ask why they believe the actions included will bring about the results they seek. Program designers articulate not only the components of a program but also an explanation of how the change is expected to occur (Anderson, 2005; Connell & Klem, 2000; Organizational Research Service, 2004; Weiss, 1972). A program's theory of change can be based on existing research, current practice, or program developers' implicit theories of action.

A program's theory of change specifies how a program's goals and objectives are logically related to its inputs (resources) and activities. The theory of change is a comprehensive representation of how the program is intended to work. Patton (1997) describes it as a "straightforward articulation of what is supposed to happen in the process that is intended to achieve desired outcomes" (p. 223). A program's theory of change specifies the goals and the activities—the series of actions that are likely to lead to the attainment of both the short-term outcomes and the long-term goals (the results).

Figure 4B A Simple Theory of Change for Staff Development

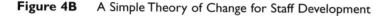

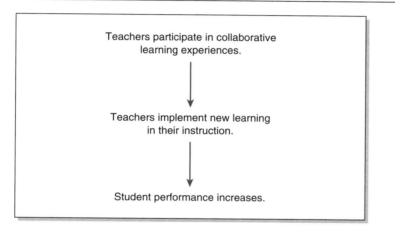

Possible Theories of Change

The field of staff development has proposed several commonly accepted theories of change. Some of these theories have emerged from research and successful practice in adult learning, school improvement, or staff development. These theoretical and practical approaches to improving educator and student learning can assist program developers as they design their programs.

One theory of change draws on research by Joyce and Showers (2002). They identified four components of training that relate to a participant's ability to apply new information to solve real-life problems. These components are presentation of theory, demonstration, low-risk practice, and study groups, coaching, or other forms of follow-up (Joyce & Showers, 2002). If a program developer were designing a staff development program with the goal of developing and transferring new instructional or leadership practices, she might choose to use this research to construct the theory of change of her program so that it incorporated knowledge, skill building, and support as prerequisites to application of new learning.

If, however, she believes that people move through stages of concern and various levels of use before they are able to focus on the consequences of their work and collaborate with others, she might use the research that emerged from the Concerns-Based Adoption Model (Hall & Hord, (1987) to design her program. In this way she would ensure that her program design incorporated ways to address stages of concern (from awareness to refocusing) and to move participants through levels of use from nonuse to routine use.

The levels of evaluation (discussed earlier) are another theory of change. Program managers may view the levels as a sequence of actions: Teachers enjoy their learning, acquire knowledge and skills, and apply them, and student learning increases. Adopting this theory of change assumes that educators will follow this process: First, they engage in a learning experience that they enjoy or find valuable. Second, they increase their understanding, as demonstrated by an increase in knowledge and skills. Third, they have the necessary organizational context to implement the new practices. Fourth, they apply their learning in the classroom. Last, their actions produce changes for students.

Figure 4C   Theory of Change—Staff Development in Reading

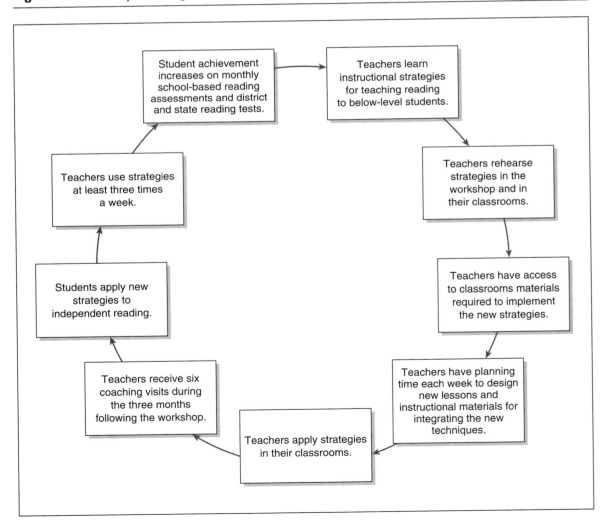

The theory of change depicted in Figure 4C is based on these assumptions:

- Teachers' understanding of various instructional strategies precedes their use of them.
- In order to use new instructional strategies, teachers have the appropriate material, human, and time resources.
- Success builds with an increase in practice and support.
- Classroom-based coaching is the best way to support teachers as they apply new practices.
- Consistency and accuracy in implementation of new practices come over time.
- Student achievement comes from consistently applied, research-based instructional practices delivered by teachers who have in-depth understanding of content and content-specific instructional strategies.

Various choices of theory are possible, the choice depending on the assumptions of the staff development leader about how his or her program works. The measure of good theories of change, according to Connell & Kubisch (1998) and Connell & Klem (2000), is fourfold: (1) they are plausible—evidence and common sense suggest that the specified activities will lead to the desired results; (2) they are doable—the initiative has adequate financial, technical, political, institutional, and human resources to implement the strategies; (3) they are testable—the pathways of change are specific and complete enough, with measurable indicators and specified preconditions for tracking the progress in a credible and useful way; and (4) they are meaningful—stakeholders perceive that the results are important and that the magnitude of change the program will bring about is worthwhile.

Some current programs do not have a clearly designed or articulated theory of change. In such cases, an evaluator might use the inductive approach to develop the program's theory of change. To do this, data are collected, and then a model based on those data is designed to depict the relationship between a program's activities and its outcomes.

Why Articulate a Program's Theory of Change?

Clearly articulating a program's theory of change is beneficial for several reasons. It clarifies what the program is and creates a common understanding among all stakeholders. Both program directors and participants will have a big picture of the scope of the program and their respective responsibilities related to it. They will also have an understanding of the results the program intends to achieve. The evaluator will be able to work with the program stakeholders to establish what they want to learn by conducting an evaluation at this point of the program and determine those aspects of the program on which to focus the evaluation's data collection.

When the program's theory of change is fully developed, many implementation problems are eliminated from the planning stages. The theory of change will identify the sequence of activities that will logically lead to the desired results. If any of the activities cannot be fully supported or implemented with available resources or do not achieve their intermediate outcomes, then program developers must seriously consider whether the overall program is likely to produce the intended results. In this case, program developers may need to discontinue plans for an evaluation until all essential components of the program are planned. Attainment of the intended results will depend upon implementation of the entire program plan.

A program's theory of change helps with the ongoing evaluation of a program. With a theory of change articulating how the program results are achieved, the evaluator can better determine what aspects of the program to examine in ongoing evaluations. The evaluator is in a better position to focus on the particular components that may need closer examination to determine their contribution to the program's results. Program designers may alter or refine the program's theory of change as the program evaluation occurs to best reflect what occurs throughout the program and to better depict the causal assumptions of the program.

A program's theory of change can be beneficial to the field of staff development by providing models for others to consider in the design of their staff development efforts. Since each situation is unique, program designers alter theories of change to adapt to the particular context of each innovation. Having a larger pool of possible theories of change to examine and compare contributes to conceptual understanding about staff development and prevents the need to reinvent the wheel with the development of each staff development initiative.

The following case study illustrates the value of a theory of change.

A Case Study: Articulating a Theory of Change

A middle school adopted teaming to increase students' academic achievement. Before it implemented teaming, the school planning team designed an extensive staff development program for the school year. The team worked with students, parents, and the community to help them understand teaming and its advantages to middle-grade students. In addition, they agreed to help the principal place teachers on teams. They developed a simple theory of change for their work. This theory of change is based on the teachers' understanding of adolescent development, the Carnegie Corporation's *Turning Points 2000*, and their past experience with developing and designing new programs.

In the spring before the scheduled implementation of teaming, the district announced a massive budget reduction. As a result of the budget reduction, the middle school lost all its extra funding to implement teaming. Consequently, the extra team planning time that had been allocated had to be eliminated. In consultation with the staff, the school planning team unanimously agreed to move forward with implementation, even though teams would not have common planning time during the school day to meet as a team. The principals asked teams to designate time before or after school to meet and promised to keep faculty meetings to a minimum to allow time for team meetings. Some teams were able to meet; some met without those members who had extracurricular responsibilities; some teams did not meet.

When the district staff developer came to assist the school planning team in designing an evaluation of their pilot, he questioned the value of conducting the evaluation because a critical step of their planned program was missing.

Figure 4D   An Example Theory of Change

1 Teachers develop a deep understanding of the principles of learning.	2 Teachers describe characteristics of a team they would work well with.	3 Learning is implemented.
4 Teachers have regular team planning time.	5 Teachers use planning time for instructional design and analysis.	6 Teachers closely monitor students' academic progress in all content areas.
7 Students' sense of belonging improves.	8 Students know where to get help.	9 Students' academic achievement increases.

He asked the planning team how likely it was that the intended results had occurred, since the intended plan had not happened. He wanted them to consider the value of conducting the evaluation of a clearly defined program that was only partially implemented. While the school planning team was still enthusiastic about their teaming efforts, he wanted them to understand that there were several potential problems with continuing the evaluation as it had been planned.

One problem was related to the likelihood of having achieved the intended results. Adding common planning time to the program's theory of change was not accidental. It was done intentionally to strengthen the implementation of the teaming program. Teachers' commitment to teaming was largely based on the expectation for common planning time. If teachers' commitment was based on planning time and planning time was no longer feasible, teachers' commitment might wane. If teachers' commitment waned, then it might be unreasonable to expect that the program would produce the student results as outlined in the original plan.

What teachers at this school had done was not teaming as they had defined it. It may have been labeled teaming, but because it lacked one of the key elements of teaming (collaborative planning time), it should not be considered teaming. Nevertheless, it would not be surprising to hear teachers at this school say, "Been there, done that," as frequently happens when staff development initiatives or other reforms are poorly implemented. If district officials concluded that teaming was ineffective after conducting an impact evaluation of the teaming pilot at this school, they might discontinue any further discussion of teaming in the entire district. This would be an unfortunate occurrence because the program's theory of change was sound, logical, and well supported by research, and if the program had been fully implemented, would likely have produced results for students.

The staff developer in this district worked with the school planning team to redesign the evaluation. Instead of determining how teaming affected student achievement, he helped them think about evaluating the components that they had implemented—the degree to which teachers understood teaming and were able to implement it on each of their teams, students' sense of belonging and knowledge about how to get help, and needs for additional organizational support and staff development to support ongoing implementation and improvement of teaming.

Program developers do not always clarify or articulate their assumptions about how their programs should work. In many cases, they focus their attention on just one aspect of the program, such as the training aspect, and neglect the many other essential components that ensure that new learning is transferred to the classroom. Some of these other components include changes in the organizational context, leadership development, and providing essential resources. Results-based accountability to produce initial, intermediate, and intended outcomes requires evaluators to establish their theory of change and identify indicators or benchmarks of progress throughout the intended sequence of events.

EXAMINE THE PROGRAM'S LOGIC MODEL

Sometimes the terms *theory of change* and *logic model* are used interchangeably. Other times, their definitions overlap. For example, Wholey (1987) states, "A program's theory of change identifies program resources, program activities, and intended program outcomes and specifies a chain of causal assumptions linking program resources, activities, intermediate outcomes, and ultimate goals" (p. 78). Patton (1997) also blends the two: "The full chain of objectives that links inputs to activities, activities to immediate outcomes, immediate outcomes to intermediate outcomes, and intermediate outcomes to results constitutes a program's theory of change" (p. 218).

In this book, a theory of change is distinguished from a logic model. A *theory of change* identifies the chain of causal actions that will lead to the intended results. It is a strategic picture of how the program actions will produce results. A *logic model* includes the theory of change and outlines the program resources or inputs and the actions or strategies program designers plan to use to produce the results (theory of change), and the outputs each action produces. A logic model serves to guide the evaluation design and particularly the formative evaluation because it identifies both the initial and intermediate outcomes of the action contained in the theory of change. These initial and intermediate outcomes serve as benchmarks of the program's progress toward its goals. A logic model is a tactical explanation of the process of producing results (Shapiro, 2005).

A logic model is one way to expand a program's theory of change (see examples in Figure 4E and in Table 4.4). A logic model is a flowchart that sequences the critical components of a program.

Table 4.3 A Logic Model for a Staff Development Initiative in Reading

GOAL: Students will become proficient lifelong readers who read both for learning and enjoyment.				
Inputs	*Activities*	*Initial Outcomes*	*Intermediate Outcomes*	*Intended Results*
Full-time literacy coaches for each low-performing school and half-time coaches for middle- and high-performing schools.	Principals hire literacy coaches. Central office staff develops and implements professional development for coaches.	Coaches develop knowledge and skills for coaching teachers.	Coaches conduct regularly scheduled professional development and coaching sessions with new teachers.	Year 1: 60% of the students score proficient or above on the state reading test in Grades 3-8. Students read at least 30 minutes a week for pleasure.
Human and fiscal resources to provide teacher professional development and follow-up support.	Central office staff develops and implements professional development for all classroom teachers. Literacy coaches provide bi-weekly coaching to all teachers.	Teacher knowledge and skills for teaching reading to all students increases.	Teachers apply strategies in their classrooms on regular basis with support from coaches. Teachers have monthly study groups to refine their understanding of the reading process.	Year 2: 80% of the students score proficient or above on the state reading test in Grades 3-8. Students read at least 60 minutes a week for pleasure.
Ongoing assessment of student progress.	Teachers collect and report student progress data every six weeks.	Teachers, principals, and literacy coaches use student progress data to identify students needing extra assistance.	Teachers and coaches use student data to design instructional interventions for those students who need extra assistance.	
Human and fiscal resources to provide principal professional development in observation and coaching.	Central office staff designs and implements professional development for principals. Principals conduct monthly walk-throughs in each classroom.	Principals develop knowledge and skills for conducting walk-throughs and coaching teachers. Principals gain familiarity with new instructional strategies.	Principals provide support and monitor teachers' use of instructional strategies and review student progress data. Uninterrupted blocks of time for reading are created.	Year 3: 100% of the students score proficient or above on the state reading test in Grades 3-8. Students view reading as a life-long tool for learning and enjoyment.
Additional reading materials for all schools.	Reading materials are selected and purchased.	Students and teachers use new reading materials.	New reading materials are used in classrooms.	

(Continued)

Table 4.3   (Continued)

Inputs	Activities	Initial Outcomes	Intermediate Outcomes	INTENDED RESULTS
High-quality instruction for students.	Teachers apply reading strategies they learned in their classrooms.	Students learn strategies for improving their reading performance.	Students apply the new strategies in reading for both learning and pleasure.	

Figure 4E   An Example Logic Model

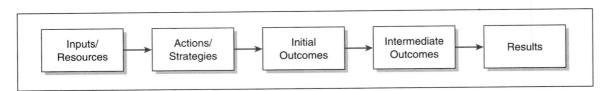

The components of a logic model

Inputs

The resources, personnel, facilities, equipment, etcetera used to accomplish the program's activities. Inputs are essential to consider early in the program's design because program activities may be limited by available resources. One common reason staff development interventions fail to produce results for students is that they have inadequate resources to deliver what is necessary to promote educator learning and support the implementation of that learning.

Activities

The services a program provides to accomplish its goals; activities may be the focus of formative or process evaluations. After implementation, some program activities may be found to be more beneficial than others, and program developers may alter their theory of change to reflect that. Activities may appear to be discrete events, but they are not. They are implemented with coherence with the intention of working together to produce results for adults and students.

Initial Outcomes

Products of a program's activities or services; they include changes in participants' knowledge, attitudes, and skills. These changes have little inherent value in themselves yet are important because they lead to the desired results.

Intermediate Outcomes

Benefits to participants during or after their involvement with the program; these benefits can be defined in terms of changes in aspirations or behaviors that result from the changes in knowledge, attitudes, and skills.

Results (Goals)

Intended, desired impact on students' learning; the ultimate goals of the program.

Context

The conditions under which the program is operational, including the external factors that might influence its success; characteristics of the program participants or staff; or other social, economic, or political factors that may intentionally or unintentionally influence the program's results.

Developing a Theory of Change and Logic Model

This information is adapted from "Logic Models: A Tool for Telling Your Program's Performance Story" (McLaughlin & Jordan, 1999). Developing a program theory of change is a collaborative effort that is best done by a representative group of stakeholders. Including multiple perspectives and ideas is beneficial and enriches the outcome.

Determine the Program Needs and Context

A design team that typically includes the program director, representative stakeholders, and the evaluator begins with a clear understanding of the program needs and the problem to be addressed by the program. Clarifying the problem, the context, and the limitations will help the design team be more focused and realistic in the design of the program.

Determine the Type of Theory of Change

Sometimes a program director, together with a stakeholder team and the evaluator, will develop a tentative theory of change they want to assess and modify as the program is implemented. Other times, a firm theory of change will depict the entire operation of a program and be used as a monitoring vehicle. Other times, the assumptions on which a program is based will be delineated and examined throughout the program for their correctness.

Determine What Is Known

One way to develop a theory of change and logic model for a program is to begin with what exists and what is known about the resources, activities, initial and intermediate outcomes, and results. By sketching those out first on a large piece of chart paper, the design team will see the gaps.

Brainstorm Elements

Sometimes the design team examines the categories described above and brainstorms elements that would fall into each category. For example, what are all the possible resources we might need? What are all the activities we could do?

Create Logical Sequence

Then, using a flowchart, the design team maps the logical sequence of the elements, linking those that go together. For example, if one of the activities is to provide classroom coaching, a necessary resource is classroom coaches. The diagram helps stakeholders understand the underlying assumptions and connections among various components of the program.

Verify the Model

Those who create the program's theory of change and logic model will want to share their draft with their colleagues for their reaction and input. The broader the perspectives of stakeholders who will review the model, the more likely the model will address all stakeholders' needs and be successful in guiding the program to achieve its intended results.

ASSESSING THE THEORY OF CHANGE AND LOGIC MODEL

One of the evaluator's tasks is assessing the program's theory of change and logic model. After working with the stakeholders to clarify the theory of change and logic model, the evaluator might use the rubric in Table 4.4 to assess the program's design and determine that it is ready to be evaluated.

If, after a careful assessment of evaluability of a staff development program, both the evaluator and the program stakeholders agree that the staff development program is well conceived, logically planned, and likely to produce the intended results and the evaluation is warranted, the next step is to design the evaluation questions and framework. To decide that a program is not evaluable and the evaluation is not warranted at this point should not be considered a sign that the program is ineffective or a failure. In fact, it is better to postpone an evaluation when the conditions for success are not present.

The flaws or deficiencies most likely indicate that further clarification of the program is necessary before initiating the evaluation. Addressing the deficiencies at this stage would ensure that the evaluation produces the most useful information and that any investment in the evaluation is well spent.

Table 4.4   Evaluability Assessment Rubric

Area	Redesign Before the Program Begins	Revise Before the Program and Evaluation Begins	Ready to Evaluate
Goals	Program goals are fuzzy or unclear.	Program goals state the desired results in vague terms and/or are means-focused only.	Program goals state clearly the desired end result in specific terms and are focused on student results.
Objectives	Objectives are stated in imprecise terms.	Objectives identify some of the changes needed to produce the results.	Objectives specify the specific changes desired and expected for both the clients and the agents.
Standard of Success	Standard of success is expressed in terms of increase or decrease only, with no specific targets.	Standard of success is set too low or too high, resulting in a standard that is either uninspiring or unreasonable.	Standard of success is challenging, motivating, and reasonable.
Theory of Change	Theory of change is missing.	Theory of change identifies key actions without underlying assumptions, the actions are insufficient to produce the desired results, or the assumptions offer little explanation about the selection of actions.	Theory of change identifies the key actions of the program in a causal process and is accompanied by the underlying assumptions that explain why the actions were included and how they will produce the expected results.
Logic Model	The logic model is missing.	The logic model is missing components, or the components are not aligned with one another. The logic of the logic model is fuzzy.	For each action of the theory of change, the logic model identifies the inputs necessary to conduct it, the initial and intermediate outcomes each action will produce, and the desired or intended result (goal).

Planning Phase

- Assess evaluability
- Formulate evaluation questions
- Construct the evaluation framework

Conducting Phase

- Collect data
- Organize, analyze, and display data
- Interpret data

Reporting Phase

- Disseminate and use findings
- Evaluate the evaluation

Formulate Evaluation Questions

5

Thoughtfully crafted evaluation questions give structure and focus to the evaluation framework. Evaluation questions specify what information the intended users hope to gain from the evaluation. Knowing the intended use of the information helps the evaluator make other critical decisions for the evaluation framework. Well-defined evaluation questions facilitate both design of the evaluation and use of the findings.

At this stage, the evaluator seeks to answer several key questions:

1. What questions does the evaluation seek to answer? Are they clear and understood by key stakeholders?

2. Are the questions logically aligned with the program's goals, objectives, and activities?

3. Do the questions guide decisions about design, data collection, and analysis?

4. Can the questions be answered?

5. Do the questions accurately reflect the understood purpose of the evaluation?

6. Are the intended uses and users of the evaluation evident?

TYPES OF EVALUATION QUESTIONS

Preparing focused evaluation questions will prevent problems during the evaluation. Too many questions may distract from what is most important, may place an added burden on the evaluator or the informants and those who provide the data, and may cause problems with data analysis (Weiss, 1998). In an evaluation, stakeholders typically have more questions than can be answered.

Table 5.1 Approaches for Focusing Evaluation Questions

Intended User	Information Desired	Type of Evaluation Question	Possible Evaluation Question
Staff Development Director	Program need	Need for program	*What do we know about elementary teachers' current content knowledge in science?*
Staff Development Director	Program operation	Linking process and outcome	*What aspects of the program are most salient in producing intended results?*
Principal	Accuracy of implementation	Program process	*How accurately is the program being implemented?*
Teachers	Impact on teaching behavior	Program intermediate outcomes	*How is the program influencing my teaching decisions?*
School Board Members	Impact on student results	Program outcomes (results)	*Is the program increasing student achievement?*

This is particularly true when there are many intended users who are searching for information for very different purposes. For example, a staff development director may want to know whether the program design is working; principals may want to know whether the program is being implemented correctly in classrooms; school board members may want to know what impact the program is having on student learning; teachers may want to know how the program affects their teaching decisions; others in the field of staff development or those responsible for developing programs themselves may want to know what worked and why. Each of these uses suggests the need for a different evaluation question. Table 5.1 shows such differences in focus. Each question is distinct, and the evaluation may require that different data be collected and analyzed to answer all of them.

Evaluation questions fall into several categories, and they parallel the purposes of evaluations. The categories—program need, program design, program process, program impact, and multiple reforms—offer evaluators a way to help stakeholders clarify what they want to learn from the evaluation.

Program Need Questions

Before planning any program, both staff development leaders and providers assess the context and characteristics of the environment and the participants. This initial activity is the planning evaluation; it will often yield more details about the evident problem or need. Without this type of information, program planners might miss the mark completely. Conducting a thorough needs assessment allows staff development leaders to make specific recommendations for program activities and resources to stakeholders.

Program Design Questions

Evaluations related to program design focus on the program's theory of change, its perceived logic, and its potential to produce results. Discussed extensively in Chapter 4, "Assess Evaluability," this form of evaluation increases the likelihood that the planned resources and activities will lead to the immediate and intermediate outcomes as well as the program's intended results. Before they implement a program fully or even conduct a pilot study, evaluators can conduct a program design evaluation. By this process, minor or major revisions can be made either before any implementation takes place or before implementation moves to full scale.

Program Process Questions

Program process evaluations, or formative evaluations, focus on implementation and the operation of the program and can improve or strengthen a program's design. Knowing the extent to which a program is carrying out its intended functions with fidelity to the design is important for several reasons. First, program directors will want to know whether the program process is working and, if not, how to improve it. Second, to determine whether the program has merit or worth, it will first be necessary to know whether the program is operational.

Those involved with staff development efforts often form conclusions about a program's effectiveness without substantial information about the status of the program's implementation. Uninformed conclusions can lead to the elimination of a program with implementation problems yet still has strong potential for producing results. Numerous educational innovations have been abandoned without adequate evaluation of the implementation phase of the intervention.

Some evaluations of programs often merely monitor the process. Monitoring is a systematic documentation about program components or features and allows the evaluator to make judgments about the operation of the program but not about the effects of the program. This distinction is essential. Program process evaluations are designed to assess whether the program is operating as planned or intended. If done well, however, they can contribute other useful information.

Program Impact Questions

An evaluation that focuses on outcomes seeks to determine consequences or impacts of the program. Specifically, it attempts to determine what has changed as a result of the program. Changes can occur in knowledge, skills, attitudes, behaviors, or circumstances. Questions for program outcome or impact evaluations usually relate to the program's goals and what the program is ultimately expected to achieve. Because goals change during a program's implementation, program designers may need to modify program goals to reflect those changes. At other times, outcomes of the program may be unexpected. Evaluators must be open to learning about both anticipated and unanticipated outcomes.

In evaluations of staff development, program staff can examine changes in educators' and students' knowledge, attitudes, skills, aspirations, and behaviors. The premise of this work is that changes in educators are intermediate outcomes and only changes in student achievement are the intended results of any staff development program. Other program directors and evaluators may disagree and consider changes in educators or schools as appropriate results of staff development.

A danger in impact evaluations is the tendency to suggest a causal link between the program and its intended outcome. Evaluators must be cautious about implying causality when the evaluation design or data do not support the inference of causality. To establish causality requires rigorous research design that is often not feasible in schools. Rather than focusing on whether staff development caused an increase in student achievement, evaluators can help staff development leaders and policy makers understand how staff development contributes to student achievement.

Questions to Guide Multiple Reforms

In complex systems such as educational institutions, a mixture of factors work together to produce results. If we accept this premise, we will need to know how to strengthen each factor and improve how it interacts with all other factors.

Most new initiatives, in reality, incorporate multiple reforms at a single time. If a school or district has significantly strengthened its staff development program, some of the following hypothetical changes may have taken place. More time may be devoted to professional development. The improvement plan may be more focused. There may be more distributed leadership; more financial and human resources for staff development; or a new curriculum, assessment, or instructional program—perhaps all of these. Some leaders in the district may think it is important to identify which of these reforms *alone* caused an increase in student achievement. Answering this question might be a multiyear endeavor and could be a very expensive and complex process. Is it important to know whether one factor caused the change? And, even if one factor were eventually shown to be the cause, are the other factors then irrelevant? Is it possible to have high-quality staff development without any of these other elements and expect significant results? Evaluators and staff developers will want to help policy and decision makers understand how their questions are related to the design and feasibility of any evaluation.

What *is* important for a school or district to know is the degree to which the intended results are being achieved and how staff development is contributing to that end. Guskey and Sparks (1996) proposed a model that depicts the complex relationships of multiple factors that influence student academic success. The model acknowledges that staff development, along with other systemic factors, such as the quality of staff development, administrator support, school culture, teacher knowledge and practices, parent involvement, and parent knowledge and skills, work together to affect student achievement.

The questions guiding the evaluation of staff development, then, should focus on what it is useful to know and possible to know. Good evaluations of professional development require the "ability to ask good questions and a basic understanding about how to find valid answers. Good evaluations provide information that is appropriate, sound, and sufficiently reliable to use in making thoughtful and responsible decisions about professional development processes and effects" (Guskey, 2000, p. 2).

Table 5.2 provides a list of sample evaluation questions that can be tailored to any specific staff development initiative. Some definitions will help readers understand the table. *Stakeholders* are those who have an interest in a program and its success. *Participants* are educators who are involved in professional learning. *Clients* are the students who benefit from educators' learning.

A Case Study

As a part of the implementation of standards-based education, a small district wanted to improve student success by increasing teachers' use of performance assessments. The district accepted the principles of standards-based education that specified (1) a strong curriculum that included content standards, (2) the use of assessment to determine students' progress toward the standards, and (3) instructional strategies that supported depth of content, active engagement, and differentiation. The district's goal was to have all students achieve standards through high-quality teaching, differentiated learning opportunities for students, and organizational support for teaching and learning.

Below are sample evaluation questions related to this situation.

Program Needs

How many teachers understand and use content standards?

To what extent are current teaching practices addressing standards, providing differentiation, and engaging students actively in classroom learning experiences?

What do teachers, principals, and central office personnel believe they need to learn and do to be able to assist their students to achieve standards?

Program Design

Do the planned professional learning experiences meet the standards for high-quality staff development (see Appendix A1)?

Are the program activities logically sequenced?

Are the resources adequate to implement all aspects of the program?

Table 5.2 Types of Evaluation Questions

Type	Sample Evaluation Questions
Need	What is the problem?
	What is the magnitude or scope of the problem?
	What are all the significant characteristics (or features) of the context in which this problem exists?
	Who is most affected by the problem?
	What are the characteristics of the participating educators?
	What services are needed to address this problem?
	What services do participants perceive will address this need?
	What related problems also exist?
	Whose needs are best to address first (e.g., teachers or principals)?
Design	Who is being served by this program?
	Are the planned activities reasonable for those participating?
	Are these activities the best possible ones for this situation?
	To be successful in their role, what qualifications do program staff need?
	How has the staff been prepared?
	What resources are necessary to implement this program?
	Have those resources been allocated?
	What resources have been allocated to this program? Are they sufficient to implement the program?
	What assumptions are being made about the participants, the activities, the resources, or the context?
	Are key personnel in place to monitor, direct, and coordinate the program's activities?
	Has the program's evaluation plan been developed and approved by program stakeholders?
	To what degree is there consensus among key stakeholders about the program's need, design, implementation plan, and evaluation plan?
	Will staff members essential to the program receive the necessary preparation for their new roles?
	Does the sequence of the program's activities seem reasonable?
	What assumptions did program developers make in the development of this program?
	What research supports these design decisions?
Process	Are the program activities being implemented as planned?
	Which clients are being served by the program?
	Who is the program not reaching?
	Are all educators completing all aspects of the program?
	What problems are arising during implementation? How are they resolved?

Type	Sample Evaluation Questions
	Are all participants satisfied with the program's services?
	Are the managerial services being performed well?
	Are resources adequate to implement the plan as intended?
	Are any participants affected more than others?
	What differences occur in implementation?
	How are those differences affecting participant satisfaction and implementation?
	How does the program work?
	What are the most salient features of the program?
	What function does each aspect of the program serve?
	What modifications are necessary to improve the program?
Impact	Are the intended results being achieved?
	What results did the program produce?
	What changes occurred in program participants?
	What impact did the program have on student achievement?
	Do the program activities have a beneficial impact on students?
	Do the program activities have a detrimental impact on students?
	To what degree do participants believe the outcomes are being achieved?
	What contributed to the program's results?
	What explains the program's outcomes?
Multiple Reforms	What are the factors at work in this school or district?
	How are the factors interacting to support or hinder student achievement?
	How does staff development align with curriculum, assessment, and instruction?
	How does leadership support or hinder the implementation and impact of staff development?
	What policies, practices, and procedures support professional learning?
	Do the program activities have a beneficial impact on students?
	Do the program activities have a detrimental impact on students?
	To what degree do participants believe the outcomes are being achieved?
	What contributed to the program's results?
	What explains the program's outcomes?

Program Process

Is the program being implemented as designed?

How many teachers are participating in the professional learning experiences?

Are teachers implementing the practices in their classrooms?

Are teachers seeking and receiving follow-up support?

Are resource materials readily available to teachers?

What teaching practices are changing?

How is teacher content knowledge changing?

Program Impact

Is student achievement increasing?

Is the program producing any results that were unintended?

CHARACTERISTICS OF GOOD QUESTIONS

Good evaluation questions have several characteristics:

Reasonable: Is doable within the scope of resources available, including the evaluator's and staff's time, skill, and the budget.

Appropriate: Aligns with the program's goal and design.

Answerable: Data can be collected to construct answers to the questions.

Specific in its focus on measurable or observable indicators of program success or performance: Guides the evaluator in knowing what success looks like; sets a standard against which to judge success.

Specific in its focus on measures of program performance: Guides the evaluator in selecting appropriate measures of success.

When evaluation questions accurately reflect the purpose of the evaluation and its planned use, and meet the criteria above, the evaluation design can proceed.

EXAMPLES AND COMMENTARY

Four examples of program goals and evaluation goals appear below with some commentary about how each meets the criteria recommended: reasonable, appropriate, answerable, specific about the standard and the measure.

Example One

Program Goal: Increase student achievement in reading and mathematics by 10% on the state reading and math tests in three years.

Program Objective: Increase teachers' repertoire of instruction and assessment options to increase differentiation in instruction and assessment.

Formative Evaluation Question: Did teachers benefit from the multiple intelligences training program?

The question is probably *reasonable* and even *answerable.* The evaluator could ask teacher participants whether they found any benefits from the training. It is not, however, appropriate as a question. One program objective is to increase teachers' repertoire of instruction and assessment options. This question does not specify what kind of "benefit" and it does not suggest a way to measure whether anything has "increased" in relation to the "benefit."

Example Two

Program Goal: Increase students' performance on the state science assessment in scientific inquiry and knowledge.

Summative Evaluation Question: Did students' performance on the fourth- and eighth-grade state science assessments indicate improvement over last year's results?

This question meets the criteria. It is *reasonable* because the state assessment was obviously given the previous year and will be given again; it is *appropriate* because it aligns with the program's intended goals; it is *answerable* because an increase can be measured easily; it specifies the standard, *improvement,* although this criterion could be strengthened; *it specifies the measure,* the state's fourth- and eighth-grade science assessment.

Example Three

Program Goal: Increase students' reading performance by 20% in two years as measured by the state reading tests.

Program Objective: Increase teachers' implementation of guided reading in the daily literacy block.

Formative Evaluation Question: Did student achievement in reading as measured by the Informal Reading Inventory (IRI) increase by one grade level during the school year?

The question focuses on *student achievement,* yet the program is focused on *teachers' implementation* of reading strategies. The question *may be reasonable* for a summative evaluation question, *yet not appropriate* as a formative question because the objective and question are not aligned. It is *answerable*; however, answering it may produce invalid conclusions about the effect of the staff development initiative. The question *does specify the standard,* one grade level. It also *specifies the measure,* the IRI.

Example Four

Program Goal: Increase students' performance on the state test in social studies by 5% annually for the next three years.

Program Objective: Fully implement new social studies curriculum in Grades 5–8.

Formative Evaluation Question: What is the degree to which the new middle school social studies curriculum is fully implemented as measured on the implementation rubric?

This question *may or may not be reasonable.* The implementation rubric may require evaluators to visit each school and collect observations or conduct interviews to determine the level of implementation. There may be unanticipated costs, such as paying staff or consultants to make visits or train for interrater reliability. If these costs have been anticipated and planned, then the question is reasonable. Alternate data-collection methods, such as a survey, could be administered to reduce visitation costs. Another consideration about the reasonableness of this question is the rubric. Whether the rubric has been developed and field-tested or whether it needs to be developed and field-tested will affect the cost of obtaining an answer to this question. If costs for rubric design and data collection have been anticipated and planned for, the question is reasonable. If not, this question may be too expensive to answer.

The question is *appropriate* because it reflects the program's purpose. It is *answerable* if a level or stage of implementation can be assessed, especially if an implementation rubric is available or can be developed. The question *specifies the standard*—full implementation or the highest level on the rubric. The question does not imply that all schools will be at the highest level of implementation. Knowing where they are along a continuum of implementation stages is feasible if "full implementation" and other benchmark stages have been defined by the rubric. The *rubric will be the measure* of implementation.

ESTABLISHING PRIORITIES IN PURSUING QUESTIONS

Various stakeholders in any staff development initiative may believe that answering questions about program need, design, process, and impact are all important. And, although there indeed may be value in answering all the questions, sometimes it is not reasonable or even appropriate to do so. Therefore, the evaluator may prioritize questions to reflect what the stakeholders believe is most important to know at this time. Narrowing or prioritizing the questions can help the evaluator design an evaluation that is more doable and useful.

The evaluator might want to engage in several prioritization exercises with the stakeholders to determine which questions would be most helpful.

Weiss (1998) suggests the considerations in Table 5.3 about selecting or prioritizing questions.

Before moving to the next step, the evaluator probably wants to cull the questions, producing a narrower set to focus the evaluation and ensure that it will be successful. With clear, focused, and prioritized evaluation questions, the evaluator is ready to begin building a framework for conducting the evaluation. Without good questions, the evaluator risks not only resources but also the integrity of the evaluation itself.

Table 5.3   A Process for Prioritizing Questions

Consideration	Notes
Timeline for Decisions	How will the findings from the evaluation be used? Are there deadlines for decisions such as budget planning to consider?
Power of Stakeholders	Who has the most positional power related to deciding which questions are answered? Who is funding the evaluation? What do they want to know? What obligations do the stakeholders have to policy makers, funders, and others?
Gaps in Knowledge Base	What can we learn that hasn't been fully addressed in other evaluations or in the literature? What do we already know fairly well? Where are our uncertainties?
Practicalities	What do we have the knowledge and skill to do? What do we have the resources to do? What do our current data allow us to do?
Program's Theory of Change	What components of the program are most critical or essential for increasing the probability of positive results? What components are not as essential as we thought?
Use of Findings	Who will use these findings, and what will they be used for? Who is invested in the evaluation?
Evaluator Professional Judgment	What do I, as the evaluator, think is most beneficial at this time?

Planning Phase

- Assess evaluability
- Formulate evaluation questions
- Construct the evaluation framework

Conducting Phase

- Collect data
- Organize, analyze, and display data
- Interpret data

Reporting Phase

- Disseminate and use findings
- Evaluate the evaluation

Construct the Evaluation Framework

6

This chapter provides an overview of the tasks in planning a framework for an evaluation and the steps necessary to accomplish this work. The chapter also includes discussion of whether the evaluation should be planned and supervised by an external evaluator or by personnel within the school district or organization providing the staff development program.

INTERNAL OR EXTERNAL EVALUATOR

Because impact evaluation requires specialized knowledge, program designers decide early on whether to use an internal or external evaluator. Reading through the next section may provide some guidance, although some may want to read the entire chapter and return to the next section before making this decision.

Before the step of planning an evaluation framework can begin, the program director and stakeholders collaboratively and carefully consider whether to have an external or internal evaluator. The information in the following section summarizes the pros and cons of both approaches and suggests ways for program leaders and the evaluator to share responsibilities.

Conducting an evaluation requires competency in the field of evaluation. Some of the decisions about the evaluation framework and conducting the evaluation can be technical, and so it is important early in the process for the person responsible for the evaluation to acknowledge his or her strengths and limitations and to identify the support system available to assist at this stage.

Several options are available for conducting evaluations with either an internal or an external evaluator. Each has its advantages and disadvantages. When making decisions about who conducts the evaluation, the following questions and guidelines adapted from *The Program Manager's Guide to Evaluation* (Administration of Children, Youth, and Families, n.d.) might be helpful (see Table 6.1). Table 6.2 will also assist with this decision. If there is a preponderance of *noes* checked in response to the questions in Table 6.3 it may be best to wait until there are adequate funds to hire an outside evaluator. If there is a balance of *yes* and *no* responses and the answer to Question 1 is *yes*, an in-house staff member can serve as the evaluator. Weighing the response to each of these questions and considering the advantages and disadvantages of each type of evaluator will help program directors make the decision about who should conduct the evaluation.

Some programs have a greater cost or perceived significance than others (because of the nature of the program or the source of funding) and may require the objectivity of an external evaluator even though there may be might in-house expertise for conducting the evaluation. When programs have large price tags, are controversial, have divided support, or are viewed as the "silver bullet" for solving problems, it may be best to have an outside evaluator lead the evaluation.

If the stakeholders decide to hire an external evaluator, program directors will want to work closely with the evaluator to establish some parameters and expectations for the work to be done. Often a written contract between the external evaluator and the program director specifies important agreements, such as the purpose of the evaluation, timeline, payment, involvement of participants, and deliverables. One expectation should be for strong collaboration between the evaluator and the program stakeholders. When evaluators work closely with program directors and engage them in the decisions about the evaluation, the evaluation will be more valuable and useful. In addition, evaluators will be building the capacity of the program staff to conduct their own evaluations and appreciate the value of evaluations.

Responsibilities of both the program directors and the evaluator are listed on pages 68 and 69. If program directors act as evaluators, with or without support of colleagues, they will assume the responsibilities of the evaluator in addition to the responsibilities of program director.

Table 6.1   External Versus Internal Evaluation

Independent or external evaluation is best when	• Funders, sponsors, or governing agencies require it. • Concerns about credibility of the evaluation process may arise. • Concerns arise that the decision making during the evaluation may be influenced by the self-interest of the stakeholders. • Using an external agent can increase the objectivity or the perceived validity of the decisions about the evaluation. • Decisions cannot be made internally for some reason.
Participatory or empowerment evaluation is best when	• Participants want to ensure that the evaluation is useful for them. • A sense of ownership among the stakeholders is important. • There is an intent to engage in continual improvement throughout the program. • Building the capacity of others to conduct evaluations or use evaluation processes is a priority.

Table 6.2   Internal Versus External Evaluator

Options for Evaluators	Advantages	Disadvantages
Outside evaluator without support from the program staff	Expertise available Objectivity Credibility of results Efficient process May offer new perspective May save time	May disenfranchise program stakeholders. May not be as useful as possible to program stakeholders. Incurs a cost to hire evaluator. May not have access to essential data or sources. Evaluator may not have investment in the program or its evaluation.
Outside evaluator with support from the program staff	Expertise available Objectivity Credibility of results Useful results Efficient process May offer new perspective	May take time away from program services. Staff may feel burdened. Incurs a cost to hire evaluator and may incur costs from involving staff.
In-house evaluator with support from the program staff, in-house experts, and other technical experts	Technical assistance available Useful results May not require extra costs Builds capacity	Greater time commitment of program staff. Coordination of services from different people. Objectivity may be compromised. Cost of staff time and reassignment of current responsibilities.
Program director with support from an outside evaluator or consultant	Useful results May not require extra costs Builds capacity	May detract focus from program implementation. May take time from program management. Staff may feel burdened by extra responsibility. Evaluator may be less committed to evaluation. Objectivity may be compromised.
Program director without support	Less expensive Useful results Builds capacity	Time commitment may detract from implementation. Objectivity may be compromised. Credibility of results may be questioned. Experience may limit evaluation options and quality.

Table 6.3 Questions for Determining the Need for an Internal or External Evaluator

Program Resource Questions	YES	NO
1. Does the program being evaluated have significant cost or a perceived importance?		
2. Will an internal evaluation have the necessary credibility?		
3. Are additional funds available, or can existing resources be redirected for the evaluation of this program?		
4. Are evaluation data collected as a regular part of the program's operation?		
5. Are there colleagues in-house, such as an assessment coordinator or a research and evaluation expert, who can lend expertise to the evaluation?		
6. Have you or your staff conducted similar evaluations previously with success?		
7. Do you or your staff members have the appropriate expertise for this evaluation?		
8. Is the program design aligned with the evaluation's purpose?		

Responsibilities of Program Directors in Evaluation

- Work closely with the evaluator to ensure that he or she understands the program, the context, the goals of the evaluation, the audience(s) for the evaluation report, and how the evaluation will be used.
- Provide feedback to the evaluator about
  ○ the evaluation design
  ○ the data-collection tools

- Keep program staff and other stakeholders informed about the progress of the evaluation.
- Keep evaluator informed about modifications in the program.
- Meet regularly with the evaluator to stay informed about the evaluation process, solve problems related to it, discuss its progress, and contribute to the data interpretation.
- Coordinate any in-house evaluation responsibilities.
- Review the draft report for clarity and usefulness and help the evaluator write for the intended audience.

Evaluator Responsibilities

- Work collaboratively with the program director, staff, and key stakeholders.
- Design the evaluation framework and present a written agreement about the evaluation framework to the program director.

- Meet regularly with the program director to review the progress of the evaluation, solve problems related to the evaluation, and provide updates on the evaluation.
- Protect confidentiality and anonymity of data sources as appropriate.
- Adhere to *Program Evaluation Standards* and *Guiding Principles for Evaluators* (see Appendix A).
- Complete all aspects of the evaluation framework according to the written plan.
- Present the evaluation findings as appropriate and as requested by the program director.

VISUALIZING THE EVALUATION FRAMEWORK

Once the decision has been made and an internal or external evaluator has been designated, the evaluator can begin to visualize the evaluation framework by asking these questions:

- What are the key constructs that will be measured?
- What change am I hoping to find in student achievement? How will I know whether student achievement has occurred?
- Do I need to know whether the change is a result of the staff development program?
- What source of information will allow me to know whether the planned changes in student achievement occurred? Do I need multiple sources and types of data to answer this question or to strengthen my findings?
- What change am I hoping to find in educators? How will I know those changes have occurred?
- What do I need to know about the nature of educator practice before and after the staff development program?
- What do I need to know about the strategies and content used in the staff development program to encourage changes in practice?
- Who has this information? Which people or documents can provide this information?
- How will I gather or collect the information from each source? What tools or process will I use to gather the information I need?

The Big Picture: Evaluation Framework Components

The evaluator will need to answer these questions in order to construct the framework. The worksheet in Appendix D may help the evaluator plan. Consider Table 6.4, which provides some examples of how the evaluation framework may begin to evolve (see page 71).

Evaluation Framework Components

Program Goals

What does the program intend to accomplish?

Measurable Objectives

What changes are anticipated for students? To what degree? What changes are anticipated for educators? To what degree?

Information/Data Needed

What is the best way to determine whether the change has occurred? What information will tell us that?

Data Source

What/Who is the best source of information about the intended change? What is already available? What might have to be created to gather the information needed?

Data Collection

How will the data be collected?

Data Analysis

How will the data be examined to determine whether change did occur? Will descriptive or inferential statistics be needed?

Timeline

When will data be collected?

Location

Where will data be collected?

Making Decisions About the Framework

After gaining clarity about the evaluation questions and the purpose of the evaluation, the evaluator decides whether the evaluation is worth doing and, if so, how to construct an evaluation framework that will serve as the action plan for completing the evaluation. The evaluation framework serves to provide a big picture of what the evaluation looks like. "The word *design* doesn't mean 'plan' in the broad sense. It refers to the specification of which groups to study, how many units in a group, by what means units are selected, at what time intervals they are studied, and the kinds of comparisons that are planned. As questions refer to the content of the study, design is its structure" (Weiss, 1998, p. 87). The framework includes tasks to be completed, a timeline, and resources to help the evaluator map out his or her responsibilities. The success of the evaluation depends upon effectively planning what data to collect, when to collect them, and how to collect them.

Deciding How to Answer the Evaluation Questions

In preparing the evaluation framework, the evaluator determines the type of evaluation he or she is conducting, based on the evaluation questions that have just been formulated. In most cases, the evaluation questions will ask

Table 6.4 Beginning Steps of an Evaluation Framework

I need to know	By collecting the following kinds of information	Information will be most useful if it comes from	The data will need to be collected by
Has the staff development program impacted student achievement?	Change in students' academic (cognitive) achievement	Students Teachers Documents (test scores)	Tests Performance tasks Portfolios Document analysis Teachers' judgments about student achievement Students' judgments about their own achievement
How have students been impacted by the staff development program?	Changes in student cognitive/academic achievement Changes in behavior (participation/attendance) Changes in attitude Changes in aspirations	Students Teachers Documents Principals	Tests Performance tasks Documents/records Surveys Observations
How have teachers been impacted by the staff development program?	Changes in teacher knowledge or skills Changes in behavior, such as participation in leadership roles attendance, morale, or job performance Changes in attitude Changes in aspirations	Students Teachers Documents Principals	Tests Performance tasks Documents/records Surveys Observations
What components of the staff development program have been most influential in impacting student achievement?	Weight of components of the staff development program	Trainers Coaches Teachers	Surveys Interviews Focus groups
Has the staff development program changed teachers' instructional practices?	Change in teacher instructional practice	Teachers Principals Coaches	Observations Surveys Interviews Rating scales
Is the staff development program being implemented accurately?	Comparison between what was planned and what is occurring	Program manager Program designer Teachers Students	Records Surveys Observations Interviews Focus groups

about the impact of the staff development program on student learning. Impact evaluations require different kinds of data from planning or implementation evaluations. They require the use of comparison groups to determine whether the staff development program is responsible for the change.

Choosing an Evaluation Design

The evaluator carefully examines the purpose of the evaluation and the questions to be answered to determine a "line of inquiry." What key concepts will be measured? How will they be measured? How will the data from those measures be analyzed to construct the answer to the evaluation questions? To construct the evaluation design and corresponding data plan (the line of inquiry) the evaluator revisits this particular program's identified theory of change. The evaluator identifies the key concept(s) related to each step of the theory of change and identifies the best possible method and source for obtaining that information. The evaluator also decides what method he or she will use to obtain descriptive, exploratory, or explanatory information that will serve as the basis for inferences or conclusions about the relationship between the program and the results observed.

Evaluators choose from among several designs for the evaluation. They are experimental, quasi-experimental, descriptive, naturalistic, and mixed method. Each will be described briefly.

Experimental design allows the evaluator to form a conclusion about whether the changes that occurred can be attributed to the program. That is, did the program cause the changes? Using random assignment of participants to either a control or a treatment group, the evaluator looks at the differences that occur between the two groups after the treatment. Quasi-experimental design uses comparison of the program participants and nonparticipants when they have not been randomly assigned. The comparison allows the evaluator to determine whether the program had an effect. Descriptive evaluations provide a description of the program's actions and the results obtained. Sometimes descriptive evaluations include perceptions of program participants or observations of their behaviors, often from results of a survey. Naturalistic evaluations provide an in-depth analysis of the behaviors, motivation, and attitudes of a small number of participants. Case studies are the most common form of naturalistic evaluations. Mixed-method evaluations use both qualitative and quantitative techniques to answer the questions the evaluation poses. Multiple methods strengthen the validity of an evaluation by overcoming the weaknesses of any one design.

Sometimes evaluators are more concerned about the methodology than about the information they are gathering. But it is crucial that the design selected aligns with the program's goals, evaluation questions, the evaluator's skill, and the resources available for the evaluation. Frequently policy makers want evaluators to prove causality, but it is not frequently the case that they understand the complexity of the design needed to answer questions about causality.

Finally, with key concepts and measures for each step of the program's theory of change, the evaluator has designed a data plan (the detailed line of inquiry) for the evaluation. That data plan will reveal how the components of the program interact to produce results for students. The evaluator can also determine which data are more critical, which are less essential to answer the questions, and how to streamline the data-collection process.

Determining What Kind of Data to Collect

The evaluator wants to prevent needless data collection and infringing on program participants or taxing program staff. Expecting program participants to produce data can create a data burden that by itself will act as a barrier to the program's success. The evaluator wants to consider what types of data already exist within the system and to determine whether they might be a source of evidence before he decides that he will create and implement a new data-collection process. Too often evaluators enter the data-analysis phase awash in data, only some of which are useful to the specific evaluation questions. On the other hand, an evaluator may find when she is beginning the data analysis that she is missing essential data. Time invested in creating a focused evaluation framework prevents such frustrations.

Near the end of an evaluation process, the evaluator and all key stakeholders want to determine whether a program has had an impact. They will look at available data to determine whether something has changed from the time the program began until the present. But what can change? What kind of data must be collected? What data will allow an eventual analysis of changes? Although many changes can occur, such as changes in status, conditions, circumstances, the changes that are most important in staff development are changes in knowledge, attitudes, skills, aspirations, and behaviors. Collected data should provide evidence about the changes that occur in these areas for the target audiences. In results-based staff development, changes in students are expected. But program staff also need to know how to improve a program, or what changes have occurred in educators' knowledge, attitudes, skills, and aspirations or how educators' behaviors influence students. These changes will be the focus of formative evaluations, while changes in students will be the focus of summative evaluations.

Selecting Suitable Formats of Data

Data come in two formats: quantitative and qualitative. Quantitative data are those that can be represented by numbers, while qualitative data are those that are represented by words or images. In this guide, *qualitative* and *quantitative* refer to how the data are represented.

Quantitative data result in scores. Sometimes those scores are from tests, surveys, or other instruments. Whenever data are represented numerically, they are quantitative. Quantitative data are usually analyzed with descriptive or inferential statistics and presented in the form of tables, graphs, charts, or models (Weiss, 1998). Most quantitative data comes from administering an instrument; therefore, the evaluator rarely has personal or direct contact with participants.

Qualitative data, on the other hand, are represented in words, such as in case studies, vignettes, or direct quotes. They result from data-collection methods such as observation, interviews, and focus groups. In analyzing qualitative data, the evaluator typically searches for meaning and analyzes the data for recurring trends, patterns, or themes as a way to make sense of the data. Collecting qualitative data usually places the evaluator in the midst of the program, and his or her presence may have an impact on the results.

Sometimes data from interviews, focus groups, or open-ended surveys are numerically coded, transforming what might appear to be qualitative data into quantitative data. For example, if an interviewer talked with students to ask about the various teaching strategies they recall their teachers using, the data might be left in the words of the children or coded using an established coding system that determined how often children spoke about particular teaching strategies.

The age-old argument about the value of quantitative versus qualitative data continues. The recently adopted guidelines for research by the National Research Council and the U.S. Department of Education exacerbate this argument. It is further compounded by the confusion that occurs when one applies guidelines for research to the field of evaluation, as is happening. The guidelines for federally supported research call for more rigorous quantitative and experimental research in education to counteract what some perceive to be decades of soft (qualitative) research. There is a strong drive to increase the amount of experimental and quasi-experimental research in education. Clinical trials or double-blind studies in medicine are identified as the gold standard for research in education.

The desire for more scientifically based research has impacted the field of evaluation. Greater accountability is driving many evaluators and their clients to opt for evaluation designs that are less descriptive and more quasi-experimental or experimental. In some cases, the use of these designs is both appropriate and doable. Using experimental or quasi-experimental designs increases both the rigor and the validity of the evaluation. But in some cases, and frequently in public education, these designs are inappropriate and unmanageable.

Policy makers and decision makers admittedly have preferences for the kind of data and evaluation designs they find convincing. School boards, superintendents, and central office personnel may find quantitative data more credible. Principals and teachers are pressured by accountability demands to present quantitative data. Yet not all evaluation questions can be answered exclusively with quantitative or qualitative data alone and may require some of both.

DETERMINING WHETHER THE CHANGE IS A RESULT OF THE PROGRAM

If the evaluator wants to answer questions about attribution—that is, "Did the changes occur because of the staff development program?—he or she will set up an experimental or quasi-experimental design for the evaluation. This means that there will be a comparison group, a group of subjects who did not receive the treatment, as well as the group who received the intervention. In staff development, some teachers or principals will not participate in the professional learning experiences, and their students or teachers therefore will not benefit from changes in their practices. For example, an evaluator might compare the performance of those students whose teachers participated in the staff development program with the performance of students whose teachers did not have access to the staff development intervention. Using a comparison group allows the evaluator to rule out, to some degree, other factors that may influence the change and, therefore, to say with some certainty that the changes that occur can be attributed to the staff development program.

Preparing to Compare

Impact evaluation requires knowing whether change did occur. There are several ways to determine change. All involve comparison. Evaluators can make comparisons within the group of participants or with other groups who have not participated in the program. Choosing the basis for intended comparison depends on a number of factors that include time, financial resources, expertise of the evaluator, and availability of nonparticipants.

Ensuring the Ability to Determine Whether Change Occurred

Table 6.5 summarizes the various ways comparisons can be made.

Table 6.5   Types of Comparisons for Impact Evaluations

Type	Advantages	Disadvantages
Individual Comparison Match and compare the scores for the same individuals before and after the intervention.	Looks at individuals rather than the group and may give a more accurate picture of the change. Provides information about changes that occur.	Individual scores may not be available. Does not allow conclusions about attribution. Potentially may have attrition from pretest to posttest in both students and teachers so that it is not possible to form valid conclusions based on the remaining data.
Cohort Group Comparison Compares the pretest and posttest scores of the same group of students.	Provides a view of the entire group. Provides information about the impact of the program.	Will not provide information about individual performance. May not account for differences present in the groups <u>before</u> the staff development intervention or interventions that may have been used in the comparison group <u>during</u> the period of interest.
Panel Group Comparison Compares the posttest scores of the same groups from two different years (e.g., eighth-grade students from one year with eighth-grade students from the next year).	Provides information about the impact of the program.	May not account for differences present in the groups <u>before</u> the staff development intervention or interventions that may have been used in the comparison group <u>during</u> the period of interest.
Selected Comparison Group Compares pretest and posttest scores of different groups, one the group receiving the intervention and another selected for group comparison.	Provides information about the impact of the program. Accounts for differences in the group <u>before</u> staff development. May allow for conclusions about attribution.	Will not provide level of confidence in generalizations without random assignment. May not account for differences present in the groups <u>before</u> the staff development intervention or interventions that may have been used in the comparison group <u>during</u> the period of interest.

Individual and Cohort Comparison Group

One way to measure change is to know the characteristics of the target group before the intervention and after. When comparing individuals or groups to themselves, it is not possible to answer the question "Is the staff development program solely responsible for the change?" Rather, the evaluator can answer the question "Did the staff development contribute to the change?" For example, a teacher might want to know whether using differentiated instructional strategies in mathematics helped students with different learning rates improve. She might look at each student's performance before she used the differentiated strategies and compare it with the student's performance afterward. She can look at individual students and at the class as a whole. Table 6.6 is a graphic representation of this example.

Table 6.6   Cohort Group Comparison of Individual Student Scores

Students	Score Before	Score After	Difference
A	83	92	+9
B	56	62	+6
C	75	84	+9
D	91	94	+3
E	24	39	+15
Mean	65.8	74.2	+8.4

Looking at the student's scores individually helps the teacher develop a better understanding of how the strategies influence different students. Looking only at the class mean does not allow the teacher to see whether the strategies worked better for certain learners. This has some advantages in allowing the evaluator to know whether the change was evenly distributed across those who were involved or whether the change was stronger for some and less so for others. If a classroom teacher were to look at the scores in Figure 6A (below), he might notice that students who scored the highest on the pretest made the least growth and that students who scored the lowest had the highest growth. The teacher who was implementing new instructional approaches to teaching reading in the content area might want to discuss ways to differentiate the strategies in order to accommodate the needs of all students, both high- and low-achieving students equally.

These same results, if examined not by individuals but rather by the group, would tell the teacher that the new instructional strategies were impacting students' learning but would not tell him about how individual students with different performance levels in the pretest phase performed in the posttest phase.

Although Figure 6B shows the difference between the pretest and posttest scores of the entire group, the comparison of individual students in Figure 6A is far more informative. Over time any group is likely to show improvement. Examining how individual students perform and knowing how the teacher

Figure 6A   Difference in Individual Student Scores From Pretest to Posttest

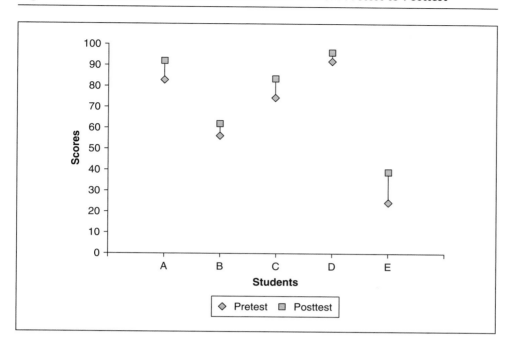

Figure 6B   Difference in Mean Scores From Pretest to Posttest

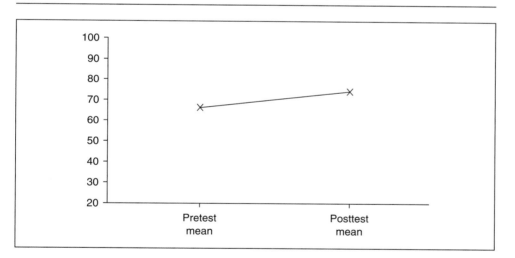

used his or her new knowledge and skills to help individual students will help teachers make sense of the results.

Time-Series Evaluation

Evaluators can make another form of comparison with time-series evaluation studies. Time series means gathering a series of performance indicators or observations from the same group before, throughout, and after the intervention to determine whether there is a difference in the observed variable. Usually time-series evaluations involve a large number of participants, although they can be used effectively by teachers in classrooms to assess the impact of a change in teaching behavior or practice.

English teachers charted their students' errors in usage for two months on classroom assignments and homework. They noticed significant errors in usage. To address this issue, they researched several ways to teach usage to high school students without making the lessons "drill and kill." They piloted several approaches to learn which worked best and then implemented their own customized lessons on usage. After a series of lessons that they planned together and implemented, they continued to chart their students' errors and noticed a significant drop in the occurrence of usage errors in each classroom while continuing to see similar occurrence rates for other errors. They concluded that the lessons helped their students and decided to investigate strategies to address other common errors; they also continued to track usage errors to see whether improvements were sustained.

This example of a time-series evaluation was practical at the classroom level but could obviously be more complex to implement at a district level. A time series may not be feasible if the evaluator has to collect new data from a large number of participants in a short period of time. If either archival or extant data are available, it would be easier to use this design (then the time needed for data collection would not interfere with the observed actions). If the likelihood of collecting a series of similar data is not possible because occurrences of the observed behavior may be sporadic, time-series design may be inappropriate.

Multiple-Interventions Evaluation

A variation of the time-series approach is the multiple-interventions study. If a comparison group is not feasible and the possibility exists to repeat the intervention, the evaluator may want to compare two or more implementations of the intervention. The evaluator might compare the impact of the program in two schools, two districts, or across multiple schools or districts.

An Example: Staff Learns Guided Reading

An elementary school staff participated in a schoolwide professional development program on using guided reading. The district reading coordinator taught the course and worked with the school principal to help her observe classrooms for occurrences of guided reading techniques. Both the district coordinator and the principal were interested in knowing whether the principal's observations influenced teachers' implementation of the guided reading strategies.

To clarify her expectations and increase pressure on teachers to put the new strategies into immediate practice, the principal announced to the staff that she would be observing classrooms during the following week using walk-throughs, a process of making brief targeted observations. This monitoring process was purposeful: The principal and reading coordinator believed that continual application of the strategies would bring about fluency of practice and comfort with the strategies. The walk-throughs served three purposes. Doing them conveyed to the staff the importance of implementing guided reading in their classrooms. Second, they served as a data source for knowing whether guided reading was being implemented. Third, they helped the coordinator and principal determine whether there were problems with implementation that needed to be addressed. The use of guided reading, in turn, would eventually translate into an increase in student proficiency in reading.

With the reading coordinator, the principal made observations using a list of "look fors" that indicated the characteristics of guided reading. Together they noted an average of 18 occurrences in a two-day period in the 20 classrooms they visited. The second week, the principal did not announce that she would visit classrooms, and only the reading coordinator visited. She observed 14 occurrences in the 20 classrooms (not all the same as in previous observations) she visited. The third week the principal announced that she would again observe classrooms using the walk-through process. The principal observed 26 occurrences in the same two-day observation with 20 classroom visits. The walk-through was repeated four weeks later, and occurrence rates increased with each announced walk-through. The principal and reading consultant hoped that increasing the announced visits would encourage more use of the strategies. They predicted (1) that there would be a corresponding increase in teacher reports that they "felt more comfortable with the strategies"; and (2) that teachers would begin to see results in the form of an increase in students' reading performance.

The principal and reading coordinator discussed the findings from the two sets of observations (two distinctly separate trials). They concluded that the principal's expectations and announcements increased the occurrence of guided reading strategies in classrooms. The principal committed to continuing the announcements of walk-throughs as a way to encourage teachers' use of the strategies and eventually to increase student achievement in reading.

Figure 6C   Intervention 1: Number of Occurrences of Guided Reading by Announced and Unannounced Visits

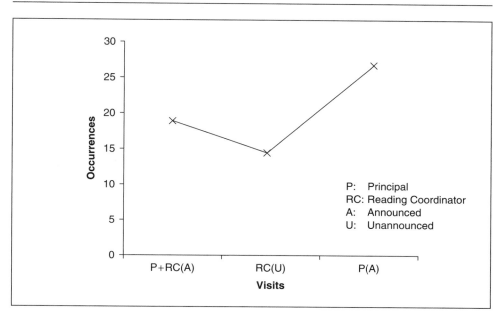

Figure 6D   Intervention 2: Number of Occurrences of Guided Reading by Announced and Unannounced Visits

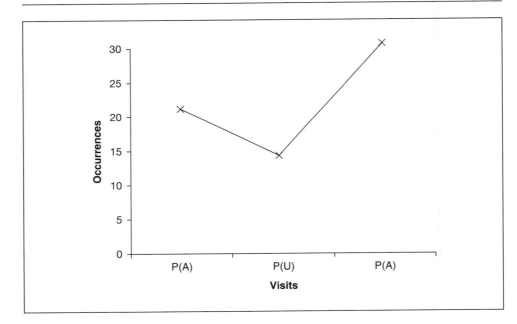

Panel Group Comparison

The district science coordinator offers an intensive staff development program in science. The program involves training, expert observations with feedback, demonstration lessons, peer observations, new instructional resources, and lesson study. Now the coordinator wants to know whether the achievement of eighth-grade students whose teachers participated in the staff development program increased on the annual state test. She examines last year's eighth-grade scores and this year's eighth-grade scores. Since scores increased by more than 9%, she is confident that the staff development program is making a difference. Naturally, this year's eighth-grade group is not composed of the same students, but the comparison is still feasible because she is comparing eighth-grade students to eighth-grade students and the composition of the population of students is adequate to making such a comparison valid. Examining trend data over multiple years increases the validity of the conclusion that the staff development program contributed to the increases in eighth-grade students' science performance. Understandably, there are possibilities that the two groups are not comparable; however, because the group is large and typically representative of the range of students, the comparison is permissible. A panel group comparison can be done if the state test is unchanged year to year or if the scores have been adjusted to account for differences.

Creating or Selecting Comparison Groups

There are three other types of comparison groups that can be created or selected for the purpose of knowing whether the staff development program influenced the results. These three groups are random, matched, and generic.

Table 6.7   Comparison of Mean Scores for Eighth Grade Across Two Years

Grade	Content	2005 Mean Score	2006 Mean Score	Change Score
8th Grade	Science	562	593	+31

Random Comparison

One way to create a comparison group is random assignment of participants either to the group that receives the staff development program or to one that does not. This type of comparison creates the conditions for an experimental study if the group size is sufficiently large. By randomly assigning members to groups, the evaluator is able to assume equivalency of the groups. That is, the groups will essentially have the same characteristics before one receives the intervention. This type of comparison group allows the evaluator to make well-supported conclusions about the impact of the intervention. Using experimental design with random assignment of participants into either the treatment or the control group allows the evaluator to draw conclusions about causality—that is, whether the staff development program caused the changes. It is the only form of comparison that allows such a conclusion.

If the number of classrooms, schools, or districts is large, the evaluator can randomly assign them to comparison or intervention groups. For example, the 120 elementary schools in one district could be randomly assigned. Or the 1,075 classrooms could be randomly assigned. Even though random assignment is possible, an evaluator may choose to use another method for determining comparison and treatment groups. Establishing randomly assigned groups provides evaluators the best possible conditions for drawing conclusions about the program's responsibility for changes that occur.

Yet creating comparison groups by random assignment is difficult in most school settings. Classrooms and schools are intact groups, which makes assignment of individual students, teachers, principals, or schools to a treatment group or a control group difficult. Denial of services to a student or educator who is in need of the particular services the program is providing also creates a potential ethical concern about randomization.

Matched Groups

Selecting similar groups for comparison is another option available for evaluators. Selected comparison groups are perhaps the second-best way to determine whether a program is responsible for the intended impact. This evaluation design is quasi-experimental because the evaluator cannot or chooses not to randomly assign participants to the treatment or control group. Selected comparison groups are often used in educational settings because pure experimental conditions are difficult to create. The quality and validity of the results of this quasi-experimental design vary by the rigor of the comparison established. Rossi, Freeman, and Lipsey (2003) acknowledge that "designing impact assessment, therefore, is generally a matter of weighing the importance of scientific rigor against the practical constraints inherent in the evaluation context" (p. 332).

Equivalent or matched-group comparisons occur when a comparison group resembles the group receiving the treatment. Constructing a comparison group is sometimes possible if there are groups who are qualified to participate but who are not participating for some reason.

The characteristics used to establish the match are critical to the integrity of the comparison. The evaluator must thoroughly know the context and understand the variables and processes that could affect the impact of the program. If the variable to be assessed is "student achievement," then the matched group should have similar achievement levels before the intervention occurs. Matching on other student demographic factors—such as socioeconomic status, mobility rates, gender, age, family background, number of schools attended—sometimes strengthens the basis for the comparison. The extent of the program's overall impact is also clearer in the final analysis of data if both the student's and the teachers' characteristics are matched.

Another consideration in matching is to decide whether there will be individual or aggregate matching. That is, will the entire group of participants be compared and matched with the entire group of nonparticipants? Or will individuals in the nonparticipating group be matched with individuals in the participating group? Matching individuals creates pairs for the purpose of comparison.

Group matching is somewhat easier than individual matching. In education, group matching can be easily accomplished because so many potential, intact nonparticipating groups exist. Classrooms can be matched with classrooms, schools with schools, and districts with districts. These intact comparisons make finding a matched pair more likely.

But evaluators tend to believe that individual matching is preferable to group matching, especially when there are a number of factors used as criteria (Rossi, Freeman, & Lipsey, 2003). The advantages of individual matching are similar to those discussed earlier about individual scores rather than group means but might not be worth the possible additional effort, time, and expense.

Regardless of the method of comparison, it is important to remember that serious problems can occur with either method. What is critical for the evaluator to determine is how rigorous the impact results need to be for the intended use of the information. Sometimes it is possible to approximate impact results through the use of matching groups. For the evaluator, practicality often outweighs what is desirable. The feasibility of a rigorous, purer experimental design often has to give way to practical issues.

A *Case Study:* Increasing Writing Performance

Teachers in one large urban district participated over five years in an intensive staff development program designed to improve teachers' understanding of writing, how children learn to write, and students' performance in writing on both the district's writing sample and on related subtests of the standardized achievement test. The staff development program involved extensive training, demonstration teaching, resource material development and dissemination, classroom coaching, and individual- and grade-level consultation. To support the change in instruction in writing, writing labs were created in the middle and high schools, lay graders were hired to assist teachers with grading writing, and student writing was published annually in a collection of student literary works. The district also instituted a pre- and posttest writing sample in each grade and required students to construct portfolios of their writing to carry with them through their educational career.

Schools were randomly assigned to participate in a three-year rotation with the unwritten assumption that all schools would participate. In the first two years of the program, schools were matched with other schools on the basis of student achievement on standardized achievement tests and district criterion-referenced tests, and also on socioeconomic status. The comparisons made were as shown in Table 6.8, and because of the evaluation results, the program was continued and received additional resources.

Table 6.8   Comparison Groups for Evaluating Staff Development Program in Writing

Year 1

   Year 1 schools compared with nonparticipating schools and the state

Year 2

   Year 2 schools compared with Year 1 schools, nonparticipating schools, and the state

   Year 1 schools compared with nonparticipating schools and the state

Year 3

   Year 1 schools compared with Year 2 and Year 3 schools and the state

   Year 2 schools compared with Year 3 schools and the state

   Year 1, 2, and 3 schools compared with the state

Generic Comparison Groups

When a specific group is not identified as the matched group or a randomized comparison group is not feasible, using a generic, nonprogram comparison group is another option for an evaluator. A generic comparison group is one in which the typical performance of those who did not receive the benefit of the intervention serves as the basis for comparison. For example, one school might choose to compare its mean scores to district or state mean scores. A district might choose to compare its performance to state or national results.

Evaluations using generic comparison groups are less rigorous than those using other comparison groups. Using generic groups suggests that the target population is similar to the typical group. In fact, an intervention program is often designed specifically for a population because it is different from typical groups. It is particularly important to acknowledge that the use of generic comparison groups may underestimate the impact of a program, particularly if the program is intended to provide support to those who are not typical. For example, a staff development program in literacy might be implemented to address the needs of students in high-poverty schools. If achievement levels in the high-poverty schools already lag substantially below typical levels, comparing their student performance to on-grade-level reading performance might suggest that the program was not effective. To the contrary, the program may have been very effective—progress may have been considerable for these students, who originally had very low achievement levels.

Two ways to overcome this problem are by comparing gain scores rather than the performance scores and by comparing the scores of a particular subset of the generic population such as the lowest quartile. Another option is to compare only a portion of the generic population, such as schools that have similar characteristics. Still another option is comparing only a portion of the generic population such as schools that have similar characteristics (e.g., comparable socioeconomic status or comparable percentage of students with limited English proficiency).

ATTRIBUTION AND CONTRIBUTION

Some evaluations are designed to allow the evaluator to draw conclusions that changes that occur are the result of the program and nothing else. *Attribution* implies the program or some aspect of it is solely responsible for the changes that occur. Making claims of attribution is possible only if a comparison can be made with a nonparticipating group when subjects are randomly assigned to participating and nonparticipating groups. Such claims are strengthened if both a pre- and a posttest comparison is made between the two groups. Attribution claims are possible if the changes that occur always occur with the particular intervention and not with any other intervention and if removing the intervention returns the observed change back to its previous condition.

In complex systems such as schools, it is likely that staff development contributes to such changes as improvements in student achievement. Most evaluation studies are not designed to provide evidence to suggest that the program is completely responsible for the changes. Claims of contribution acknowledge there are other factors that might have an impact on student achievement gains, such as new curriculum, improved student test-taking skills, different cohort of students, other professional development the teachers experience, new teachers, or new principal at the school.

An evaluator may identify the changes that occur from the staff development program (contribution) but may not be able to say that the program is solely responsible for the changes (attribution). Even when comparison groups are used, it still may be impossible to draw conclusions about attribution if the evaluation design does not include random assignments of participants to treatment and control groups.

The various evaluation designs are summarized in Table 6.9.

Table 6.9   Summary of Evaluation Designs

Design	Description
Experimental	Random assignment of program participants into treatment and control groups; used to determine cause-effect relationships; allows conclusions about the attribution of the program to results for clients; requires careful control that no other participants other than those included in the control group are accessing the treatment.
Quasi-experimental	Is less restrictive than pure experimental design; used when participants are not or cannot be randomly assigned to treatment and control groups; requires some form of comparison group; usually easier to implement in an educational setting than an experimental design; time-series studies fall into the category of quasi-experimental design.
Descriptive	Used to collect descriptive data about a program, such as how many people participate, characteristics of the participants; typically use surveys, interviews, or focus groups as data-collection methods; permit conclusions about contribution, not attribution, although those conclusions are not particularly strong unless coupled with other data sources and other forms of data collection; in this case, the evaluation becomes a mixed-method evaluation.
Ethnographic	Uses techniques such as observation, interviews, focus groups, and case studies to develop an in-depth understanding about behaviors, attitudes, and aspirations; more flexible than experimental and quasi-experimental designs; used often in exploratory research so the evaluator can become familiar with the problem before generating hypotheses; usually involves a small number of participants.

DATA SOURCES AND COLLECTION METHODS

Once the evaluator knows what the program's desired changes are, he begins to specify how he will know whether they occur. This leads to decisions about the sources of data and data-collection methods. The success of the evaluation largely depends upon three essential tasks: (1) identifying what data to collect, (2) choosing the appropriate source of the data, and (3) selecting the most appropriate data-collection process to gather the data necessary to determine whether a change has occurred. Table 6.10, at the end of this section, offers a sample data-collection plan.

Data Sources

Selecting the appropriate data-collection method is an important decision evaluators make, because the quality of their conclusions rests on the quality of the data they have gathered to support the conclusions. Data sources include students, teachers, principals, central office personnel, parents, others within the community who influence the learning of students, partner organizations such as institutes of higher education, outside experts, national, state, and local databases, documents, records, and reports. When the evaluator knows what data she needs in order to answer the evaluation questions, she will decide on the best source of the information and what the best method of collecting that information is. Sometimes multiple sources of data are preferable to single sources of data.

To improve the support for their conclusions, evaluators seek to find evidence from multiple data sources and to answer their questions through multiple data-collection methods. This process, called triangulation, results in stronger, more valid conclusions. Using multiple data sources and different data-collection methods offsets some of the potential for measurement error or biases in the evaluation. Generally, the more data sources and the greater the variety of data-collection methods, the more credibility in the evaluation results.

An Example: Mannsfield Middle School

Mannsfield Middle School wanted to improve students' literacy performance on the state reading assessment and on a norm-referenced test. To do this, both the principal and teachers wanted more strategies for teaching literacy and reinforcing literacy in all content areas. First of all, teachers needed to know more about the reading process. As middle school teachers, most had taken only one course in reading in the content areas. Consequently, they did not understand how children learned to read or how to teach adolescents the basic reading processes they lacked.

The school staff engaged in more than 30 hours of professional development that included a workshop, coaching, observations with feedback, and study groups. The administrative team conducted weekly walk-throughs of classrooms to examine teachers' practices and provide information to the entire staff about how the various strategies were being implemented. The principal met with each staff member to help him or her develop a personal professional development plan to identify target areas for growth and strategies for achieving those targets. Coaches worked one-on-one with teachers in their classrooms and with grade-level and department teams, devoting most of their time to assisting new staff members. The evaluator worked with the leadership team in the school to establish various ways to collect data about changes in teacher knowledge and practices and student learning without disrupting classrooms or burdening teachers or students with additional testing.

Table 6.10 summarizes the data the evaluator will use in this evaluation.

Multiple types of data sources and data-collection methods allow the evaluators to look at the impact of teachers' increased knowledge and skills on student achievement from different perspectives. The program leaders and evaluator would know whether (1) student achievement increased as it was measured by the selected tests, (2) students' attitudes about reading are more positive, (3) teachers are regularly using the strategies (their behaviors), and (4) students can describe their reading behaviors. With this information, the evaluators are able to determine whether teachers' acquisition of knowledge and additional practice in literacy positively influence students' literacy achievement.

Selecting sources for data is a pivotal decision. The evaluator may have determined the most appropriate data to collect and the best method for collecting but, if the source is not accurate, the entire data set and evaluation can be compromised. It may seem appropriate to ask teachers to recall information about their lessons, but actually checking their classroom lesson plans or student work may be more accurate. When selecting the data sources to use, the evaluator considers whether the data from each source are likely to be accurate, which sources might be more expedient to tap, and whether the actual data collection will pose any excessive burden, potential harm, or threat to the source.

Table 6.10   Data-Collection Plan for the Mannsfield Middle School Evaluation Framework

Data	Data-Collection Methods	Timeline
Student achievement	Pretest and posttest reading scores on Gates MacGinitie	September and May
Teacher behavior	Walk-through logs	Weekly
Student behavior	Student interviews	Quarterly with representative sample of students
Students' attitudes about reading	Pretest and posttest student surveys	Twice a year: in the fall and spring

Data-Collection Methods

Evaluators have a number of options for data collection. Sometimes they choose to use methods to strengthen the validity and reliability of the data. Evaluators strive to select data-collection methods that most authentically capture the desired data. Below are descriptions of some data-collection methodologies.

Tests

Tests come in a variety of formats. Some formats are standardized norm-referenced: criterion-referenced (designed to measure particular predetermined criteria and used in many states to measure students' acquisition of the state-adopted curriculum) and classroom-based (designed by teachers or groups of teachers to assess students' learning about some particular aspects of the curriculum). Tests typically measure knowledge, and in a limited way can measure skill and behavior. The test selected for measuring student learning should closely align with the staff development practices that have been applied in the classroom so that a valid conclusion can be drawn about the link between staff development and student achievement.

Consider this scenario: The staff development program focuses on deepening teachers' understanding of problem solving in mathematics and expanding their strategies for teaching problem-solving skills. But the current measure of student achievement used in the district focuses on a different key concept, math computation. This mismatch between what the staff development program emphasizes and what the district test measures will not allow the evaluator to determine the impact of the staff development program. So a different test is necessary. Evaluators and program directors need to take adequate time to determine what key concepts need to be measured to answer the evaluation questions and the best way to measure those key concepts.

Some evaluations call for assessments of educator learning in the formative evaluation. Information about student assessment techniques offers guidance for designing assessments of educator learning as well as student learning.

Several excellent resources are available that deal with measuring student learning. Those wishing to find, construct, or adapt measures of student achievement that align with their staff development program will have no difficulty accessing the numerous resources available. The box offers some excellent resources on student assessment.

Recommended Resources on Assessing Student Learning

Beers, B. (2006). *Learning-driven school: A practical guide for teachers and principals.* Alexandria, VA: Association for Supervision and Curriculum Development.

Bernhardt, V. (2003). *Using data to improve student learning in elementary schools.* Larchmont, NY: Eye on Education.

Bernhardt, V. (2005). *Using data to improve student learning in high schools.* Larchmont, NY: Eye on Education.

Bernhardt. V. (2005). *Using data to improve student learning in middle schools.* Larchmont, NY: Eye on Education.

Bernhardt, V. (2006). *Using data to improve student learning in school districts.* Larchmont, NY: Eye on Education.

Brahier, D. (2001). *Assessment in middle and high school mathematics: A teacher's guide.* Larchmont, NY: Eye on Education.

Costa, A., & Kallick, B. (2000). *Assessing and reporting habits of mind.* Alexandria, VA: Association of Supervision and Curriculum Development.

Council of Chief State School Officers. (n.d.). *State Collaborative on Assessment and Student Standards.* Retrieved August 7, 2007, at www.ccsso.org/projects/ SCASS/

Earl, L. (2003). *Assessment as learning: Using classroom assessment to maximize student learning.* Thousand Oaks, CA: Corwin Press.

Gronlund, N. (2005). *Assessment of student achievement* (8th ed.). Boston: Allyn & Bacon.

Spinelli, C. (2005b). *Classroom assessment for students in special and general education.* Englewood Cliffs, NJ: Prentice Hall.

Stiggins, R. (1997). *Student-centered classroom assessment* (2nd ed.). Columbus OH: Merrill.

Stiggins, R. (2000). *Student-involved classroom assessment* (3rd ed.). Upper Saddle River, NJ: Prentice Hall.

Walker-Wilson, L. (2004). *What every teacher needs to know about assessment.* Larchmont, NY: Eye on Education.

Wiggins, G. (1998). *Educative assessment: Designing assessments to inform and improve student performance.* San Francisco: Jossey-Bass.

Wiggins, G., & McTighe, J. (1998). *Understanding by design.* Alexandria, VA: Association of Supervision and Curriculum Development.

Surveys

Surveys are measures of personal opinion, beliefs, knowledge, behaviors, or values and can be done orally or in writing. Oral surveys are often called interviews. The difference between a survey and an interview is that a survey tends to use multiple-choice questions with predetermined responses, although it doesn't always. Interviews are more open-ended. Online surveys are increasingly being used because they don't require budget for postage, paper, and personnel, and they make tabulation of responses easier. The box gives resources for example surveys for educators. Resources for student surveys are also available at some of these sites.

Interviews

Interviews are oral data-collection methods in which an interviewer typically uses standard predetermined questions and follow-up questions (probes) to ask respondents about their knowledge, skills, attitudes, behaviors, or aspirations. Interviews can be done in person, over the phone, or through other electronic media. Interviews can be recorded for further analysis. Some interviews are less structured and more free-flowing, although there are limitations in compiling data from multiple interviews where there are no standard questions.

Focus Groups

A focus group is a group discussion moderated by a facilitator who uses a prepared set of three or four questions to engage a small group of 6 to 10 participants in a discussion of the questions. The questions are limited, as is the size of the group, to ensure that all participants have the opportunity to share their views. Focus groups are usually recorded for later analysis.

Resources for Evaluation Instruments Related to Staff Development

Online Evaluation Resource Library (OERL)
    (www.oerl.sri.com)
    OERL contains plans, instruments, and reports used to evaluate projects funded by the Directorate for Education and Human Resources (EHR) of the National Science Foundation (NSF). The OERL Web site also contains glossaries of evaluation terminology, criteria for best practices, and scenarios illustrating how evaluation resources can be used or adapted.

    The Evaluation Center
    (www.wmich.edu/evalctr/)
    The center's mission is to provide national and international leadership for advancing the theory and practice of program, personnel, and student/constituent evaluation, as applied primarily to education and human services. The center's principal activities are research, development, dissemination, service, instruction, and leadership.

    The National Center for Research on Evaluation, Standards, and Student Testing
    (www.cse.ucla.edu)
    This national center has information related to testing and the use of test results and research on assessment and instructional tools, among other areas.

    The National Science Foundation
    (www.nsf.gov)
    NSF has resources on evaluation of math, science, and technology programs.

Logs

Logs are used to document occurrences of particular behaviors or practices. Logs may be kept by program participants, by other noninvolved stakeholders who may be beneficiaries of the participants' services, or by trained observers. Logs may record actions that occur such as particular teaching strategies used, time invested, or reactions.

Observations

Observations are visitations to the site of implementation. Usually observers have a tally or check sheet, a list of specific items to look for, or some other way to record their observations. Sometimes observers write scripts of the observation, recording what is happening and what participants are saying. These scripts are later analyzed in a structured process. In other cases, observers record their perceptions about the situation or combine their perceptions with anecdotal data. This type of observation is often referred to as field notes. Observations are best done by trained observers. Sometimes observations can be audiotaped or videotaped for later analysis. Even though recording observations may be difficult, the process helps the evaluator obtain a complete picture of what occurred.

Rating Scales

Rating scales come in a variety of forms and guide the data collector to rate the observed situation on the established scale. Innovation Configuration Maps (ICMs) and rubrics are sophisticated forms of rating scales. Rating scales require an observer or evaluator to make a judgment about a situation with prepared descriptors to guide the judgments. The descriptors usually provide a continuum of strong practices to weak practices to help the rater determine how to score the situation.

Extant Data Sources: Documents and Artifacts

Documents and artifacts are data resources found in the educational system. They can provide information about the context, knowledge, and skills of program participants and students. Some examples are attendance records, disciplinary actions, library checkout rates, meeting agenda and minutes, and schedules. For example, students' products that serve as demonstrations of their knowledge or skills are often collected and assembled in portfolios and are available to others for review. Such artifacts are valuable if they demonstrate growth or the occurrence of significant events.

Expert Judgments

Expert judgments rely on the use of an expert to provide his or her observations, opinions, or information about the program. Experts can be internal or external to the program and may be content area experts, process experts, program administrators, participants, or supervisors of the participants. Experts may use a set of standards or guidelines as the basis for their judgments and program directors will want to request that standards appropriate to the program be used. For example, experts might want to use *NSDC's Standards for Staff*

Development, Revised (or similar standards) to serve as the criterion against which to evaluate their staff development programs.

Role-Playing or Simulations

Role-plays, or simulations, are processes in which program participants demonstrate their knowledge and skills in simulated situations. They can be recorded for later analysis. While these are not common forms of data collection, they do permit the evaluator to see the learning in action, at least in a simulated situation. When done in authentic situations, that is, those that are as close to real as possible, they can provide opportunities to examine both student behavior and educator practice.

Selecting Instruments

When selecting a data-collection method that involves an instrument such as a test or a survey, the evaluator decides whether to use an existing one or construct a new one particular to the staff development program being evaluated. Constructing instruments requires extra time for development and field-testing. While there are advantages to using previously developed instruments, there are also disadvantages. Existing instruments are usually field-tested and determined to be valid and reliable. In some cases they will be normed and standardized. But they may not align with the constructs of the evaluation at hand or be appropriate for the context or the population who will be completing them.

When the evaluator chooses to develop new instruments, he must be certain they are valid and reliable. Do they measure the constructs identified as important? Are they appropriate for the age and language of the population completing them? Are they free from bias? Are they clear and can they be completed in a reasonable amount of time?

Table 6.11 Advantages and Disadvantages of Developing New Instruments Versus Using Available Instruments

Instrument	Advantages	Disadvantages
Existing	• Field-tested • May be standardized and normed • May be more valid and reliable	• May not be appropriate for the construct • May not be appropriate for the population
Newly Developed	• Specific to the program, context, and audience	• May not be appropriate for the construct • Time and expense for development and field-testing • Reliability is unknown until it is used

Choosing an Appropriate Data-Collection Method

The choice of the data-collection strategy depends on what information is needed. While some data-collection strategies are more time-consuming and costlier than others, decisions should be made on the basis of their potential for collecting the best data. For example, an interview is more time-consuming and can be costlier than administering a survey. But if the evaluator believes the quality and depth of the information from interviews may be better, she should use that data-collection method rather than compromise the integrity of the evaluation.

Some data-collection methods require more resources than others. But making decisions about data collection on the basis of what is preferred rather than what is affordable will ensure the integrity of the evaluation. If resource limitations require modification of these decisions later, they should always be considered in light of what the evaluation questions, purposes, and uses are.

CAUTIONS FOR EVALUATORS AND STAKEHOLDERS

Cost of Evaluation

Since evaluations cost money, either in paying for direct services of an evaluator or in staff time invested in the evaluation or a combination of both, decisions about the evaluation framework must consider the resources available for the evaluation. The cost of evaluations is one reason that educators do not conduct more of them. Yet valuable information can result from low-cost evaluations. When designing an evaluation framework, evaluators will want to consider what is achievable with various levels of fiscal support for an evaluation. Some program directors realize that cutting corners too closely may not provide the information they, decision makers, and policy makers want from a program. If done with an inadequate budget, the evaluation will be less useful to them. When program directors have options about what is possible at different levels of funding, they may opt to budget more for the evaluation to produce the results that will be valid, reliable, and useful.

The cost of conducting evaluations varies widely and depends on the evaluation questions, the requirements of the evaluation, the cost of the program, and the rigor required. While a range of 10% to 20% of total program budget is usually recommended by granting agencies for evaluations, there is no universally accepted standard for funding evaluations (see Table 6.12).

Seeking Permission

Evaluators, both internal and external, must follow policies or procedures that exist within a school district for evaluation studies and must be sure to follow them. One guideline typically involves informing or seeking permission for involving students and staff in any evaluation or research studies.

Evaluators respect the security, dignity, and self-worth of the respondents, program participants, clients, and other stakeholders with whom they interact. Where applicable, evaluators must abide by current professional ethics and standards regarding risks, harms, and burdens that might be engendered to those participating in the evaluation; regarding informed consent for participation in evaluation; and regarding informing participants about the scope and limits of confidentiality. Examples of such standards include federal regulations about protection of human subjects, or the ethical principles of such associations as the American Anthropological Association, the American Educational Research Association or the American Psychological Association. Although this principle is not intended to extend the applicability of such ethics and standards beyond

Table 6.12 General Guidelines for Evaluation at Different Cost Levels

Range of Cost	Characteristics
Low Cost	Allows for collection of existing data about program implementation such as numbers of participants, participant satisfaction with the program.
	Permits description of program implementation.
	Provides little in-depth information about program information or impact on which to base decisions.
	May not provide impact information.
	Can be used for some compliance requirements.
	Provides little information about changes that occur in the program.
Low to Moderate Cost	Allows for collection of existing data about program implementation, such as numbers of participants, participant satisfaction with the program.
	Permits description of program implementation.
	Provides little in-depth information about program information or impact on which to base decisions.
	May not provide impact information.
	Can be used for some compliance requirements.
	Provides little information about changes that occur in the program.
Moderate to High Cost	Permits in-depth information about program implementation and impact.
	Permits conclusions about whether change occurred.
	Permits conclusions about whether the program is responsible for the changes.
	Focuses on short-term rather than long-term changes.
High Cost	Allows all the information from other evaluations, as well as the ability to determine whether changes are sustained over time.

Adapted from Administration of Children, Youth, and Families (n.d.). *A program manager's guide to evaluation.* Retrieved on December 21, 2006, from www.acf.hhs.gov/programs/opre/other_resrch/pm_guide_eval/index.html.

their current scope, evaluators should abide by them where it is feasible and desirable to do so. (See *Guiding Principles for Evaluators,* Appendix A.)

Sometimes schools and districts ask parents to sign blanket permission forms granting permission to use student records or routine classroom practices for research and evaluation. If this is not the practice, districts can inform parents that their children's records will be a part of an evaluation study and at least give them an opportunity to exempt their child from involvement.

Similar procedures are required for staff members who are asked to participate. They minimally must be given an overview of the evaluation and its purpose, told how information from them will be used and if the information will be confidential and anonymous, and be given an opportunity to not participate without sanction. Some district contracts and state policies include specific guidelines about the involvement of staff and students in research and evaluation. Evaluators must adhere to these guidelines in all circumstances unless specific exemptions are granted.

A SUMMARY: MAKING DECISIONS ABOUT THE FRAMEWORK

An evaluator has significant choices about possible designs for the evaluation study; but the options are often limited by a number of factors. Some of the most significant determining factors are resources, including time, personnel, and money; intended use of the evaluation findings; and the stage at which the evaluator became involved. One major challenge a program director and evaluator have is knowing the degree to which the evaluation study itself is worth the investment. If resources are limited, the evaluator's choice of design may be limited. Simple designs such as the self-evaluation or expert evaluation may be necessary. Simple pretest/posttest designs are usually relatively inexpensive. Rossi, Freeman, and Lipsey (2003) state

> Our position is that evaluators must review the range of design options to determine the most appropriate one for the particular evaluation. The choice always involves trade-offs; there is no single, always-best design that can be used universally as the "gold standard." Rather, we advocate using what we call the "good enough" rule in formulating research [evaluation] designs. Simply stated, the "good enough" rule is that the evaluator should choose the best possible design from a methodological standpoint after having taken into account the potential importance of the results, the practicality and feasibility of each design, and the probability that the design chosen will produce useful and credible results. (p. 240)

If the evaluation is integral to making significant decisions related to program continuation or resources, the staff development leader and evaluator will want to lobby for the resources they believe are essential to conducting a credible evaluation. If they are obligated to cut too much, the credibility of the entire evaluation and ultimately any decisions based on it are compromised.

A Case Study: Writing Case

Hubbard Middle School staff could no longer ignore their students' deficiency in writing after the last state assessment. Their scores were substantially below the state means on the two writing assessments. The state's holistic scoring system gave them little information about why student scores were so low. Some teachers voluntarily analyzed the writing samples using the district's writing rubric to determine where their students had not performed well and determined that all students, and especially those considered at risk, lacked the ability to organize ideas and employ language conventions correctly (grammar, punctuation, capitalization, spelling, etc.).

To address these problems, teachers decided to work together as a staff to improve students' writing performance. They created a plan that included the following components:

- Administer a writing sample in the fall and spring
- Keep writing portfolios for all students throughout the year

- Work with the district language arts coordinator to explore current research about writing and acquire strategies for teaching language conventions and organization of ideas
- Examine student writing samples several times during the year, observe other teachers in other schools, watch videotaped lessons from another state where a similar school had dramatically improved student writing scores, establish three study groups on adolescent writing, and develop collaborative lesson plans as a team at least once a week to ensure that students are writing every day in at least one class

The assistant superintendent commends them on their extensive plan to improve student writing. She asks several hard questions that they need to answer in order to gain her support to establish a student writing center at the school. The writing center is designed to provide additional support to students on writing skills and will be staffed before and after school by a teacher and student editors who will help their fellow students with their writing skills.

The assistant superintendent wants answers to these questions:

1. How do you know you are making a difference in student performance in writing and especially in organization and language conventions?

2. Which of the many interventions you are implementing had the greatest impact on classroom instruction?

To construct a framework for the evaluation process, ask these questions:

1. Is this evaluation worth doing?

2. How rigorous does the evaluation need to be to satisfy the intended use and users?

3. What kind of information is needed to answer the evaluation question(s)? Are multiple sources and types of data needed to answer the questions or to strengthen the findings?

4. Who has this information? What people or documents can provide this information?

5. How will the data be gathered or collected from each source? What tools or processes are necessary?

6. What is the plan for gathering the information, including timeline, necessary resources, and support?

7. What resources are available for the evaluation?

8. Does this evaluation require an external evaluator?

9. How do cost, time, and credibility of result, and so on, affect decisions about the evaluation framework?

Table 6.13   Evaluation Framework for Hubbard Middle School Writing Staff Development Evaluation

Types of Changes	Question	Data Source	Data Collection Method	Data Analysis Method	Timeline	Responsible Party
Improved student writing in areas of organization of ideas and language conventions	Did student writing scores in the areas of organizing ideas and language conventions improve on the state writing assessment by 10% from the spring 2008 to spring 2010 testing?	State writing assessment in Grades 4, 7, and 9	State test	Difference in scores in panel groups	Spring 2008 through spring 2010	Principal and Staff Development Committee
Language arts teachers' teaching practices in language conventions and organization of ideas	Are all language arts teachers implementing explicit instruction in organizing ideas and language conventions into their classrooms at least once a week?	Review of teachers' lesson plans	Document collection	Counting	Fall 2007 through May 2010	Principal
All teachers' teaching practices in organizing ideas	Are all teachers providing authentic opportunities for students to practice writing and to use writing to learn at least once a week?	Review of teachers' lesson plans	Document collection	Counting	Fall 2007 through May 2010	Principal
Types of writing assignments students have	Do students' writing assignments provide varied and challenging opportunities for students to generate and organize ideas?	Review of six-week writing prompts for all content areas	Document review and coding by type of writing	Coding by type of writing (e.g., narrative, persuasive, explanation)	Fall 2007 through May 2010	Staff Development Committee
Teachers' analysis of student writing	How often are teachers examining student writing in departments and teaching teams? What are teachers learning from examining student work?	Meeting summary logs	Document review	Counting; finding patterns	Fall 2007 through May 2010	Staff Development Committee
Teachers' efficacy in writing instruction	To what degree do teachers in all content areas feel competent to teach writing? What is contributing to their increase in efficacy and competence?	Survey	Pre- and posttest difference scores	Descriptive statistics	Fall 2005 (pretest) and May 2007 (posttest)	Staff Development Committee

Planning Phase

- Assess evaluability
- Formulate evaluation questions
- Construct the evaluation framework

Conducting Phase

- Collect data
- Organize, analyze, and display data
- Interpret data

Reporting Phase

- Disseminate and use findings
- Evaluate the evaluation

Collect Data

7

In this stage, the evaluator is gathering data as planned and being vigilant about the need to collect additional data or, if necessary, alter the data-collection process to ensure that the data needed to answer the evaluation questions are collected. Many decisions that will facilitate this step of the evaluation process are made while designing the evaluation framework.

Questions the evaluator asks at this stage are

1. Are the data being collected those that were planned?

2. What problems are occurring in the data-collection process and how can they be resolved?

3. What other data might need to be collected?

4. How do I manage the data during this time?

5. How can I ensure accuracy and precision in the data-collection process?

PILOT TESTING INSTRUMENTS AND PROCESSES

To ensure that the data-collection process runs as smoothly and unobtrusively as possible, it is advantageous to pilot all instruments, directions, and processes with a trial group. Sometimes the smallest problems may create major problems for participants. If evaluators know these problems in advance of the full-scale data-collection process, they can be corrected.

The pilot test helps the evaluator determine whether the instruments are effective in collecting the needed data, the directions are clear, and the time allocated is appropriate and whether participants encounter any problems in implementing the process that the evaluator did not anticipate. The evaluator should analyze instruments and processes used in the pilot test to see whether the responses parallel what he or she expected and whether there are any items or questions that were consistently skipped or caused confusion. Asking participants to comment on their experience during the pilot data collection is another way to learn about the effectiveness and efficiency of the data-collection process.

TRAINING FOR DATA COLLECTORS

Those people in the field collecting data may need to be trained. Training increases data collectors' accuracy and the consistency among data collectors.

Training for data collectors includes the following items:

- Program overview
- Review of all data-collection instructions and guidelines
- Discussion of problems that may occur during data collection
- Practice session where data collectors actually complete some or all of the data-collection processes or instruments themselves
- Discussion about respondent confidentiality
- Strategies for managing and keeping data in a safe place
- Procedures for submitting data
- Sources of help when problems occur

If the data-collection process is complex, a written manual with the information above is helpful for data collectors to have as a reference.

MANAGING DATA-COLLECTION ACTIVITIES

The ease with which the management of data collection occurs depends on the specificity of the data plan. If the plan clearly delineates who will collect the data, where the data will be collected, when the data will be collected, and how the data will be collected, the process will run smoothly. A master schedule of the data-collection process can help track the activities and provide a checklist to ensure that steps are not missed. It is advisable to have one person or a team, depending on the scope of the data-collection process, responsible for monitoring all data-collection activities. For example, one person might be responsible for collecting student data; another might collect teacher data; a third might collect school documents and artifacts.

Because data are often cumbersome, evaluators should establish a specific place and specific format for all collected data. Prepared forms, templates, spreadsheets, or logs can facilitate the data-management process. If data collectors have a computer spreadsheet into which they enter the data they collect from the field, the transfer of data is much easier than if those same data are entered on paper and sent or delivered to a specific place. If paper (rather than electronic) records are used, special care is necessary to ensure they are not lost or damaged. If possible, data records should be copied, backed up, or duplicated before transferring them, delivered in person rather than mailed, and immediately placed in safekeeping.

The evaluator monitors the data-collection process by

1. Creating a firm time line for collecting and submitting data

2. Making random observations of the data-collection process

3. Checking with respondents to determine whether the data have been collected

4. Ensuring the safekeeping of all data

5. Viewing the data-collection process as a part of the program itself

Source: Administration of Children, Youth, and Families, n.d.

Adding Data

The success of the evaluation depends on the quality of the data. Occasionally during the data-collection process, evaluators may realize that important data are not being collected. This is not unusual. The evaluator may find some unanticipated information in a series of interviews with students that leads her to wonder whether teachers' views about the same question parallel those of their students. If this seems important, the evaluator may add a question to teacher interviews to triangulate the information she is collecting from students. The evaluator may also find redundancies in the data and may consider eliminating one data source, although this decision should be made with great care so as not to compromise the ability to triangulate data.

Scoring Instruments

The data-collection process includes scoring instruments or tests. The scoring process ensures accuracy and consistency. Specialized training to ensure interrater reliability is necessary if more than one scorer is scoring instruments to ensure consistency and accuracy. If computerized scoring is used, periodic checks on the data should prevent any major problems.

Knowing the kind of scores needed for the analysis and producing those will eliminate having to repeat scoring. Table 7.1 describes the most common types of scores that can be produced from quantitative data and how those data are used.

Methodical and Systematic Process

Data collection requires methodical and systematic processes that include substantial detail and frequent cross-checks. At all phases of the data-collection process, steps must be precise and accurate. Erring at this point jeopardizes the evaluator's ability to analyze data and form valid conclusions. While timing can influence the results, those involved in gathering data need to allocate enough time to the data-collection step to ensure that the work can be done with care.

Table 7.1 Types of Scores and Their Uses

Score	Definition	Compared With
Raw score	The number of items answered correctly (assuming there are correct and incorrect responses).	Nothing
Percentile	Scores range from 1 to 99 and indicate the percentage of students scoring at or lower than the test score in question; percentiles cannot be averaged, summed, or combined because the differences between percentile points are not equal.	Norm group
Mastery scores	Notation that indicates a level of performance typically based on a range of raw scores.	Test group or defined criterion performance
Standard scores	A recalculation of the raw score that provides equal-interval scales for comparison across students and tests and for mathematical calculations; includes NCEs and scaled scores.	Norm group
Stanines	Rough approximations of an individual's performance relative to the performance of others in the group; scores are divided into nine equal groups ranging from 1 to 9, with 1 being the lowest.	Norm group
Rubrics	Descriptors representing a range from excellent to poor performance to guide scoring of tasks or products.	Criterion performance
Gain scores	Score indicating how much a student has improved or progressed; typically a problematic score because the reliability and validity of the pre- and posttest may doubly impact the gain score; gain scores may have different meanings at different points on the scale.	Self; cohort group

Planning Phase

- Assess evaluability
- Formulate evaluation questions
- Construct the evaluation framework

Conducting Phase

- Collect data
- Organize, analyze, and display data
- Interpret data

Reporting Phase

- Disseminate and use findings
- Evaluate the evaluation

Organize, Analyze, and Display Data

8

Organizing, analyzing, and displaying data collected are the initial process in transforming words and numbers into something meaningful. The goal of data organization and analysis is to create a set of manageable information by sorting, arranging, and processing the data collected (Weiss, 1998). The consistent use of thorough and methodical processes is the hallmark of a successful data analyst. Since each analysis is a unique, dynamic, evolving process, the process is usually more time-consuming than anticipated. Throughout the data-analysis process, the evaluator is constantly looking at new ways to combine data, slice data, or connect data to understand the program being evaluated.

The evaluator answers several questions in this step:

1. How will I organize, sort, and arrange the data collected to prepare it for analysis?

2. What types of data analysis will I use to examine the data?

3. How can I display the analyzed data to facilitate data interpretation?

4. How will I involve stakeholders in the analysis process?

Data analysis is often done in two phases. The first phase usually results in a general overall view of the program. The second phase involves a closer look, taking some aspects of the program and placing them under the microscope for a deeper, more detailed examination to reveal other important information. For example, the evaluator might decide to take a closer look at data from two schools, one where the results were high and one where the results were not, and attempt to uncover any factors that might have influenced the difference in the results.

ORGANIZING DATA

Evaluators can drown in data. The more streamlined and condensed the data processes are, the easier the analysis will be. If, for example, the evaluator is reviewing archival data, it may make more sense to extract the informative sections, sort them, and work solely with the extracted sections than to work with the entire document. Spreadsheets make the management of multiple data simpler and easier. While reducing the data set can make them more manageable, evaluators should be careful not eliminate any useful data. The evaluator may lose the ability to triangulate or conduct an in-depth analysis if any data are lost or eliminated. For example, the evaluator may decide to take a closer look at one school's data to understand better what occurred in the program. The evaluator should always have such options at any point in the data analysis and interpretation processes.

Spreadsheets, folders, labels, codes, and files are great tools in the data-organizing stage. Sorting data to make categories of information, formulating and testing various grouping systems, and developing coding systems for organizing data are all processes in which the evaluator needs proficiency. Being flexible early in the data-organizing process and testing the categories will ensure that the final categories are the most logical for further analysis.

Another task during the data-organization stage is making decisions about how to handle missing data. If half the sample of third-grade teachers did not respond to a survey to report how often they use a new instructional strategy, the evaluator will decide what to do about the missing survey responses. Sometimes, despite a well-planned data-collection system, data are missing that may be needed. The evaluator decides whether to fill in the information gaps and how to do so, whether to seek the missing data, whether to devise a method to indicate that the data are missing, or perhaps some combination of tactics. These decisions will be reported in the evaluation report.

The last step of the data-organization process is to examine any abnormalities in data that may influence or affect the analysis process. The evaluator is particularly looking for any illegitimate or irrelevant data. Some of these abnormalities are incorrect codes, typographical errors, or information that fall beyond the scope of the evaluation. Sometimes the information that falls beyond the scope of the evaluation may be useful to the program directors, even if it is not useful to the evaluator. Careful organization of the data ensures that the data analysis is based on the most complete and accurate data rather than spurious information.

For example, if a series of interviews was used, the evaluator would list all the responses to a particular question together and carefully review the list to determine whether any response is not related to the topic of the question. The response might be related to another question in the interview or irrelevant and should be discarded. Or, in looking at a set of numerical scores, the evaluator might notice that one response is a 6 from a range of *five* possible responses. The evaluator returns to the original data set to find the correct response and replaces the incorrect response with the correct one.

DATA-ANALYSIS METHODS

While the data-analysis process can be complex, it need not be. The evaluator has to assess the best type of analysis to use on the basis of the evaluation question, the type of data collected, and the intended use(s) and user(s).

There are two types of data analysis, quantitative and qualitative. Quantitative analyses are required in experimental and quasi-experimental evaluations. Quantitative analyses can be either complex or simple. Descriptive statistics, such as numbers, counts, percentages, means, or ranges, are simpler forms of quantitative data analysis. A common data-analysis method is calculating the mean or mean differences. Means are best when reported with both the range of scores and the standard deviation. Standard deviation is a measure of the variation among scores.

More sophisticated forms of quantitative analyses are inferential statistics for use in experimental and quasi-experimental evaluations. Inferential statistics require that certain conditions be met, such as the size of the treatment and control groups. The use of inferential statistics such as the t-tests or analyses of variation allows the evaluator to determine whether the difference that occurs between the pretest and posttest or between the treatment and control group is a significance difference, meaning that it happened not as a result of chance. A test for significance allows the evaluator to determine whether something more than chance produced the differences that occurred.

Qualitative analyses are used in ethnographic evaluations. Qualitative analyses seek patterns or themes across the various data sources. Sometimes qualitative data, usually in the form of words, can be aggregated into numbers, such as how many program participants identified the support of a coach as a valuable aspect of the program. To conduct a qualitative analysis, the evaluator usually starts by identifying categories, patterns, themes, or commonalities and then uses one of several analysis techniques to complete the data analysis.

Evaluators do not always need to conduct sophisticated statistical analyses. Simply providing a narrative description of the program with descriptive statistics might be sufficient. Descriptive statistics are usually easier for most audiences to understand and use than inferential statistics are. Sometimes more complex statistical analysis is necessary, however. If sophisticated analyses are needed and the evaluators' skills in that area are inadequate, they should seek the assistance of someone skilled in statistical analyses.

Data can be analyzed in several ways. Weiss (1998) provides a comprehensive list of these analysis techniques, and some are given below.

Describing

Narrative description of the program often accompanied by descriptive statistics, such as mean, median, mode, and range, for example, changes in the frequency with which teachers use a particular instructional methodology, or the changes that occur from pre- to posttests of student test scores when teachers use particular instructional strategies.

Counting

Numerical description of the program; allows the evaluator to compare the program to some standard or other programs, for example, the number of students who achieved proficiency on the state test.

Factoring

In the algebraic sense, breaking down aggregates into their parts; for example, the factors contributing to student academic success, such as attendance, previous academic work; parents' involvement in school activities.

Clustering

Putting things together by forming classes, categories, or groups based on some common feature; for example, students whose reading level has increased more than or less than one grade level.

Comparing

Examining the similarities and differences in the features of the participants before, during, and after the program; for example, students' ability to complete a classroom performance task in geography before their teachers began examining student work with their peers measured against students' ability to complete a similar task after their teachers regularly examined student work with their peers.

Seeking Trends/Patterns

Identifying recurring patterns, trends, or commonalities; for example, students' use of the language of science to describe their actions in the lab activity.

Examining Outliers

Looking at the situations at the extreme ends of the data set to determine what, if any, information can be learned that does not appear in the data tending more toward the mean.

Finding Covariation

Noting the pattern where changes in one feature occur in tandem with changes in another feature; for example, the increase in teachers' use of journal writing in social studies and math and the increase in students' proficiency on the schoolwide writing sample in language arts.

Eliminating Rival Explanations

Using the data to rule out other plausible explanations for the changes observed; for example, the improvement in students' performance in history is better explained by increased attendance than by new instructional strategies used by teachers.

Modeling

Depicting how a program works with a graphic display, including relationship, sequence, and importance of the program's components or features.

Univariate Analysis

Univariate analysis is the analysis of single variables or single information items. Univariate analysis can show the overall level of a response, the variability of responses, or atypical responses.

Bivariate and Multivariate Analyses

Bivariate and multivariate analyses bring together multiple variables to determine whether any relationship exists between and among variables. Bivariate analyses, for example, would permit the evaluator to determine how the implementation of a staff development program related to results for students. Evaluators who use multivariate analyses look for associations among three or more items of information and compare reported performance levels with acceptable levels of performance. Multivariate analysis allows comparison of results. Comparisons are essential for impact evaluations.

Evaluations of staff development might include comparisons of

- teachers' frequency of use of particular instructional methodologies with student performance
- set or expected performance levels such as Adequate Yearly Progress targets to achieved performance levels
- work products such as assignments or lesson/unit plans of teachers who participated in the staff development program to work products of teachers who have not participated in the staff development program
- the content knowledge of teachers who participated in the staff development and their students' performance on benchmark to the content knowledge of teachers who did not participate in the staff development program and their students' performance
- performance of the same group students before their teachers participated in the staff development program and after their teachers' participation

One example of a way to examine the impact of a staff development program using a bivariate analysis is by comparing teachers' level of proficiency (as determined through classroom observations or self-report) with a particular behavior as defined by a specific set of descriptors with their students' performance. A display of this analysis technique appears in Table 8.1.

Searching for relationships among variables is another way to conduct multivariate analyses. These analyses are conducted statistically with quantitative data and visually with qualitative data. Statistical techniques such as correlations, t-tests, chi-square, or analysis of variance require certain conditions to be valid and provide useful information to the evaluator if those conditions can be met. Visual techniques include contingency tables, matrices, differences in percentages, and various graphing processes, such as scatter plots.

Table 8.1   Sample Bivariate Analysis for the Evaluation of Staff Development

Teachers' Level of Proficiency	Student Performance Scores
High	x
Medium	x
Low	x

One caution associated with bivariate or multivariate analysis is the tendency to want to infer a causal relationship among the items of information or data when the data and analysis permit only an inference of relationship. When evaluators move into the interpretation phase, they carefully describe relationships among variables accurately.

DISPLAYING DATA

How the evaluator displays data often determines how the data will be interpreted. The data displays created by the evaluator help others to make sense of the data in order to prepare the final evaluation report. It is helpful if the evaluator displays the same data in multiple formats rather than a single one. In this way, during the interpretation step, stakeholders can identify which display best conveys the data for the intended audience so that the data are most useful.

Data displays typically include charts, graphs, and tables. They might also include models, diagrams, relationship charts, organization charts, communication pattern diagrams, checklists, theories of change, flowcharts, logic models, decision trees, timelines, and process maps. The goal of these data displays is twofold: (1) to create a way to display the data to make sense of them, and (2) to use them to form conclusions about the staff development program.

INVOLVING OTHERS IN ANALYSIS

To involve program directors or stakeholders in the data-analysis process increases their understanding of the data and increases the value they place on the analysis process. Ultimately they will be "the ones who must translate data into decisions and actions" (Patton, 1997, p. 302). Involvement of others in data analysis depends on their level of competence with data analysis. Evaluators may decide that it is more appropriate to involve others in the interpretation phase rather than in the data-analysis phase.

Patton (1997) recommends increasing stakeholders' comfort with and ability to analyze data. He suggests mock analysis with "prepared" data before the data collection begins. This helps participants establish realistic expectations about the data, prepares them to engage productively in the actual data analysis, builds commitment to use the data, and helps the evaluator refine the data-collection process.

The second strategy is to have participants guess what the data will tell them before they begin the data analysis. Patton believes this helps build participants' interest in the data analysis by creating anticipation for the results. It gives the evaluator a concrete basis for knowing whether the results are similar to those expected by participants. Comparing their expectation with the actual results often provides new insights and an appreciation for the evaluation process.

Recommended Resources for Further Exploration on Data Analysis

Bernhardt, V. (2004). *Data analysis for comprehensive school improvement* (2nd ed.). Larchmont, NY: Eye on Education.

Creighton, T. (2001). *The educator's guide to using data to improve decision making.* Thousand Oaks, CA; Corwin Press.

Holcomb, E. (1999). *Getting excited about data: How to combine people, passion, and proof.* Thousand Oaks, CA: Corwin Press.

Johnson. R. (1996). *Setting our sights: Measuring equity in school change.* Los Angeles: Achievement Council.

Leithwood, K., & Aitken, R. (2001). *Making schools smarter: A system for monitoring school and district progress* (2nd ed.). Thousand Oaks, CA: Corwin Press.

Love, N. (2001). *Using data/getting results: A practical guide for school improvement in mathematics and science.* Norwood, MA: Christopher-Gordon.

Parsons, B. (2001). *Evaluative inquiry: Using evaluation to promote student success.* Thousand Oaks, CA: Corwin Press.

Reeves, D. (2000). *Accountability in action: A blueprint for learning organizations.* Denver: Advanced Learning Press.

Schmoker, M. (2001). *The results fieldbook: Practical strategies from dramatically improved schools.* Alexandria, VA: Association of Supervision and Curriculum Development.

Wahlstrom, D. (1999). *Using data to improve student achievement: A handbook for collecting, organizing, analyzing, and using data.* Virginia Beach, VA: Successline.

Questions to Guide Data Analysis

A data analyst often uses a series of questions to make sense of the data and guide the analysis. Evaluators commonly ask some of the questions below as they examine data and figure out their importance. This is not an exhaustive list but does include samples of questions that can initiate the process. This list of questions is not sequential. Sometimes answering one question will lead the evaluator to answer other, similar questions.

The evaluator may use the questions below when analyzing data.

What percentage of the total population is represented?

Were particular subgroups adequately represented?

What patterns or trends exist in the data?

What are the results for the overall group? various groups?

How consistent are the patterns across a group, such as grade levels, schools, departments?

How do the data compare with other similar data sets (such as last year's or the last several years') or with other schools with similar students?

How does the performance of various groups differ, that is, gender, socio-economic status?

What are the outliers, those responses that fall far from the modal response? How do they differ?

What strengths and weaknesses are evident?

What changes occurred in knowledge, attitudes, skills, aspirations, or behaviors?

What unexpected events or outcomes occurred?

Encouraging a Collaborative Analysis Process

Organizing and analyzing data require methodical, detail-oriented work, understanding of and ability to conduct various data analyses, and ability to display data analyses visually to facilitate understanding. During this step of the evaluation process, the evaluator is advised to collaborate with stakeholders frequently to ensure that the data analyses and displays are useful and easily understood. The more stakeholders understand and participate in the organization and analysis of data, the less suspicious they will be of the data and how they are used to draw conclusions.

Creating a Safe Place for Data Analysis

If the evaluator chooses to include stakeholders in the data-analysis process, he or she will need to create a safe context for data analysis. This will increase the likelihood that educators, particularly classroom teachers, will want to engage in collaborative analysis of the data about their teaching and their students' performance. If stakeholders feel that they are being judged, singled out, or embarrassed, they will be less objective and less open to examining the data. To create a blame-free environment that allows stakeholders to participate without fear, the evaluator might set clear norms or agreements for participants, such as confidentiality, focusing on the issues not the people, and working on the problem rather than finding blame. The evaluator may choose to remove identifying marks, such as names, or have stakeholders analyze only group rather than individual data. By creating a safe environment for both data analysis and interpretation in the next step, stakeholders will be more fully engaged and willing to identify both strengths and weaknesses evident in the data.

Planning Phase

- Assess evaluability
- Formulate evaluation questions
- Construct the evaluation framework

Conducting Phase

- Collect data
- Organize, analyze, and display data
- Interpret data

Reporting Phase

- Disseminate and use findings
- Evaluate the evaluation

Interpret Data

9

Closely linked with analysis is the interpretation of data. Many, in fact, view analysis and interpretation as a single step. Interpretation is the meaning-making process that comes after the data have been counted, sorted, analyzed, and displayed. According to Patton (1997), "interpretations go beyond the data to add context, determine meaning, and tease out substantive significance based on deduction or inference" (p. 307). The interpretation phase of the evaluation process has two parts. Making a judgment about the success of the staff development program is the essential task; making recommendations for future actions can be optional.

The questions evaluators answer in the interpretation process are

1. What do these data mean?

2. What worked, what didn't, and why?

3. Which aspects or components of the program seemed to contribute the most or the least to the outcomes the program produced?

4. What are the implications of these findings?

5. Does this program have merit?

6. Does this program have worth?

7. What recommendations can I make about the program based on these findings?

8. Did this program make a difference?

SUPPORTING A FINDING

The process of interpreting data and forming conclusions is largely an inductive process in which the evaluator takes discrete data and pools them together to form broad statements of finding. One way to think about this process is grouping independent, isolated bits of information (data) into a more meaningful, yet broader, finding. Table 9.1 is a useful format for constructing findings based on data. The table demonstrates how the evaluator uses data to arrive at a finding.

Another approach to interpretation is clustering data to form a multileg support for each finding. The examples in Figure 9A will clarify how using multiple data supports increases the credibility of the findings. The more data that can support a finding, the stronger the finding and the more likely decision makers will be to act on the results of the evaluation.

Figure 9A   Simple Finding With Limited Support

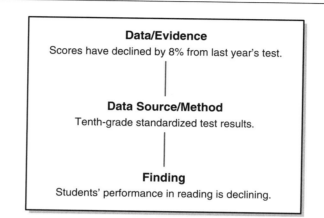

Data/Evidence
Scores have declined by 8% from last year's test.

Data Source/Method
Tenth-grade standardized test results.

Finding
Students' performance in reading is declining.

With only one data point to support this finding, most decision makers will be less likely to believe the finding is credible and will more quickly dismiss it. In the example in Figure 9B, the finding is stronger because it has more support.

Figure 9B   Well-Supported Finding With Triangulated Evidence

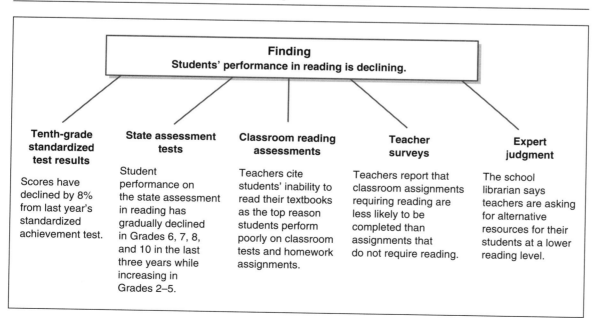

Finding
Students' performance in reading is declining.

Tenth-grade standardized test results

Scores have declined by 8% from last year's standardized achievement test.

State assessment tests

Student performance on the state assessment in reading has gradually declined in Grades 6, 7, 8, and 10 in the last three years while increasing in Grades 2–5.

Classroom reading assessments

Teachers cite students' inability to read their textbooks as the top reason students perform poorly on classroom tests and homework assignments.

Teacher surveys

Teachers report that classroom assignments requiring reading are less likely to be completed than assignments that do not require reading.

Expert judgment

The school librarian says teachers are asking for alternative resources for their students at a lower reading level.

Table 9.1   Sample Findings From Data

Data Source	Data/Evidence	Method	Finding
Performance assessment scores	360 data points (3 individual scores of 59 students from last year and 3 individual scores of 61 students from this year).	Aggregated scores on the three classroom performance assessments (given and scored by teachers) increased by 10 percentage points over scores on first year's assessments.	Students' performance increased on the schoolwide performance assessments in mathematics.
Teachers' class records	17,833 data points (95 individual homework scores for 100 student from last year and 101 individual homework scores of 83 students from this year)	Grades for homework completion increased 8 percent (77 to 85 percent) over last year's homework scores.	Students completed more mathematics homework.
Teacher surveys **Staff developer logs** **Principal surveys**	10,166 data points* (40 individual survey questions for 220 teachers; 82 pages of logs from 3 staff developers; 28 principal surveys with 40 questions each) *Logs often contain multiple data points.*	Survey responses indicate that teachers' understanding of math concepts they teach increased. Coaches' logs indicate that teachers seek help more on problem solving and number sense than any other area of the math curriculum.	Teachers are more knowledgeable about and comfortable with the math concepts they teach.
Principal observations	More than 313 data points* (96 principal observation reports contain multiple data points) *Observation reports contain multiple data points.*	Teachers' use of "reasoning out loud" strategies increased from an average of 0 per class to an average of 5 per class from September to May.	Teachers incorporated more "reasoning out loud" strategies in their classrooms.

Individual data sources and information items are clustered in the example in Figure 9B to make the finding more robust. Robust findings are those that are both accurate and persuasive and therefore deserve confidence. Triangulation, having data from more than one source to support the finding, is one way to ensure that the findings are robust. If a teacher survey, student achievement data, and an expert all report that student achievement is declining and teachers are seeking new ways to address student needs, the finding about student performance is more supportable. Looking for quantitative data that can be supported with qualitative data is another way to triangulate data sources and strengthen the interpretation process.

Of course, alternative interpretations are possible with other combinations of data or information items. The evaluator can make greatest sense of the findings by trying out a number of possible interpretations, engaging program stakeholders in dialogue about which interpretations might be most feasible from their perspective, and examining the analyzed data to determine which interpretations are most supportable.

More support makes the finding more credible and harder to ignore and gives the program stakeholders more information to examine possible implications and potential actions as a result of the evaluation. Patton suggests the use of a claims matrix to categorize claims or findings from an evaluation as either major or minor, strong or weak. The claims matrix is a useful tool to help the evaluator determine which findings are more important to present to stakeholders. Patton recommends that evaluators seek to make major claims with strong support.

The most powerful, useful, and credible claims are those that are of major importance and have strong empirical support (Patton, 1997).

Claims Matrix

Rigor of Claims	Importance of Claims	
	Major	*Minor*
Strong	*	
Weak		

Source: Michael Quinn Patton, *Utilization-focused evaluation: A new century text* (3rd ed.). Claims Matrix from pp. 322–323. ©1997 by SAGE. Reprinted with permission.

*GOAL: Strong claims of major importance.

The most powerful, useful, and credible claims are those that are of major importance and have strong empirical support.

Characteristics of a Claim of MAJOR IMPORTANCE

- Involves making a difference, having an impact, or achieving desirable outcomes
- Deals with a problem of great societal concern
- Affects large numbers of people
- Provides a sustainable solution (claim deals with something that lasts over time)
- Saves money
- Saves time, that is, accomplishes something in less time than is usually the case (an efficiency claim)
- Enhances quality
- Claims to be "new" or innovative
- Shows that something can actually be done about the problem; that is, claims the problem is malleable
- Involves a model or approach that could be used by others (meaning the model or approach is clearly specified and adaptable to other situations)

Characteristics of a STRONG CLAIM

- Valid, believable evidence to support the claim
- Follow-up data over time (longer periods of follow-up provide stronger evidence than shorter periods, and any follow-up is stronger than just end-of-program results)
- The claim is about a clear intervention (model or approach) with solid implementation documentation
- The claim is about clearly specified outcomes and impacts: behavioral outcomes are stronger than opinions, feelings, and knowledge
- The evidence for claims includes comparisons:
  - To program goals
  - Over time (pre-, post-, follow-up)
  - With other groups
  - With general trends or norms
- The evidence for claims includes replications:
  - Done at more than one site
  - More than one staff person attained outcomes
  - Different cohort groups of participants attained comparable outcomes over time
  - Different programs attained comparable results using comparable approaches
- Claims are based on more than one kind of evidence or data (i.e., triangulation of data):
  - Quantitative and qualitative data
  - Multiple sources (e.g., kids, parents, teachers, and staff corroborate results)
- There are clear logical and/or empirical linkages between the intervention and the claimed outcomes
- The evaluators are independent of the staff (or where internal evaluation data are used, an independent, credible person reviews the results and certifies the results)
- Claims are based on systematic data collection over time

(Continued)

(Continued)

CAVEAT

Importance and rigor are not absolute criteria. Different stakeholders, decision makers, and claims makers will have different definitions of what is important and rigorous. What staff deem to be of major importance may not be so to outside observers. What is deemed important and rigorous changes over time and across contexts. Making public claims is a political action. Importance and rigor are, to some extent, politically defined and dependent on the values of specific stakeholders.

Related Distinctions

1. Program *premises* are different from but related to and dependent on program *claims.*

   Premises are the basic assumptions on which a program is based, for example, that effective, attentive parenting is desirable and more likely to produce well-functioning children who become well-functioning adults. This premise is based on *research*. The program cannot "prove" the premise (though supporting research can and should be provided). The program's claims are about the program's actual implementation and concrete outcomes; for example, a program might claim that the program yielded more effective parents who are more attentive to their children. The program does not have to follow the children to adulthood before claims can be made.

2. Evidence is different from claims—but claims <u>depend on</u> evidence.

   Claim: This program trains welfare recipients for jobs, places them in jobs; as a result, they become self-sufficient and leave the welfare rolls.

   Evidence: Numbers and types of job placements over time; pre-, post-, and follow-up data on welfare status; participant interview data about program effects; employer interview data about placements.

Source: Michael Quinn Patton, *Utilization-focused evaluation: A new century text* (3rd ed.). Claims Matrix from pp. 322–323. ©1997 by SAGE. Reprinted with permission.

FORMING JUDGMENTS ABOUT THE PROGRAM'S SUCCESS

At this stage, the evaluator determines whether the program is successful from the data, its analysis, and its interpretation. Success can be determined by comparing the results of the program to the standards for success that were established for the program. Standards serve as the criteria of success against which the program is measured. The evaluator is determining whether a program achieved its intended results or improved other related and unanticipated conditions. If student achievement is the target, and the evidence collected and analyzed demonstrates that student achievement has increased and the increase meets or exceeds the standards established for acceptable performance, the evaluator can conclude that the program has achieved its intended outcome. Without the standard, any judgment becomes arbitrary and suspect.

Standards can be arbitrary themselves or they can have empirical or practical support. A standard is a statement of desired impact of the program and seeks to answer the question "How good is good enough?" If the program's objective was to raise student achievement by 10% on the standardized test of mathematics and the data indicate only an 8% gain, the evaluator will find that the program did not achieve its intended results. Nevertheless, the evaluator may want to use the data to suggest ways to increase the effectiveness of the program or question the reasonableness of the standard, the program timeline, or the program's structure. With specific standards of desirable results in place, the judgment process is less capricious and less subjective. The standards will reflect expectations for the program's results and, therefore, the actual results will be more meaningful and useful to program stakeholders.

The value of glass-box evaluations is particularly evident at this stage of evaluation. Programs may or may not achieve their intended results; to suggest that a program is a failure, however, and bypass the opportunity for finding ways to improve the program or learn from the program is a huge loss to students, educators, and the field of staff development. To end an evaluation with a finding that the program has not met its anticipated results, without understanding possible reasons why, leaves program stakeholders empty-handed. The evaluator who has conducted a black-box evaluation lacks the information or data to understand what might have contributed to or been responsible for the results.

If a program falls above or below the established standard, the program is not automatically a success or failure. If a program has not met its expected standard but is close to achieving the intended results, the evaluator may examine factors that prevented the program from reaching the desired success. Perhaps the original timeline was too brief. Perhaps program staff lacked the skills to deliver the program. Perhaps program participants were reluctant to get involved in the early stages. Whatever the reasons, evaluators who have data about how the program worked and information about the program's operation and implementation will be better able to offer explanations for the program's results and to recommend ways to improve it. Formulating explanations is best done in collaboration with representatives of the program stakeholders. Their perspectives and insights expand the evaluator's reasoning.

Claims of Attribution or Contribution

It is important to revisit the concepts of attribution and contribution discussed in Chapter 6. There is an intense desire and demand to show that there is a cause-effect relationship between staff development and increases in student achievement. Perhaps because the argument is so intuitively strong, the desire to assume or suggest causality is stronger than a fear of misrepresenting evaluation findings. Policy makers and other decision makers often ask advocates for staff development to show that there is such a cause-effect relationship and that investments in professional learning are more valuable than other reform or improvement efforts. Evaluators must be careful in making claims of attribution, that is, saying that a staff development program solely is *responsible for* the changes that occurred. In education, most evaluation and research studies are not designed to result in conclusions about the cause-effect relationship. The design of most staff development evaluations makes this finding virtually impossible. When staff developers are confronted with policy makers or their publics who want evaluations that will make this claim, a rich opportunity exists to teach the difference between attribution and contribution.

Contribution suggests that the staff development program was *involved,* yet it was *not solely responsible* for the change in teacher practice or increase in student achievement. It acknowledges that other factors act to influence student achievement. One factor that we know influences student achievement is students' socioeconomic status. Poverty has been identified as a significant influence in students' academic success in a number of studies. A number of other factors, such as familiarity with the tests, improved test-taking skills, different cohorts of students, other learning experiences the teachers participate in, new teachers, or a new principal at the school may also contribute to the increases in student achievement. For example, a study of staff development in high- and low-performing schools in Georgia (Harkreader & Weathersby, 1998) worked back and forth between qualitative and quantitative data and discovered that certain characteristics of professional development were common in high-performing schools but noticeably absent in lower-performing schools. They inferred that those characteristics were making a contribution to student achievement, or conversely that the absence of those characteristics was related to low performance. Within the group of high-performing schools, specific professional development activities varied widely, so the results could not be attributed to specific training activities, suggesting that it wasn't what they did but how they decided what to do that made a difference (M.J. Taylor, personal communication, October 8, 2001).

Attribution, on the other hand, suggests that *nothing other than* the staff development program was responsible for the change in student achievement. Claims of attribution imply a cause-and-effect relationship and also imply that measurable and identifiable changes can be attributed solely to the staff development program. But claims of attribution are possible only in strictly controlled experimental studies, something rarely done in the real-life context of education. For example, professional development training in 6 + 1 Trait writing results in improved student writing scores at School A. The same training in School B resulted in no change in student performance. Since neither School A nor School B was randomly assigned to the treatment or control group, an attribution claim that the changes in student writing performance are the result of 6 + 1 Trait writing training is not possible. It is possible to say that "in School A, 6 + 1 Trait writing training *contributed to* improvement in student performance in writing." An evaluator would want to hold both schools under the microscope to identify other differences between the schools that may have influenced the success of the staff development program (M.J. Taylor, personal communication, October 8, 2001).

This distinction is critical for evaluators. Because many who question the link between staff development and student achievement do not value evaluation claims of contribution, they question or even discount evaluations that do not result in claims of attribution. Many educators and staff developers want more from an evaluation of staff development than is possible. Understanding the difference between attribution and contribution and accurately reflecting this distinction in evaluations of staff development will add to a broader understanding of these two important concepts.

Determining Merit and Worth

Ultimately the evaluator is determining whether the program is valuable to those who participate (worth) and if it produces the intended results (merit). Guskey (2000) defines merit as "a property of the program, judged by comparing its performance against an established standard of excellence in the profession" (p. 43). Worth, he explains, is "the extent to which the program is essential to the organization's mission, its perceived value to various constituents, its payoff in terms of the benefits to a single individual as in the case of an individually guided professional development activity" (p. 43). Patton (1997) defines merit as "the intrinsic value of a program, for example, how effective it is in meeting the needs of those it is intended to help" (p. 65). He defines worth as the "extrinsic value to those outside the program, for example to the larger community or society" (p. 65). Sometimes programs have high perceived worth and little merit. Occasionally the opposite is true. A program may produce the intended results and be perceived by program participants as cumbersome, too costly in terms of their time and effort, inappropriate, or unsuccessful.

When the latter occurs, it is even more important to share the evaluation findings with the participants. When they are so closely engaged in a staff development program, burdened by new expectations, confronted with their attitudes and aspirations, and overwhelmed with the challenge of changing years of habits and practice while juggling new knowledge and skills, both the evaluator and the program director might reasonably expect participants to experience dissonance and disequilibrium. Sharing the evaluation findings may offer encouragement and evidence of the impact of the hard work participants are engaged in to increase student achievement.

The goal of evaluating results-based staff development programs is to know whether the program does contribute to increases in student achievement and how. Not all programs will be successful immediately. Abundant opportunities emerge for improving those programs that may have been less than successful initially. The role of the evaluator is to help program stakeholders use the evaluation information to move ahead more informed about effective staff development, armed with evidence about their current practices, and with a clear commitment to improve student achievement.

Making Recommendations

Another part of the interpretation process is formulating recommendations about the program's design, operation, or impact. Recommendations identify the next steps for the program and its stakeholders or suggest changes that might strengthen the program or its results. Recommendations can focus on changes in the program's operation, policies, resources, personnel, or activities. Well-developed recommendations can serve to solidify the evaluation process, while poorly crafted ones may discredit the value of an evaluation (Patton, 1997). Not all evaluations include recommendations. Evaluators and program stakeholders should determine whether to include recommendations in the final evaluation report.

The evaluator is in a unique position to offer recommendations. She may have evidence that suggests that in schools where principals were actively engaged in professional learning alongside their teachers, students' performance was higher. She may see that, in schools with little clarity about the purpose of staff development, teachers were less likely to sustain usage of a new instructional practice. Therefore, she may recommend that schools' leadership teams make the purpose of staff development more explicit and expectations clearer.

Sometimes the data available do not offer information on the programs' process and the evaluator cannot as easily make recommendations for improving the program. In these cases, he can turn to research and best practices, experts in the field, and other evaluation of similar programs to develop helpful and useful recommendations (Weiss, 1998). In addition, he might invite program participants and other stakeholders to suggest their own recommendations.

Decisions about a program's continuation or discontinuation are usually not a part of recommendations an evaluator makes. Program directors and policy and decision makers typically make those decisions on the basis of the evaluation.

The following questions may assist evaluators in the interpretation process:

1. What do these data tell program personnel?

2. What are the implications of these findings?

3. What do the findings mean for this program in practical terms?

4. What are the limitations of these findings?

5. Does this program have worth, that is, is it seen as a valuable part of the school's or district's mission, or is it perceived as valuable to the program participants?

6. What recommended actions can either improve the program or its results?

Planning Phase

- Assess evaluability
- Formulate evaluation questions
- Construct the evaluation framework

Conducting Phase

- Collect data
- Organize, analyze, and display data
- Interpret data

Reporting Phase

- Disseminate and use findings
- Evaluate the evaluation

Disseminate and Use Findings

10

Disseminating the findings of the evaluation requires the evaluator to prepare and disseminate interim and final reports about the evaluation study. Reports can be offered in a variety of written and oral formats. In this step, the evaluator considers answers to several questions:

1. Will there be interim reports or only a final report?

2. Who are the various audiences with whom the evaluation report will be shared?

3. Who is the primary audience for the evaluation report?

4. What does the primary audience for the evaluation report want and need to know in the report? For example, how much do they want to know about methodology, data sources and collection tools, and other technical aspects?

5. Will the final report be written, oral, or oral supported with graphics or other presentation aids?

6. What is the best format for presenting the written report to the primary audience, that is, brief text with bullets, more charts, tables, or graphs than text, technical?

7. When the various audiences receive the report, will those presentations permit the audience members to interact with the evaluator, the evaluation team, and the program staff about the findings?

8. What voice or tone is best for the written report, that is, conversational, authoritative?

9. Will other audiences want to read the evaluation report?

10. Will there be one, or multiple, evaluation reports tailored to various audiences?

11. Who else will be disseminating the report? speaking about the evaluation? What information or materials will they need to speak both accurately and effectively about the evaluation?

12. Will the report be disseminated widely or to a limited audience? Primarily to internal stakeholders? to external stakeholders? to members of the community? to the media?

13. What layout or design issues must be considered in preparing the final report? For formal publication, will the evaluator need to adhere to certain specifications in word processing? Or if the report will be translated to pdf or html files for Web-based distribution, what is the best way to format the document?

14. Will there be a formal press release?

15. What will be the role of the evaluator beyond the presentation of the final report and the completion of Step 8: Evaluate the Evaluation? Will the evaluator have any ongoing relationship with the program, program staff, or organizations?

INTERIM VERSUS FINAL REPORTS

Sometimes evaluators prepare interim reports about the progress of the program and final reports about the impact of the program. The two differ in that the interim report does not attempt to assess impact, but rather focuses on the process, implementation, or operation of the program. The interim reports are formative evaluations that present status reports on what is occurring. Interim reports may include recommendations for fine-tuning, modifying, or changing some aspect of the program to improve implementation.

One or more interim evaluation reports may be required by the program manager or funder. Typically, programs funded by federal, state, or local agencies or foundations require at least one interim report documenting the program's progress. Interim reports may include documentation about the number of clients served, the occurrence of program activities, and budget expenditures.

Final reports most often focus on a staff development program's impact and use the intended results or overall program goals as their focus. Rather than emphasizing the program's operational aspects, a summative report focuses on the impact of the program, detailing what happened and why.

Although final reports most often focus on the impact of the staff development program, some evaluations are conducted for different purposes. Some evaluations are done to determine need. Some are done to assess a program's theory of change. Some are done to improve implementation. In these cases, the final reports naturally will focus on what the evaluation was intended to do. In other words, not all final evaluation reports will focus on a program's impact.

FORMAT OF THE EVALUATION REPORT

Most evaluators submit a written report of the evaluation study, although this is not always necessary. Sometimes an oral presentation with supporting graphics, charts, tables, or graphs may suffice to inform the audience about the findings. Other times, a more formal and extensive evaluation report is necessary. The evaluator should make decisions about the format, style, and structure of the final report with the stakeholders to ensure that it will be delivered in the most useful format. Occasionally the evaluator will be asked to provide multiple forms of an evaluation report, such as an executive summary, a simple one- to five-page report with bullets and highlights for wider distribution or posting on a school or district's Web site, and a technical and comprehensive report as well.

Simplicity and clarity are the goals of both oral and written reports. The evaluator strives to ensure that the language and tone of the evaluation are neutral, unbiased, and informative. Reports should be easy to understand and free of jargon or technical terms not widely known to likely audiences. Preparing the report is not the time for the evaluator to impress an audience with his or her technical knowledge about evaluation, but rather to become the teacher. Evaluators are trained to clarify and simplify a complex process so that others can understand it and use the results effectively in making decisions for improving both the program and its results.

Patton (1997) begs for simplicity in evaluation reports and presentations so that the information will be accessible and understandable to those who intend to use its results:

> Simplicity as a virtue means that we seek clarity, not complexity. Our presentations must be like the skilled acrobat who makes the most dazzling moves look easy, the audience being unaware of the long hours of practice and the sophisticated calculations involved in what appear to be simple movements. Likewise evaluators must find ways of so perfecting their public performances that those participating will understand the results, though unaware of the long hours of arduous work involved in sifting through the data, organizing it, arranging it, testing out relationships, taking the data apart, and creatively putting it back together to arrive at that moment of public unveiling. (p. 310)

Clarity is another attribute of evaluation reports that evaluators want to address. What is said will have a long-term impact on the program stakeholders. The way it is said will also influence the degree to which people will be able and willing to hear the message.

Mary Jean Taylor, a program evaluator and colleague, shared the story below with the author via e-mail:

> I was coming back from meetings in Washington, DC, and happened to be seated next to a scientist from Ball Aerospace. We got into a fairly lengthy conversation about the organizational behaviors that led to the *Challenger* disaster, writing, and rocket design. You would have enjoyed it. I made some comment about the importance of writing clearly so you could be understood, and he noted that they used a different criterion for clear writing—to write so that you could not be misunderstood. I immediately liked the idea and try to use it as my standard. (personal e-mail, September 9, 2001)

The standard used at Ball Aerospace for writing is a high bar for written work. Preparing the evaluation report sometimes seems anticlimactic; but the report stands long after the work is completed as evidence of the thought, effort, and energy that went into the entire evaluation.

The evaluators and all those who help to write the report should be aware of the need to remain concise, unbiased, and accurate. According to the Accuracy Standards section in *Program Evaluation Standards*, "reporting procedures should guard against distortion caused by personal feelings and biases of any party to the evaluation so that evaluation reports reflect the evaluation findings fairly" (Joint Committee on Standards for Educational Evaluation, 1994). These standards appear in Appendix A. In addition to accurate reporting and concise writing, when reporting on sources of information used in a program evaluation, evaluators need to provide enough detail to make the adequacy of the information evident.

The evaluator keeps the goals of the evaluation in the forefront when preparing either an interim or a final report. Yet a secondary goal of evaluations of staff development is to contribute to the conceptual knowledge about effective staff development. Evaluation, then, becomes a mechanism to help stakeholders understand (1) how the staff development program works, (2) how change occurs, (3) what factors enhance and inhibit change, and (4) how their knowledge, actions, and beliefs influence student learning.

Evaluations can help stakeholders develop new insights and perspectives about their work. Sometimes program staff are too close to see how even simple changes dramatically increase the impact of the program. For example, teachers in one program appreciated it when the staff developer left a short note after a classroom observation and conference listing key points from the conference. Teachers referred back to these notes, they said, as reminders about implementing new practices and a way to assess their own progress. They also viewed them as motivation to move ahead. Teachers said they were sometimes flustered or anxious in the conference and didn't remember all the details. The staff developers were previously unaware of the impact of that practice and had begun using it inconsistently because they had believed the practice was not helpful. When staff developers learned the value of their notes, writing them became a part of every classroom visit.

Typical Components of a Final Evaluation Report

Evaluation reports can take a variety of formats. The list that follows includes possible components to guide discussion with the primary audience about what components they want in their evaluation report and is not intended to be a list of required components. While evaluation specialists may add other elements to these components, they most often agree on these as the essential ones (Boulmetis & Dutwin, 2000; Hendricks, 1994; Weiss, 1998; Zepeda, 1999).

Sometimes, before a final draft of a report is completed, evaluators meet with those who will use the report to talk about the findings and the "look and feel" of the report. Discussing the findings and recommendations with key program staff, the director, and others in advance of preparing the final draft of the report will increase their understanding and acceptance of it.

While an evaluation serves as a vital and formal part of the information base upon which future decisions about the program's design, status, and resources,

Table 10.1 Possible Components of Evaluation Reports

---

1. EXECUTIVE SUMMARY/ABSTRACT

   Evaluation questions

   Summary of findings

   Implications

   Recommendations

2. INTRODUCTION

   Purpose of the evaluation

   Goals of the evaluation

   Evaluation questions

3. OVERVIEW OF THE PROGRAM

   Program description and context

   Program goals, objectives, and activities

   Resources

   Stakeholders

   Participants

4. EVALUATION DESIGN

   Methods

   Data collection

   Data sources

   Data analysis

5. FINDINGS

   Interpretations

   Limitations

   Implications

6. RECOMMENDATIONS

   Future actions

   Possible resources

---

it is typically not the *sole* source of information on which future decisions are based. Evaluation serves as one part of a much broader knowledge base about the program that policy and decision makers have accumulated over time.

Disseminating the Report

The final report belongs to the organization that commissioned it. The evaluator might facilitate discussion with the program director or stakeholders to determine who will receive a copy of the report, but the ultimate decision rests with the school, district, or agency. Some suggestions for distributing the report are listed below, although they are merely ideas to consider.

Ways to Distribute an Evaluation Report

- Web site
- Presentations to groups, committees:
  - School board or accountability teams
  - Department chairs or administrative team
  - Faculties or parent organization

- Mailing
- Media coverage:
  - Newspaper
  - Television
  - Cable

- Inclusion in other reports:
  - Quarterly reports
  - Annual reports
  - Newsletters

Different versions of the evaluation reports may best serve the interests and needs of different audiences. Table 10.2 suggests kinds of evaluation reports that may be most appropriate to common audiences.

Study Groups

The evaluator can facilitate the usefulness of the evaluation to the program staff by leading study groups on the report. The study groups would include strategically selected or interested individuals. They would come together after having read the report prepared to discuss it, ask questions, and consider its implications. The protocol below is one example of how the study groups might discuss the report:

Member Identification

Identify members of the study group either by inviting strategically selected members who represent various project stakeholders or who volunteer to participate because they hold a particular interest in the results of the evaluation.

Prereading Guide

Prepare a prereading guide to accompany the report when it is sent to study group members. The prereading guide will remind participants about the time and location of the meeting, offer guidance for reading the report as in the questions in the accompanying box, and encourage participants to come prepared to the study group meeting.

Sample Prereading Guide

Thank you for agreeing to be a member of the Study Group on the Math and Science Staff Development Evaluation. Your participation is important because you can assist with the dissemination of the evaluation report and, more important, be a part of decisions about the program that will be made based on this evaluation. Our meeting will be held in the Main Office Conference Room on Tuesday, May 16, at 3:45 p.m. at Perry High School. The meeting is scheduled to last until 5:00 p.m.

Before reading the evaluation report, take a few minutes and fill out the form below:

Name:
Role:
E-mail:
Relationship to the Math and Science Staff Development Program:
Reason for volunteering to be a member of the Study Group:
Individuals/Groups you plan to share the evaluation results with:
Predictions about what the evaluation report will say. List four or five conclusions or findings
   you expect to find in the report:

As you read the report, use these codes and mark the text:
++ strongly agree
+ agree
?? not clear to me
! disagree
!! strongly disagree

Jot down questions you want to ask the following people. Mark the appropriate column to indicate whom you want to answer the questions.

Questions to Ask	Evaluator	Program Director	Program Staff	Program Participants	Policy Makers Members	Other Study Group

Submit a copy of these questions that emerge from your reading to George Markham no later than Tuesday, May 3, so the evaluation team can review them before the study group.

Table 10.2   Typical Evaluation Reports for Various Audiences

Audience	Version of the Report
• **Primary stakeholder** Program director and program's supervisor, such as the superintendent, assistant superintendent, board of education, funder or funding agency; program staff	Full report
• **Secondary stakeholder** Program participants	Executive summary and/or abbreviated report
• **Public** Community members, parents, various committees not directly involved in the project	Executive summary and/or abbreviated report
• **Other agencies, districts, schools**	Executive summary and/or abbreviated report

Study Group Protocol

Facilitator introduces himself or herself.

Members introduce themselves and state their interest in the project.

Facilitator and members make agreements for the conversation like the ones below.

- We will focus on the report and not our personal opinions or hunches.
- We will focus on the issues not people.
- We will not find fault, but rather find possibilities.
- We will listen fully to each other's comments.
- We will approach this discussion with an inquisitive mind rather than a fix-it mind-set. That is, we want to understand rather than to act. We may choose to act after we fully understand. Understanding is the focus of this meeting.
- We will refer frequently to the report when we speak, pausing to let each member find the right page before we ask questions or make comments.

Facilitator guides the discussion using the questions below.

1. What did the report tell us?

2. How did your own predictions differ from the evaluation's conclusions?

3. What data sources were most influential to you?

4. What aspects of the report did you strongly agree with?

5. What aspects of the report did you disagree with?

6. What questions do you have about the report? Let's try to get answers to those questions.

7. What did you learn today about the evaluation and the project?

8. Who else needs to know about this report?

9. How do you plan to share what you learned today with your colleagues?

10. What might be some next steps for the evaluator and project staff?

Any interim findings, as well as the final report, should be disseminated promptly so that the information can be used in a timely fashion. Stakeholders have a *right* to receive the information from the evaluation. The Joint Committee on Standards for Educational Evaluation advocates that "disclosure of findings be made accessible to the people affected by the evaluation, as well as any others with expressed legal rights to receive the results. In addition, evaluators who plan to use information from the report to inform others about the evaluation process or as references for future work will want to ask permission to share the report with others. They must protect the identity of the school or district if they use the information to advance the field of evaluation. The *Program Evaluation Standards* and *Guiding Principles for Evaluators* address the evaluator's appropriate use of evaluation results (see Appendix A).

Planning Phase

- Assess evaluability
- Formulate evaluation questions
- Construct the evaluation framework

Conducting Phase

- Collect data
- Organize, analyze, and display data
- Interpret data

Reporting Phase

- Disseminate and use findings
- Evaluate the evaluation

Evaluate the Evaluation

11

Once the evaluation report is completed and disseminated, the evaluators evaluate the evaluation. This step gives them an opportunity to gain valuable feedback on the results of their work, how the work was done, and the value or usefulness of the evaluation. This practice is the hallmark of a reflective practitioner and allows evaluators to model evaluation behaviors as a routine part of their work and to engage in continual improvement. The process of conducting an evaluation of the evaluation is helpful to those who commissioned the evaluation as well. It will give them time to reflect on the value of the evaluation process, what they learned, and how evaluation can be used in the future to strengthen the information base upon which they make critical staff development decisions.

At this stage, the evaluator seeks answers to these questions:

What can I learn about

- The program?
- The effectiveness and efficiency of this evaluation?
- The field and value of evaluation?
- My knowledge, skills, attitudes, and practices as an evaluator?
- The value of this evaluation?

There is no "right" way to conduct an evaluation of the evaluation. One strategy is to create a survey to administer to those involved; another is to conduct a focus group with representatives from the stakeholder groups; yet another strategy is to have stakeholders engage in an informal discussion about the evaluation. Evaluators may want to add a question to the study group protocol about the value of the evaluation. Evaluating the evaluation might be done best as a discussion with the key stakeholders, including the program director and staff involved in the evaluation, decision and policy makers who used the evaluation results, and program participants involved in the evaluation. (See "Questions for Your Consideration" below for appropriate questions for the evaluator to pose during this step of the evaluation process.)

When evaluators seek to improve their own work, increase the use of evaluation within an organization, and build the capacity of others to engage in "evaluation think," they contribute to a greater purpose. Through their work, they convey the importance of evaluation as a process for improvement and ultimately for increasing the focus on results.

QUESTIONS FOR YOUR CONSIDERATION

The evaluator will want to answer these questions:

Resources

Were the time, personnel, and money allocated for this evaluation adequate to conduct the evaluation as it was designed?

Design

Did the design align with the evaluation question(s) and provide the appropriate data to answer the question(s)?

Did the evaluation address the questions the program stakeholders wanted and needed answered?

How appropriate were the data-collection procedures?

Were appropriate stakeholders involved in the design of this evaluation?

Analysis/Interpretation

Were the data-analysis methods appropriate for the type of evaluation conducted?

Were the data displayed in ways that facilitated use of the data?

Were multiple, appropriate stakeholders involved in the interpretation of the analyzed data?

Findings/Interpretation

How certain are we that the findings are credible and unbiased and result from rigorous analysis of the data?

To what degree are the recommendations timely, realistic, comprehensible, and specific?

What recommendations have been implemented?

What program changes have occurred or are being planned as a result of this evaluation?

Reporting

Were the findings presented clearly and accurately in ways appropriate for the various audiences?

To what degree do the intended users find the evaluation results to be useful, informative, enlightening, and a justification for the program?

Did stakeholders have opportunities to ask questions about the evaluation report?

In what ways has the evaluation report been used? What plans are in place to act on the evaluation's recommendations or others that resulted from stakeholders?

Evaluator

Was the evaluator professional and ethical?

To what degree did the evaluator uphold the *Program Evaluation Standards* and the *Guiding Principles for Evaluators?*

Was the evaluator collaborative and responsive to the needs of the evaluation clients?

Did the evaluator engage in an evaluation of the evaluation?

Has the evaluator made public his or her learning gain from this evaluation experience?

After an extensive or even brief evaluation study, evaluators and evaluation teams may not have the energy or motivation to engage in this last step. Yet this last step of the eight-step process is most helpful to the evaluator or team. If the evaluation team neglects this final reflection, they will lose an opportunity to learn about the work of evaluation.

Shifting Perspectives About Evaluating Staff Development

12

Conducting a staff development program evaluation requires practitioners to alter an often-held negative and fearful view of evaluation. When conducted as a routine part of any program, evaluation provides valuable information to help program managers make decisions so that the program positively impacts its clients. Table 12.1 describes the shift in thinking that is needed in order to view evaluation in a helpful light and to engage more practitioners in evaluation of their staff development programs.

Table 12.1 Paradigm Shift in Evaluating Staff Development

From	To
Externally driven and designed	Internally driven and designed
Summative evaluations only	Planning, formative, and summative evaluations
Event-based	Program-based
Looking for answers/solutions from others	Discovering or creating solutions and alternatives with others
Feared	Embraced
Filed/shelved	Used
Done as an afterthought	Planned from the beginning
Documentation	Evaluation
Process-focused	Results-focused
Presentation of results	Reflective dialogue

EXTERNALLY DRIVEN AND DESIGNED VERSUS INTERNALLY DRIVEN AND DESIGNED

Specific programs receive external, independent evaluations—often with external federal, state, or private funding—to determine whether the program was successful. When only the external evaluator makes decisions about the evaluation's design, program participants tend to feel disenfranchised and uninvolved in the evaluation. When program stakeholders are involved more actively in all aspects of the evaluation, they gain these advantages:

- More investment in the program's success
- More opportunity to understand how the program works
- The ability to avert problems before they occur
- The possibility of using practical and reasonable solutions to problems that do occur
- More information to improve the program on an ongoing basis
- Increased advocacy for the program and its success

SUMMATIVE EVALUATIONS ONLY VERSUS PLANNING, FORMATIVE, AND SUMMATIVE EVALUATIONS

Planning, formative, and summative evaluations have distinct purposes. Planning evaluations, those conducted before a program is designed, help identify the social conditions or needs that the program should address. Sometimes when specific needs are not clearly articulated, a program's design may target perceived needs rather than real needs. While planning evaluations are done at the beginning of a program, formative evaluations are those done in the middle. They are designed to give information about how a staff development program is working. This type of evaluation information is essential to improving programs, preventing problems related to implementation, and ensuring that the program is fully functioning. Evaluators can also use formative evaluations to help explain how the program works and how it contributes to the results it achieves. For staff developers to be able to replicate a program and also to contribute to the broad conceptual knowledge base of the field of professional development, how the process leads to the results must be clear. Summative evaluations are done at the end of a program or at a particularly important benchmark. If a program is three years long, a summative evaluation would obviously be conducted at the end of the three years. If the intention is to continue the program, ongoing evaluation might be done every three to five years to determine whether the program continues to impact both educator and student learning.

EVENT-BASED VERSUS PROGRAM-BASED

What is thought to be staff development is often really a training event. This limited view of staff development interferes with the ability of some staff development to produce the intended results—that is, to improve student achievement. When staff development is perceived as an isolated event or even a series of isolated events, there is an inherent danger that the design may fall short of the comprehensive scope of experiences and support necessary to change practice and positively impact student achievement. Staff development is the planned, coherent actions and support systems designed and implemented to develop knowledge, skills, attitudes, aspiration, and behaviors to improve student achievement. The research is clear: Good training alone will not guarantee that information will be used, nor will good training alone produce student results (Joyce & Showers, 1982; NSDC, 2001).

LOOKING FOR ANSWERS OR SOLUTIONS FROM OTHERS VERSUS DISCOVERING OR CREATING SOLUTIONS OR ALTERNATIVES WITH OTHERS

When external forces pressure us to perform and meet expectations, there is the tendency in education, as in other fields, to look for quick fixes and convenient interventions. In schools, quick fixes often translate into the adoption of isolated programs or short-term training. The assumptions that educators hold influence these practices. Some assumptions that educators hold are

- If teachers have new knowledge, then surely student achievement will increase.
- If principals know more about instructional leadership, then student achievement will increase.
- If a program has worked somewhere else, then it probably will work in our school as well.
- If teachers attend staff development, they will then implement in their classrooms what they learned.
- All teachers and principals want to learn and grow.
- What works in one school will work in all schools.

These assumptions are faulty: Knowing does not automatically mean doing. Schools are complex social systems dependent on people whose knowledge, skills, and relationships cannot be easily transformed. What works in one may not work in another.

Confronting these assumptions may fundamentally change the way we improve schools. If we cannot simply install programs and expect long-term, deep change, then what are schools whose students are dramatically below grade level supposed to do? Merely doing what can be squeezed into the available time and budget has not produced the results we seek. Instead, the answer lies in adopting an inquiry perspective about our work. That is, we must actively seek to examine the impact of our work.

"Evaluation think" therefore becomes an important concept. We must become evaluators of our work—asking ourselves questions to elicit data so we can make decisions about what is and is not producing the impact we hope to produce. We must continually assess what we are learning, doing, believing, valuing, and wanting. We must be ruthless in asking for evidence and scrutinizing our own practices. To improve, we must get comfortable with the idea of routinely and critically examining our data to know whether our work is producing the results we desire.

FEARED VERSUS EMBRACED

Simply mentioning the word *evaluation* engenders fear and suspicion in most people. People generally associate evaluation with correction or improvement of deficit behaviors. Still others believe that evaluation suggests personal inadequacy. Personal experience or history with evaluation may support these perceptions. Rather than fear evaluations, we must embrace them, participate in them actively, and adopt evaluation think to generate the information necessary to make sound decisions about professional learning.

Evaluation should be embraced for the purposes of improving a program or the social condition and contributing to the field. Evaluation provides the analysis that informs future decisions and policies. Without periodic, objective evaluation, practices may cease to have the intended impact. Evaluation keeps us honest. By offering far more than conjecture, opinion, or individual preferences, evaluation justifies everyday or significant decisions about our work as staff developers.

Staff development leaders can improve the perceived value of evaluations by asking these questions before decisions are made:

- What do data tell us?
- What evaluation report or processes can we examine before we make these decisions?
- What evaluation process will we put in place to inform us that this is working as intended, producing the results intended, and contributing to the well-being of individuals and the organization?
- Is this a good investment of our resources?

FILED/SHELVED VERSUS USED

- Evaluations provide useful information. Three problems typically occur. First, many program managers are so involved in program implementation and design that they do not think about evaluation. Second, when external evaluators conduct the evaluation and do not purposely involve program staff, the staff perceive the evaluation as unimportant. Third, evaluation reports are so convoluted or technical that they are not useful to program staff, particularly if the staff have not been involved in the design of the evaluation. As a result of these problems, many evaluation reports sit on shelves or in file cabinets unused.
- Because evaluations are often time-consuming and expensive, program managers resort to using opinions, hunches, and guesses to answer

questions about the program. Using anything less than data or evidence collected with a specific plan and guided by clear questions to learn about the merit, worth, or impact of a program is insufficient. Evaluation data—purposefully collected, analyzed, and interpreted—will provide the most reliable basis for sound decisions about any staff development program. Every evaluation should be conducted with the interest of using the results to make decisions about the program. With this mind-set in place, evaluation will not just be shelved, but rather will become the topic of numerous meetings, dialogues, and other interactions.

DONE AS AN AFTERTHOUGHT VERSUS PLANNED AT THE BEGINNING

Sometimes evaluations are an afterthought. Well into a project or program, someone may ask what kind of evaluation is being done to determine whether the program is working. At that point, someone decides how to gather the appropriate evidence to document the program's operation and assess its impact. Inevitably, when doing evaluation planning after implementation, someone will say, "If we had gathered this information at the beginning . . ." or "If we had known, we could have . . ."

Planning evaluation in the middle or at the end of a program compromises the quality and sometimes the integrity of the evaluation. Evaluation is best planned from the inception of the program when stakeholders are beginning to articulate the possibilities for the program. An evaluator can assist the program designers in clarifying the goals, objectives, and processes of the new program. Early planning of the evaluation strengthens both the program and the evaluation.

The evaluator, who sometimes is the program director, can contribute to the program's quality during the design stage by asking these questions:

- Are the identified needs and the program's intended intervention aligned?
- Are the program's activities sufficiently powerful to produce the intended changes?
- Is the plan comprehensive enough?
- Are appropriate resources available to implement the program?

A purposeful evaluation planned before the program begins is best, but there are strategies for conducting an evaluation after the program begins.

DOCUMENTATION VERSUS EVALUATION

In current practice, much of what constitutes evaluation of staff development is actually documentation of events. Compliance regulations for some programs and funders often require program directors to report on services delivered, such as the number of training sessions held, the number or characteristics of participants, and completion rates.

The following statements lend insight into the differences between the two processes:

> Documentation is gathering and presenting data while evaluation is the systematic investigation of a program that involves data collection, analysis, and interpretation.

> Documentation is done to demonstrate what occurs in a program, while evaluation is done to assess the impact of what occurs.

> Documentation may lead to the production of lots of charts and graphs summarizing the data yet may produce little information that can help decision makers know how to improve the program or its results or understand the reasons for the numbers reported. Evaluation, on the other hand, is guided by carefully planned questions to assess a program's efficiency, impact, or return on investment.

> Both documentation and evaluation are important; without evaluation, however, decisions are based on assumptions, opinions, or preferences. Evaluations depend on good documentation yet do far more to assist staff development leaders in understanding what happened and for what possible reasons. Evaluations also provide or encourage clarity about how to improve the program and its impact on student achievement.

PROCESS-FOCUSED VERSUS RESULTS-FOCUSED

Some evaluations are structured to look at how well a program is working. While this is a worthy purpose of evaluation, even a well-functioning program can fall short in producing results. Process-focused evaluations are based on data about the way the program is functioning and how the planned program activities are being conducted. Process evaluation, more commonly called implementation (or sometimes, formative) evaluation, is helpful to those who want to know whether the program is being implemented, how well it is being implemented, or whether problems are occurring in implementation. In contrast, results-focused evaluation, also called impact, or sometimes summative, evaluation is concerned with outcomes. Results-focused evaluation asks, "Is the program producing results for students?"

Most evaluations of staff development programs focus on both implementation and impact. Process evaluation assists with ongoing revision and modification of the program to improve implementation. Yet process evaluation alone will not provide information on results. Schools need summative evaluations to keep intended results for students in the forefront. A mix of process and impact evaluation helps both program directors and stakeholders know whether the program is working and producing results. To help stakeholders know how to formulate questions that are appropriate to the task at hand, Table 12.2 gives a few examples of the differences between process-focused questions and results-focused questions.

Table 12.2   Focus of Questions

Process-Focused

How well is the program working?

How is its implementation aligned with the intended program (plan)?

Does it meet standards of operation?

Are the components in place as planned?

Results-Focused

Does the program produce results?

Does it have impact?

What unintended effects, if any, are occurring?

Powerful evaluation occurs when the conditions below are met. Given long-standing evaluation practices, these conditions are not yet widespread. Sometimes the conditions do not exist, and evaluators must conduct the evaluation simultaneously with shifting beliefs, practices, and knowledge about evaluation. Evaluation of staff development is most powerful when it

1. Focuses on results as well as on means

2. Focuses on the whole program as well as the component parts

3. Is tightly aligned with comprehensive planning of the staff development program

4. Promotes evaluation think

5. Includes tools used to measure change that are valid and reliable with a design appropriate for the questions the evaluation seeks to answer

6. Makes decisions about the evaluation that are appropriate to the context of the evaluation

7. Increases practitioners' knowledge about the evaluation process

8. Helps stakeholders view evaluation as a constructive and ongoing process

9. Builds staff development leaders' capacity to facilitate high-quality staff development

10. Has sufficient and appropriately allocated funding.

PRESENTATION OF RESULTS VERSUS REFLECTIVE DIALOGUE

Evaluators can significantly increase the perceived value and usefulness of an evaluation by doing more than presenting the results in a well-written and well-designed document or presentation. To move findings into improvements or actions, evaluators engage program staff in reflective dialogue about the evaluation findings. Reflective dialogue among program staff focuses on determining how the evaluation findings can be used to make improvements in the program and its results. The reflective dialogue on an evaluation is typically guided by a set of questions such as those below.

1. What components of the program do we want to continue as they are, revise, or eliminate?

2. What next steps does the evaluation report suggest we consider?

3. Which are immediate areas for action, and which can be delayed?

4. How will we approach these possible next steps? Whom will we involve? What resources are necessary? What will be our time frame for revision?

5. What will be our plan for reporting on these actions to the appropriate audience?

Evaluating staff development enables program managers and participants to make data-based decisions about the program. If the evaluation is done well, everyone benefits. If done poorly, it will be a waste of resources. The most useful evaluations result from a desire to improve both the program and its results and thoughtful planning, careful implementation, and use of the evaluation findings.

A Guide to the Appendices

Appendix A

Standards to Guide Evaluations

A1. NSDC'S STANDARDS FOR STAFF DEVELOPMENT, REVISED (2001)

Learning Communities

Staff development that improves the learning of all students organizes adults into learning communities whose goals are aligned with those of the school and district.

Leadership

Staff development that improves the learning of all students requires skillful school and district leaders who guide continuous instructional improvement.

Resources

Staff development that improves the learning of all students requires resources to support adult learning and collaboration.

Data-Driven

Staff development that improves the learning of all students uses disaggregated student data to determine adult learning priorities, monitor progress, and help sustain continuous improvement.

Evaluation

Staff development that improves the learning of all students uses multiple sources of information to guide improvement and demonstrate its impact.

Research-Based

Staff development that improves the learning of all students prepares educators to apply research to decision making.

Design

Staff development that improves the learning of all students uses learning strategies appropriate to the intended goal.

Learning

Staff development that improves the learning of all students applies knowledge about human learning and change.

Collaboration

Staff development that improves the learning of all students provides educators with the knowledge and skills to collaborate.

Equity

Staff development that improves the learning of all students prepares educators to understand and appreciate all students; create safe, orderly, and supportive learning environments; and hold high expectations for their academic achievement.

Quality Teaching

Staff development that improves the learning of all students deepens educators' content knowledge, provides them with research-based instructional strategies to assist students in meeting rigorous academic standards, and prepares them to use various types of classroom assessments appropriately.

Family Improvement

Staff development that improves the learning of all students provides educators with knowledge and skills to involve families and other stakeholders appropriately.

A2. AMERICAN EVALUATION ASSOCIATION: GUIDING PRINCIPLES FOR EVALUATORS

Revisions reflected herein ratified by the AEA membership, July 2004. Retrieved on August 10, 2006, from www.eval.org/Publications/GuidingPrinciples Printable.asp

Preface: Assumptions Concerning Development of Principles

A. Evaluation is a profession composed of persons with varying interests, potentially encompassing but not limited to the evaluation of programs, products, personnel, policy, performance, proposals, technology, research, theory, and even of evaluation itself. These principles are broadly intended to cover all kinds of evaluation. For external evaluations of public programs, they nearly always apply. However, it is impossible to write guiding principles that neatly fit every context in which evaluators work, and some evaluators will work in contexts in which following a guideline cannot be done for good reason. The Guiding Principles are not intended to constrain such evaluators when this is the case. However, such exceptions should be made for good reason (e.g., legal prohibitions against releasing information to stakeholders), and evaluators who find themselves in such contexts should consult colleagues about how to proceed.

B. Based on differences in training, experience, and work settings, the profession of evaluation encompasses diverse perceptions about the primary purpose of evaluation. These include but are not limited to the following: bettering products, personnel, programs, organizations, governments, consumers and the public interest; contributing to informed decision making and more enlightened change; precipitating needed change; empowering all stakeholders by collecting data from them and engaging them in the evaluation process; and experiencing the excitement of new insights. Despite that diversity, the common ground is that evaluators aspire to construct and provide the best possible information that might bear on the value of whatever is being evaluated. The principles are intended to foster that primary aim.

C. The principles are intended to guide the professional practice of evaluators, and to inform evaluation clients and the general public about the principles they can expect to be upheld by professional evaluators. Of course, no statement of principles can anticipate all situations that arise in the practice of evaluation. However, principles are not just guidelines for reaction when something goes wrong or when a dilemma is found. Rather, principles should proactively guide the behaviors of professionals in everyday practice.

D. The purpose of documenting guiding principles is to foster continuing development of the profession of evaluation, and the socialization of its members. The principles are meant to stimulate discussion about the proper practice and use of evaluation among members of the profession, sponsors of evaluation, and others interested in evaluation.

E. The five principles proposed in this document are not independent, but overlap in many ways. Conversely, sometimes these principles will conflict, so that evaluators will have to choose among them. At such times evaluators must use their own values and knowledge of the setting to determine the appropriate response. Whenever a course of action is unclear, evaluators should solicit the advice of fellow evaluators about how to resolve the problem before deciding how to proceed.

F. These principles are intended to supersede any previous work on standards, principles, or ethics adopted by AEA or its two predecessor organizations, the Evaluation Research Society and the Evaluation Network. These principles are the official position of AEA on these matters.

G. These principles are not intended to replace standards supported by evaluators or by the other disciplines in which evaluators participate.

H. Each principle is illustrated by a number of statements to amplify the meaning of the overarching principle, and to provide guidance for its application. These illustrations are not meant to include all possible applications of that principle, nor to be viewed as rules that provide the basis for sanctioning violators.

I. These principles were developed in the context of Western cultures, particularly the United States, and so may reflect the experiences of that context. The relevance of these principles may vary across other cultures, and across subcultures within the United States.

J. These principles are part of an evolving process of self-examination by the profession, and should be revisited on a regular basis. Mechanisms might include officially-sponsored reviews of principles at annual meetings, and other forums for harvesting experience with the principles and their application. On a regular basis, but at least every five years, these principles ought to be examined for possible review and revision. In order to maintain associationwide awareness and relevance, all AEA members are encouraged to participate in this process.

The Principles

A. Systematic Inquiry

Evaluators conduct systematic, data-based inquiries.

1. To ensure the accuracy and credibility of the evaluative information they produce, evaluators should adhere to the highest technical standards appropriate to the methods they use.

2. Evaluators should explore with the client the shortcomings and strengths both of the various evaluation questions and the various approaches that might be used for answering those questions.

3. Evaluators should communicate their methods and approaches accurately and in sufficient detail to allow others to understand, interpret and critique their work. They should make clear the limitations of an evaluation and its results. Evaluators should discuss in a contextually appropriate way those values, assumptions, theories, methods, results, and analyses significantly affecting the interpretation of the evaluative findings. These statements apply to all aspects of the evaluation, from its initial conceptualization to the eventual use of findings.

B. Competence

Evaluators provide competent performance to stakeholders.

1. Evaluators should possess (or ensure that the evaluation team possesses) the education, abilities, skills and experience appropriate to undertake the tasks proposed in the evaluation.

2. To ensure recognition, accurate interpretation and respect for diversity, evaluators should ensure that the members of the evaluation team collectively demonstrate cultural competence. Cultural competence would be reflected in evaluators seeking awareness of their own culturally-based assumptions, their understanding of the worldviews of culturally-different participants and stakeholders in the evaluation, and the use of appropriate evaluation strategies and skills in working with culturally different groups. Diversity may be in terms of race, ethnicity, gender, religion, socio-economics, or other factors pertinent to the evaluation context.

3. Evaluators should practice within the limits of their professional training and competence, and should decline to conduct evaluations that fall substantially outside those limits. When declining the commission or request is not feasible or appropriate, evaluators should make clear any significant limitations on the evaluation that might result. Evaluators should make every effort to gain the competence directly or through the assistance of others who possess the required expertise.

4. Evaluators should continually seek to maintain and improve their competencies, in order to provide the highest level of performance in their evaluations. This continuing professional development might include formal coursework and workshops, self-study, evaluations of one's own practice, and working with other evaluators to learn from their skills and expertise.

C. Integrity/Honesty

Evaluators display honesty and integrity in their own behavior, and attempt to ensure the honesty and integrity of the entire evaluation process.

1. Evaluators should negotiate honestly with clients and relevant stakeholders concerning the costs, tasks to be undertaken, limitations of methodology, scope of results likely to be obtained, and uses of data resulting from a specific evaluation. It is primarily the evaluator's responsibility to initiate discussion and clarification of these matters, not the client's.

2. Before accepting an evaluation assignment, evaluators should disclose any roles or relationships they have that might pose a conflict of interest (or appearance of a conflict) with their role as an evaluator. If they proceed with the evaluation, the conflict(s) should be clearly articulated in reports of the evaluation results.

3. Evaluators should record all changes made in the originally negotiated project plans, and the reasons why the changes were made. If those changes would significantly affect the scope and likely results of the evaluation, the evaluator should inform the client and other important stakeholders in a timely fashion (barring good reason to the contrary, before proceeding with further work) of the changes and their likely impact.

4. Evaluators should be explicit about their own, their clients', and other stakeholders' interests and values concerning the conduct and outcomes of an evaluation.

5. Evaluators should not misrepresent their procedures, data or findings. Within reasonable limits, they should attempt to prevent or correct misuse of their work by others.

6. If evaluators determine that certain procedures or activities are likely to produce misleading evaluative information or conclusions, they have the responsibility to communicate their concerns and the reasons for them. If discussions with the client do not resolve these concerns, the evaluator should decline to conduct the evaluation. If declining the assignment is unfeasible or inappropriate, the evaluator should consult colleagues or relevant stakeholders about other proper ways to proceed. (Options might include discussions at a higher level, a dissenting cover letter or appendix, or refusal to sign the final document.)

7. Evaluators should disclose all sources of financial support for an evaluation, and the source of the request for the evaluation.

D. Respect for People

Evaluators respect the security, dignity and self-worth of respondents, program participants, clients, and other evaluation stakeholders.

1. Evaluators should seek a comprehensive understanding of the important contextual elements of the evaluation. Contextual factors that may influence the results of a study include geographic location, timing, political and social climate, economic conditions, and other relevant activities in progress at the same time.

2. Evaluators should abide by current professional ethics, standards, and regulations regarding risks, harms, and burdens that might befall those participating in the evaluation; regarding informed consent for participation in evaluation; and regarding informing participants and clients about the scope and limits of confidentiality.

3. Because justified negative or critical conclusions from an evaluation must be explicitly stated, evaluations sometimes produce results that harm client or stakeholder interests. Under this circumstance, evaluators

should seek to maximize the benefits and reduce any unnecessary harms that might occur, provided this will not compromise the integrity of the evaluation findings. Evaluators should carefully judge when the benefits from doing the evaluation or in performing certain evaluation procedures should be foregone because of the risks or harms. To the extent possible, these issues should be anticipated during the negotiation of the evaluation.

4. Knowing that evaluations may negatively affect the interests of some stakeholders, evaluators should conduct the evaluation and communicate its results in a way that clearly respects the stakeholders' dignity and self-worth.

5. Where feasible, evaluators should attempt to foster social equity in evaluation, so that those who give to the evaluation may benefit in return. For example, evaluators should seek to ensure that those who bear the burdens of contributing data and incurring any risks do so willingly, and that they have full knowledge of and opportunity to obtain any benefits of the evaluation. Program participants should be informed that their eligibility to receive services does not hinge on their participation in the evaluation.

6. Evaluators have the responsibility to understand and respect differences among participants, such as differences in their culture, religion, gender, disability, age, sexual orientation and ethnicity, and to account for potential implications of these differences when planning, conducting, analyzing, and reporting evaluations.

E. Responsibilities for General and Public Welfare

Evaluators articulate and take into account the diversity of general and public interests and values that may be related to the evaluation.

1. When planning and reporting evaluations, evaluators should include relevant perspectives and interests of the full range of stakeholders.

2. Evaluators should consider not only the immediate operations and outcomes of whatever is being evaluated, but also its broad assumptions, implications and potential side effects.

3. Freedom of information is essential in a democracy. Evaluators should allow all relevant stakeholders access to evaluative information in forms that respect people and honor promises of confidentiality. Evaluators should actively disseminate information to stakeholders as resources allow. Communications that are tailored to a given stakeholder should include all results that may bear on interests of that stakeholder and refer to any other tailored communications to other stakeholders. In all cases, evaluators should strive to present results clearly and simply so that clients and other stakeholders can easily understand the evaluation process and results.

4. Evaluators should maintain a balance between client needs and other needs. Evaluators necessarily have a special relationship with the client who funds or requests the evaluation. By virtue of that relationship, evaluators must strive to meet legitimate client needs whenever it is feasible and appropriate to do so. However, that relationship can also place evaluators in difficult dilemmas when client interests conflict with other interests, or when client interests conflict with the obligation of evaluators for systematic inquiry, competence, integrity, and respect for people. In these cases, evaluators should explicitly identify and discuss the conflicts with the client and relevant stakeholders, resolve them when possible, determine whether continued work on the evaluation is advisable if the conflicts cannot be resolved, and make clear any significant limitations on the evaluation that might result if the conflict is not resolved.

5. Evaluators have obligations that encompass the public interest and good. These obligations are especially important when evaluators are supported by publicly-generated funds; but clear threats to the public good should never be ignored in any evaluation. Because the public interest and good are rarely the same as the interests of any particular group (including those of the client or funder), evaluators will usually have to go beyond analysis of particular stakeholder interests and consider the welfare of society as a whole.

Source: American Evaluation Association Task Force. (1995). Guiding principles for evaluators. In *New directions for evaluation (no. 66),* pp. 19–34. Copyright © 1995. Reprinted with permission John Wiley & Sons, Inc.

A3. JOINT COMMITTEE ON STANDARDS FOR EDUCATIONAL EVALUATION: PROGRAM EVALUATION STANDARDS

The Joint Committee on Standards for Educational Evaluation included representatives from the following organizations:

American Association of School Administrators

American Educational Research Association

American Evaluation Association

American Federation of Teachers

American Psychological Association

Association for Assessment in Counseling

Association for Supervision and Curriculum Development

Canadian Society for the Study of Education

Council of Chief State School Officers

Council on Postsecondary Accreditation

National Association of Elementary School Principals

National Association of Secondary School Principals

National Council on Measurement in Education

National Education Association

National School Boards Association

Utility Standards

The utility standards are intended to ensure that an evaluation will serve the information needs of intended users. These standards are as follows:

- *Stakeholder identification.* People involved in or affected by the evaluation should be identified so that their needs can be addressed.
- *Evaluator credibility.* The people conducting the evaluation should be both trustworthy and competent to perform the evaluation so that the evaluation findings achieve maximum credibility and acceptance.
- *Information scope and selection.* Information collected should be broadly selected to address pertinent questions about the program and should be responsive to the needs and interests of clients and other specified stakeholders.
- *Values identification.* The perspectives, procedures, and rationale used to interpret the findings should be described carefully so that the bases for value judgments are clear.

- *Report clarity.* Evaluation reports should describe clearly the program being evaluated, including its context and the purposes, procedures, and findings of the evaluation, so that essential information is provided and understood easily.
- *Report timeliness and dissemination.* Significant interim findings and evaluation reports should be disseminated to intended users so that they can be used in a timely fashion.
- *Evaluation impact.* Evaluations should be planned, conducted, and reported in ways that encourage follow-through by stakeholders, so that the likelihood that the evaluation will be used is increased.

Feasibility Standards

Feasibility standards are intended to ensure that an evaluation will be realistic, prudent, diplomatic, and frugal.

- *Practical procedures.* Evaluation procedures should be practical so that disruption is kept to a minimum while needed information is obtained.
- *Political viability.* The evaluation should be planned and conducted with anticipation of the different positions of various interest groups so that their cooperation may be obtained, and so that possible attempts by any of these groups to curtail evaluation operations or to bias or misapply the results can be averted or counteracted.
- *Cost-effectiveness.* The evaluation should be efficient and produce information of sufficient value so that the resources expended can be justified.

Propriety Standards

The propriety standards are intended to ensure that an evaluation will be conducted legally, ethically, and with due regard for the welfare of those involved in the evaluation, as well as those affected by its results.

- *Service orientation.* Evaluations should be designed to assist organizations to address and effectively serve the needs of the full range of targeted participants.
- *Formal agreements.* Obligations of the formal parties to an evaluation (what is to be done, how, by whom, and when) should be agreed to in writing so that these parties are obligated to adhere to all conditions of the agreement or to formally renegotiate it.
- *Rights of human subjects.* Evaluations should be designed and conducted to respect and protect the rights and welfare of human subjects.
- *Human interactions.* Evaluators should respect human dignity and worth in their interactions with other people associated with an evaluation so that participants are not threatened or harmed.
- *Complete and fair assessment.* The evaluation should be complete and fair in its examination and recording of strengths and weaknesses of the program being evaluated so that strengths can be built upon and problem areas addressed.

- *Disclosure of findings.* The formal parties to an evaluation should ensure that the full set of evaluation findings, along with pertinent limitations, are made accessible to the people affected by the evaluation, as well as any others with expressed legal rights to receive the results.
- *Conflict of interest.* Conflict of interest should be dealt with openly and honestly so that it does not compromise the evaluation processes and results.
- *Fiscal responsibility.* The evaluator's allocation and expenditure of resources should reflect sound accountability procedures and be prudent and ethically responsibility so that expenditures are accounted for and appropriate.

Accuracy Standards

Accuracy standards are intended to ensure that an evaluation will reveal and convey technically adequate information about the features that determine the worth or merit of the program being evaluated.

- *Program documentation.* The program being evaluated should be described and documented clearly and accurately so that the program is identified clearly.
- *Context analysis.* The context in which the program exists should be examined in enough detail so that its likely influences on the program can be identified.
- *Described purposes and procedures.* The purposes and procedure of the evaluation should be monitored and described in enough detail so that they can be identified and assessed.
- *Defensible information sources.* The sources of information used in a program evaluation should be described in enough detail so that the adequacy of the information can be assessed.
- *Valid information.* The information-gathering procedures should be chosen or developed and then implemented in a manner that will ensure that the interpretation arrived at is valid for the intended use.
- *Reliable information.* The information-gathering procedures should be chosen or developed and then implemented in a manner that will ensure that the information obtained is sufficiently reliable for the intended use.
- *Systematic information.* The information collected, processed and reported in an evaluation should be reviewed systematically, and any errors found should be corrected.
- *Analysis of quantitative information.* Quantitative information in an evaluation should be analyzed appropriately and systematically so that evaluation questions are answered effectively.
- *Analysis of qualitative information.* Qualitative information in an evaluation should be analyzed appropriately and systematically so that evaluation questions are answered effectively.
- *Justified conclusions.* The conclusions reached in an evaluation should be justified explicitly so that stakeholders can assess them.

- *Impartial reporting.* Reporting procedures should guard against distortion caused by personal feelings and biases of any party to the evaluation so that evaluation reports reflect the evaluation findings fairly.
- *Metaevaluation.* The evaluation itself should be evaluated formatively and summatively against these and other pertinent standards so that its conduct is appropriately guided, and on completion, stakeholders can closely examine its strengths and weaknesses.

Source: Joint Committee on Standards for Educational Evaluation, *Program evaluation standards* (2nd ed.). © 1994 by SAGE. Reprinted with permission.

A4. NSDC'S CODE OF ETHICS

PRINCIPLE I: *Staff development leaders are committed to achieving school and district goals, particularly those addressing high levels of learning and performance for all students and staff members.*

Staff development leaders make decisions based on high academic standards for all students. They ensure that staff development activities make a significant contribution to the accomplishment of school system and school goals for student learning.

PRINCIPLE II: *Staff development leaders select staff development content and processes that are research-based and proven in practice after examining various types of information about student and educator learning needs.*

Staff development leaders are informed consumers of educational research. They are familiar with and use research finding and understand the strengths and weaknesses of the research and its applicability to their settings. Consequently, staff development leaders only recommend professional practices that support high-quality teaching and learning. Staff development leaders use data to plan, assess, and evaluate the effectiveness of staff development efforts. Data may be drawn from various valid and reliable sources such as norm-referenced and criterion-referenced tests, portfolios of student work, teacher grades, and student attendance and graduation rates. These data are disaggregated to determine the effectiveness of the school program and staff development on various sub-groups of students. In addition, other sources of information, such as data on student, parent, staff, and community satisfaction with schools, are used to guide decision making.

PRINCIPLE III: *Staff development leaders continuously improve their work through the ongoing evaluation of staff development's effectiveness in achieving school system and school student learning goals.*

Staff development leaders conduct formative as well as summative evaluations of the effectiveness of staff development content and processes in achieving student learning objectives. They routinely and clearly report in writing the results of staff development to persons responsible for allocating staff development resources. Staff development leaders ensure that adequate funds are available for evaluation and that the evaluation process begins with the establishment of student learning goals and the planning of adult learning activities. They also ensure that members of school improvement teams have the necessary knowledge and skills to evaluate the effectiveness of staff development in improving student learning.

PRINCIPLE IV: *Staff development leaders continuously improve their knowledge and skills.*

Staff development leaders read widely, attend workshops and conferences, belong to appropriate professional associations, regularly consult with researchers and professional colleagues, and reflect on the effectiveness of their own practice. They contribute to the development of other staff development leaders through conference presentations, professional writing and service on professional boards and committees.

PRINCIPLE V: *Staff development leaders ensure an equitable distribution of resources to accomplish school system and school goals for student learning.*

Staff development leaders ensure to the extent of their authority that adequate resources of funding and time are available to achieve district and school goals and that the allocation of these resources reflect both fairness and need. They also ensure that resources are invested in those areas deemed most likely to promote high levels of learning for all students.

PRINCIPLE VI: *Staff development leaders advocate for policies and practices that ensure the continuous learning of all students and employees.*

Staff development leaders make certain that schools provide a culture and structures that support the continuous improvement of practice and of student learning. These organizations have norms of continuous improvement, collegiality, and experimentation. Organizational structures such as school calendars and daily schedules, labor contracts, and leadership practices advance school system and school goals for student learning.

PRINCIPLE VII: *Staff development leaders conduct themselves in a manner that avoids conflict of interest or the appearance of such conflict.*

Staff development leaders do not accept any compensation, gratuities, or favors from staff development providers that may directly or indirectly affect leaders' judgments about contracting for services with providers. In addition, staff development leaders have no financial investment in or obligation to providers with whom the school system or school contracts.

Staff Development Providers

PRINCIPLE I: *Staff development providers only offer services that are consistent with high standards of quality.*

Staff development providers are well trained in the techniques and processes they use with clients. They thoroughly understand their client's needs and honestly describe their qualifications to clients before they undertake any project. They also make available information about similar work with previous clients. Providers refuse to offer services or accept compensation for services that are unlikely to achieve the organization's goals.

PRINCIPLE II: *Staff development providers present accurate, up-to-date information and habitually and accurately explain the strengths and limitations of the practices they recommend in relation to the school or district's goals and current level of functioning.*

Staff development providers possess a deep understanding of the subjects they teach. They also understand the research base of the content and approaches they recommend and explain without bias to staff development leaders the strengths and weaknesses of these of these approaches. Providers do not make unsubstantiated claims regarding their work or other professional matters nor do they use coercive group techniques to limit critical thought or constructive dissent. They ask questions to ascertain the appropriate match between the recommended approaches and the school system or school's goals.

PRINCIPLE III: *Staff development providers select content and adult learning processes based on student learning goals and systematic assessment of participants' learning needs.*

Staff development providers use information about student and staff learning needs in determining the content and learning processes they will use. They describe to their clients the content and methods required to achieve program goals, including the school and classroom follow-up processed needed to improve teachers' content knowledge and instructional skills.

PRINCIPLE IV: *Staff development providers continuously learn and improve their performance.*

Staff development providers use a variety of kinds of evidence to determine their effectiveness in meeting program goals and seek feedback from clients, participants, and others affected by their work. In addition, staff development providers advocate the program evaluation be undertaken by their clients in relation to their work. To continuously improve their performance, providers attend relevant workshops and courses, read related research, and communicate regularly with leaders and colleagues in these areas.

PRINCIPLE V: *Staff development providers give appropriate credit to individuals or organizations whose work has influenced them.*

Staff development providers understand and recognize the theoretical and research traditions that are the basis of their work. They acknowledge these contributions when appropriate in their presentations and writing.

PRINCIPLE VI: *Staff development providers conduct themselves in a manner that avoids conflict of interest or the appearance of such conflict on the part of staff development leaders with whom they contract.*

Staff development providers do not offer any compensation, gratuities, or favors to staff development leaders that may directly or indirectly affect staff development leaders' judgments about contracting for services with providers.

Source: National Staff Development Council. (2000). *NSDC's Code of Ethics for Staff Development Leaders and Providers.* Oxford, OH. This material is used by permission of National Staff Development Council.

Appendix B

Sample Data-Collection Instruments

B1. INTERVIEW PROTOCOLS

B1a. Hilton CLASSIC, Hilton Central School District, Hilton, New York

Personal Interview

CLASSIC (Curriculum, Learning, Assessment Initiative for Children) is a long-standing project in Hilton. As part of this year's evaluation of CLASSIC, we are asking a random sample of Hilton teachers to participate in a 15–20 minute personal interview about professional development in general and CLASSIC in particular. Thank you for taking the time to help make professional development at Hilton the very best it can be.

1. What kinds of professional development have you pursued this year? Which was the best and why?

2. What are the challenges to implementing what you have learned? What have you been able to implement fairly easily?

3. How much effort do you think is reasonable to spend getting a new practice or technique to work?

4. What have you learned in professional development that has positively impacted your students' learning?

5. Let's talk about CLASSIC. How has CLASSIC changed the way you teach? (If you are not a CLASSIC participant, what do you know about CLASSIC?) What are its benefits? What are its challenges?

6. What would you like to learn from a long-term professional development initiative like CLASSIC?

7. How has CLASSIC changed the way students learn?

8. Let's talk about assessment. Do you think that student assessment is an ongoing challenge? How could the situation be improved?

9. Do you involve students in their own assessment? Should they be involved? Have you involved your students in the development and use of rubrics? How has that worked for you and the students?

10. Given the recent English Language Assessments and Mathematics Assessments (or the Regents at the high school level) and the results for Hilton, what professional development do you think is important for teachers so that they may better prepare their students?

11. Is there anything else about CLASSIC or professional development that you would like us to know?

Source: CLASSIC Interview Protocol, Hilton Central School District, Hilton, NY. Used by permission of Mark Bower.

B1b. Assessment Academy, Lawrence Public Schools, Lawrence, Kansas

Open-Ended Survey

1. As you see it, what are the purposes of the Assessment Academy? Have you taken ownership by understanding why we have assessments and how they should be used?

2. How are you using assessments?

3. What do you know now, that you didn't know six months ago, regarding assessments, standards, and data?

4. How are you aligning your instruction and assessment to the state standards?

5. Which subject area standards are you most familiar with?

6. How are district/state/national norm assessments an integral part of your teaching process?

Rubric for Scoring of Staff's Understanding and Use of Assessments, Data, and Standards

	Unsatisfactory 1	Below Expectations 2	Expected 3	Exceeds Expectations 4
1. As you see it, what are the purposes of the Assessment Academy? Have you taken ownership by understanding why we have assessments and how they should be used?	• Very limited understanding. • Provides one or no reason. Lack of ownership for using assessments and/or data	• Limited understanding regarding the purpose of the assessment academy. • Provides two or more reasons. • Lack of ownership for using assessments and/or data.	• Clearly understands why the Assessment Academy is an ongoing process in the district. • Provides three or more reasons for Assessment Academy related to the following concepts: reasons for assessment, how they can be used; a team to provide staff development at building; how to use assessments to drive instruction; understanding the "big picture" of the role of assessment. • Clear statement of personal ownership regarding assessments.	• Clearly understands why the Assessment Academy is an ongoing process in the district. • Provides four or more reasons for Assessment Academy, including concepts listed in Level 3. • Clear statement of personal ownership regarding assessments.
2. How are you using assessments?	• Little or no understanding of how assessment should drive instruction.	• Does not state an aligned connection among curriculum, instruction, and assessment. • Little mention of understanding of importance of strengths and weaknesses of students. • No mention of adjustments in teaching.	• Identifies connections among curriculum, instruction, and assessments. • Uses assessment to identify strengths and weaknesses of individual students or groups of students. • Develops and uses classroom assessments	• Adjusts units/lessons to sequence with assessments. • Personalizes instruction (that is, reteaching, reinforcement of topics). • Identifies connections among curriculum, instruction, and assessments.

162

			• that assist the teacher in determining whether students are reaching expected standards.	• Uses assessments to identify strengths and weaknesses of individual students or groups of students. • Develops and uses classroom assessments that assist the teacher in determining whether students are reaching expected standards.
3. What do you know now that you didn't know six months ago regarding assessments, standards, and data?	• No mention of change.	• Identifies the many ways teachers use assessments.	• Clearer understanding of state standards and new state assessments. • More awareness of district and state assessment results to modify instruction.	• Clearer understanding and sees the connection between state standards and new state assessments. • More use of district and state assessment results to modify instruction. • Increased awareness of appropriate test modifications and adaptations.
4. How are you aligning your instruction and assessment to the state standards?	• Knowledge of grade or course district curriculum. • Unaware of state standards and the relationship to district curriculum or the state assessments.	• Knowledge of grade or course district curriculum only. • Limited knowledge of state standards and of the benchmarks and indicators relevant to the grade level taught.	• Working knowledge of the benchmarks and indicators for the appropriate state standards. • Working knowledge of the district's curriculum and its alignment of state standards.	• Working knowledge of the benchmarks and indicators for the appropriate state standards. • Provides students feedback pertinent to the state rubrics or state indicators.

(Continued)

Rubric for Scoring of Staff's Understanding and Use of Assessments, Data, and Standards

	Unsatisfactory 1	Below Expectations 2	Expected 3	Exceeds Expectations 4
				• Working knowledge of the district's curriculum and its alignment to state standards.
5. Which subject area standards are you most familiar with?	• Not familiar with any standards.	• Mentions only standards for which he or she is responsible.	• Mention of communication standards, math standards, and standards for which he or she has responsibility.	• Mention of communication standards math standards, and standards for which he or she has responsibility. • Also aware of standards for other areas.
6. How are district/state/national norm assessments an integral part of your teaching process?	• They aren't.	• Unclear. • Not sure how to interpret tests and use data to identify strengths and weaknesses.	• Identifies why specific assessments are used as part of teaching. • Works to instruct students on the appropriate skills and information based on assessment results. • Building/department works as team to identify student strengths and weaknesses.	• Identifies why specific assessments are used as part of teaching. • Assessments are an integral part of instruction—e.g., references appropriate benchmarks and indicators to plan instruction. • Building/department works as team to identify student strengths and weaknesses.

The Assessment Academy of the Lawrence Public Schools, Lawrence, KS. The interview, rubric, and scoresheet are used by permission of Sandee Crowther.

B1c. Children's Academy North, Minneapolis Public Schools, Minneapolis, Minnesota

Informal Student Interview

Sample Questions for Children's Academy North, Minneapolis Public Schools

How do you learn to be a better reader in school?

- What kinds of things do you do to practice reading skills?
- Do you ever play games (use manipulatives)?

Do you sometimes work on reading with your whole class as one big group?

Do you sometimes read together in small groups with a teacher or an E.A.?

If *yes,* ask

- Do you meet as a group every day for reading?
- About how many kids are in your reading group?

Do you always meet with the same kids to have reading?

If *yes,* ask

- Have you been in the same reading group all year?
  If *yes,* ask
    - Do you think everybody in this classroom has been in the same reading group all year, or do you think some kids have changed groups?

Do you ever work all by yourself with a teacher or an E.A.?

If *yes,* ask

- Do you work all by yourself with a teacher or E.A. *every day?*
- What is one thing you can remember doing when working by yourself with the teacher or E.A.?

Source: Minneapolis Public Schools, Children's Academy North, Minneapolis, MN. Used by permission.

B2. SURVEYS

B2a. Rising Stars, Jefferson County Public Schools, Louisville, Kentucky

---

End-of-Training Survey Assessment

Summer 2001 **RS School Assignment:** _____ **JCPS Summer 2001** **Teacher Survey PD**

Please circle your assigned *level* and *content area* for RS 2001 as well as the *number of years* in the program.

1. Elementary   Middle High

2. Reading   Math

3. COUNTING 2001, I have been employed   1   2   3 years
   in the Rising Stars Program for:

Based on the following criteria, please rate your three-day training sessions by circling the number that best corresponds with your assessment of the experience.

	1 = poor	2	3	4	5 = excellent
1. Content was based on district and state standards.	1	2	3	4	5
2. Content was focused on best practices.	1	2	3	4	5
3. Content was organized to provide opportunities to learn new teaching strategies.	1	2	3	4	5
4. Training activities were designed for adult learners.	1	2	3	4	5
5. Training activities were designed for diverse learning styles.	1	2	3	4	5
6. Materials were organized for effective training use.	1	2	3	4	5
7. Materials were adequately covered for understanding.	1	2	3	4	5
8. Training input was received from a variety of sources.	1	2	3	4	5
9. There was an opportunity for collaborative learning.	1	2	3	4	5
10. There was opportunity to "try" instructional strategies.	1	2	3	4	5
11. I feel adequately prepared to deliver instruction during Rising Stars as "prescribed" by the training materials.	1	2	3	4	5

If there is something more you believe would benefit your immediate success with the Rising Stars 2001 program, please document suggestions here and on the back:_____

Level of Understanding and Degree of Implementation Survey

Code _____   Rising Stars Loc: _____   JCPS Summer 2000   **Elementary Reading Teacher Survey**

As of today, for each of the following categories, assess your own degree of understanding and level of implementation during the past 1999–2000 school year by circling or marking the appropriate response:

	Current Level of Understanding Little/No..........Extensive					**1999–2000 SY Degree of Implementation** Never..........Frequently				
Teaching reading by/with										
1. Activity-based approach to presenting lessons	1	2	3	4	5	1	2	3	4	5
2. Using assessments to plan instruction	1	2	3	4	5	1	2	3	4	5
3. Authentic experiences										
4. Cooperative learning groups	1	2	3	4	5	1	2	3	4	5
5. Learning stations	1	2	3	4	5	1	2	3	4	5
6. Facilitating student learning groups	1	2	3	4	5	1	2	3	4	5
7. Manipulatives to teach word recognition	1	2	3	4	5	1	2	3	4	5
8. Helping students become independent strategy users	1	2	3	4	5	1	2	3	4	5
Literacy Strategies:										
9. Letter manipulatives (letter tiles, cubes, etc.)	1	2	3	4	5	1	2	3	4	5
10. Word walls	1	2	3	4	5	1	2	3	4	5
11. Word cards	1	2	3	4	5	1	2	3	4	5
12. Word families (rhyming patterns, etc.)	1	2	3	4	5	1	2	3	4	5
13. Conferencing about book choice	1	2	3	4	5	1	2	3	4	5
Writing:										
14. Daily oral language (cap., usage, punct., spell.)	1	2	3	4	5	1	2	3	4	5

(Continued)

(Continued)

15. Writing for a purpose	1	2	3	4	5	1	2	3	4	5
16. Voyager adventure book (journal)	1	2	3	4	5	1	2	3	4	5
17. Recording knowledge	1	2	3	4	5	1	2	3	4	5

Rising Stars Program, Jefferson
County Public School

Comprehension:

18. Visualization	1	2	3	4	5	1	2	3	4	5
19. Writing for a purpose	1	2	3	4	5	1	2	3	4	5
20. Read aloud (incorp. instruct. conversation)	1	2	3	4	5	1	2	3	4	5
21. Graphic organizers	1	2	3	4	5	1	2	3	4	5
22. Fix up strategies	1	2	3	4	5	1	2	3	4	5

Please rate how you perceive your own effectiveness:

	Minimum = 1			Maximum = 5	
1. Working effectively with low-achieving students	1	2	3	4	5
2. Working with culturally diverse students	1	2	3	4	5
3. Assessing social skills in small groups	1	2	3	4	5
4. Motivating students to be excited about learning	1	2	3	4	5
5. Improving student self-confidence	1	2	3	4	5

Level of Understanding /Degree of Implementation/Level of Effectiveness Survey

Code _____   Rising Stars Loc: _____   JCPS Summer 2001   **Elementary School VOYAGER Teacher Survey**

Counting this current summer, 2001, how many years have you taught in the RS program? 1 2 3

Counting this current summer, 2001, how many years have you taught the Voyager curriculum? 1 2 3

As of today, for each of the following categories (pre- and post-), assess your own degree of understanding, level of effectiveness, and level of implementation during the Rising Stars Program by circling or marking your response.

LEVEL OF UNDERSTANDING/LEVEL OF EFFECTIVENESS/ DEGREE OF IMPLEMENTATION

	Pre-Rising Stars Little/No..........Extensive					Post-Rising Stars Little/No..........Extensive					During 2001 Rising Stars Never..........Frequently				
Teaching reading by/with															
1. Activity-based approach to presenting lessons	1	2	3	4	5	1	2	3	4	5	1	2	3	4	5
2. Using assessments to plan instruction	1	2	3	4	5	1	2	3	4	5	1	2	3	4	5
3. Authentic experiences	1	2	3	4	5	1	2	3	4	5	1	2	3	4	5
4. Cooperative learning groups	1	2	3	4	5	1	2	3	4	5	1	2	3	4	5
5. Learning stations	1	2	3	4	5	1	2	3	4	5	1	2	3	4	5
6. Facilitating student learning groups	1	2	3	4	5	1	2	3	4	5	1	2	3	4	5
7. Manipulatives to teach word recognition	1	2	3	4	5	1	2	3	4	5	1	2	3	4	5
8. Helping students use independent strategies	1	2	3	4	5	1	2	3	4	5	1	2	3	4	5
9. Letter manipulatives (letter tiles, cubes)	1	2	3	4	5	1	2	3	4	5	1	2	3	4	5
10. Word walls	1	2	3	4	5	1	2	3	4	5	1	2	3	4	5
11. Word cards	1	2	3	4	5	1	2	3	4	5	1	2	3	4	5
12. Word families	1	2	3	4	5	1	2	3	4	5	1	2	3	4	5
13. Daily oral language (cap., usage, punct., spell.)	1	2	3	4	5	1	2	3	4	5	1	2	3	4	5
14. Writing for a purpose	1	2	3	4	5	1	2	3	4	5	1	2	3	4	5
15. Voyager adventure book (journal)	1	2	3	4	5	1	2	3	4	5	1	2	3	4	5
16. Recording knowledge	1	2	3	4	5	1	2	3	4	5	1	2	3	4	5
17. Visualization	1	2	3	4	5	1	2	3	4	5	1	2	3	4	5
18. Retelling	1	2	3	4	5	1	2	3	4	5	1	2	3	4	5
19. Read aloud (incorp, instruct. conversation)	1	2	3	4	5	1	2	3	4	5	1	2	3	4	5
20. Graphic organizers	1	2	3	4	5	1	2	3	4	5	1	2	3	4	5
21. Fix up strategies ("get mouth ready," "chunk it," "ready-skip-read")	1	2	3	4	5	1	2	3	4	5	1	2	3	4	5

(Continued)

(Continued)

	LEVEL OF EFFECTIVENESS									
	Pre-Rising Stars					Post-Rising Stars				
	Minimum = 1 Maximum = 5					Minimum = 1 Maximum = 5				

Please rate how you perceive your own effectiveness:

1. Working effectively with low-achieving students	1	2	3	4	5	1	2	3	4	5
2. Working with culturally diverse students	1	2	3	4	5	1	2	3	4	5
3. Sharing effective strategies with peers	1	2	3	4	5	1	2	3	4	5
4. Motivating students to be excited about reading	1	2	3	4	5	1	2	3	4	5
5. Improving student self-confidence	1	2	3	4	5	1	2	3	4	5

Rate the 1-hour (professional development (PD) on the following criteria:

	Poor = 1			Excellent = 5	
1. Opportunities for teachers to share strategies and experiences.	1	2	3	4	5
2. Opportunities to reflect on teaching and learning	1	2	3	4	5
3. Direction for further teaching	1	2	3	4	5
4. Improved knowledge of a variety of reading assignments	1	2	3	4	5
5. Improved knowledge of a variety of reading assessments	1	2	3	4	5
6. Connection between Rising Stars curriculum and your classroom practices next year	1	2	3	4	5

From the professional development provided prior to and during Rising Stars, I was able to use the Rising Stars curriculum AS INTENDED, the following amount of time: _____ 0–25%   _____ 26–50%   _____ 51–75% _____76–100%

If program conditions were not conducive to implementing strategies as planned, please identify the primary reasons:

e.g., time constraints; # of students, level of students, space, materials)

Rate the quality of the Rising Stars program components:

	Poor = 1			Excellent = 5	
1. Student selection	1	2	3	4	5
2. Curriculum	1	2	3	4	5
3. Class size	1	2	3	4	5
4. Your hiring experience	1	2	3	4	5
5. Site appropriateness	1	2	3	4	5
6. Length of program (# of days)	1	2	3	4	5
7. Length of program day (# of hours)	1	2	3	4	5
8 Teaching/office supplies	1	2	3	4	5
9. Administrative support	1	2	3	4	5
10. Instructional support	1	2	3	4	5
11. Amount of instructional materials					

Source: Rising Stars Program, Jefferson County Public Schools, Louisville, KY. Reprinted with permission.

B2b. Powerful Learning, Accelerated School Project, Storrs, Connecticut

These two selections from the Accelerated Schools project surveys are examples of questions asked of teachers and the parallel questions asked of students about learner-centered powerful learning.

Powerful Learning Component: Learner-Centered
Selection Section From Teacher Survey

I accommodate and build upon individual students' needs, interests, and strengths.	Almost always	Frequently	Occasionally	Never
My students are involved in the planning of instruction.	Almost always	Frequently	Occasionally	Never
My instruction helps each learner to be a creator, thinker, and problem solver.	Almost always	Frequently	Occasionally	Never
I set up my classroom so each learner can independently access and use materials, books, equipment, and reference materials.	Almost always	Frequently	Occasionally	Never
Most displays in my classroom are of student work.	Almost always	Frequently	Occasionally	Never
I display individual student work that shows originality, creativity, and thinking.	Almost always	Frequently	Occasionally	Never

Powerful Learning Component: Learner-Centered
Selection Section From Student Survey

LEARNER-CENTERED	Often	Sometimes	Never	Unsure
I have the opportunity to experiment, write, speak, and produce art in school.				
What I learn and how I learn it are based on my strengths and interests.				
I am involved in planning what I will learn and how I will learn it.				
I have opportunities to be a creator, a thinker, and a problem solver.				
The classroom has materials, books, equipment, and references that I can easily use.				
I demonstrate what I have learned in ways that make sense to me.				
My classroom(s) and the school display student work that shows individual creativity and thinking.				

Source: National Center for Accelerated Schools at the University of Connecticut. Reprinted with permission.

B2c. Strategic Thinking Program, Children's Academy North, Minneapolis Public Schools, Minneapolis, Minnesota (Self-Assessment Survey)

Teacher Behavior Survey

Using Exemplary Reading Grant Instructional Practices
Children's Academy North Self-Assessment Survey, Minneapolis Public Schools

Learning to use new instructional practices usually entails acquiring new knowledge and resources, and changing some established practices, as well as developing and refining new skills and procedures. The purpose of this survey is to help characterize your development in acquiring skills and using exemplary reading instructional practices in the classroom. The four instructional practices that are the focus of your school's Exemplary Reading Grant for the 1999–2000 school year are defined below, as they have been operationalized at your site.

Small-Group Instruction refers to 2 to 5 students of similar reading ability meeting as a group to work with a teacher or E.A. These groups are formed to better match instruction with students' needs.

Flexible Group Structure refers to the practice of systematically making changes in the make-up of the small groups to reflect changing student needs.

One-on-One Instruction refers to individual students meeting with a teacher or E.A. Instruction sessions are typically brief, lasting 10 to 15 minutes, and are used to provide reinforcement for students who need extra help.

Assessments Help Shape Instruction refers to teachers reviewing student work and modifying instruction based on student need.

Directions: These four instructional practices are listed down the left side of the attached survey. Descriptions of various levels of use of these practices are listed across the top of the survey. For each instructional practice place an X under the one description that best characterizes your present use of that practice in your classroom. Then at the bottom of the sheet write your name (after circling the appropriate title to indicate whether you are a teacher or an E.A.) and specify the grade level at which you teach. After that, indicate the estimated total number of minutes students spend in small-group instruction for reading. Next specify the amount of time you spend in one-on-one instruction and the number of different students you work with one-on-one each day for reading. Then indicate the fraction of students (the number of students out of all your reading students) who are receiving one-on-one instruction this grading period. Finally, estimate how frequently small-group membership has changed based on students' needs during this grading period.

Thank you for taking time to complete this task.

Using Exemplary Reading Grant Instructional Practices

	I have little or no knowledge about this teaching practice and have no plans to use the practice.	I am gathering general information about this instructional practice through reading, discussions, observations, or workshops.	I have established a time to begin implementing the instructional practice. I am preparing to use the practice through preuse training and by organizing resources and schedules.	I am using the instructional practice. At this point, I am primarily dealing with logistical issues such as planning appropriate activities, and/or figuring out how to fit them into the curriculum.	I routinely use this instructional practice, and I am satisfied with how the practice is being implemented.	I use this instructional practice, and I am beginning to modify its implementation to enhance the practice's impact on students.	I use this instructional practice, and I am working with colleagues to combine my effort with theirs to achieve a collective impact on our students.
Small groups							
Flexible groups							
One-on-one Instruction							
Assessments help shape Instruction							

Average minutes per day each student spends in a small group for reading instruction _____

Total minutes (on average) you spend per day providing one-on-one reading instruction _____

Average number of different students you work with per day on a one-on-one basis _____

Fraction of students receiving one-on-one instruction for reading this grading period _____

Small group membership changes were made _____ times during this grading period.

Teacher/E.A. _____

Grade level _____

Source: Minneapolis Public Schools, Children's Academy North, Minneapolis, MN. Used by permission.

B2d. North Central Regional Education Laboratory

North Central Regional Education Laboratory Online
Course Participant Posttest

Last Name _____ First Name _____
Date _____ Course Title _____

Please rate how much you understand and use the principles and techniques described below as a part of your teaching (either as part of your lessons or in helping you prepare your lessons).

Your frank self-assessment at the end of the course will show what you have learned. Your answers will be kept completely confidential; only group summaries will be reported in an evaluation of the course.

Read the following statements and check the box of the response that most closely matches your knowledge and use of the concept.

1. How well do you understand the principles of engaged learning?
   - ☐ Unsure what is meant by this term
   - ☐ Some understanding
   - ☐ Good understanding
   - ☐ Very good understanding

2. How often do you apply the principles of engaged learning in your teaching?
   - ☐ Never or almost never
   - ☐ Infrequently
   - ☐ Frequently
   - ☐ All the time

3. How well do you understand how to apply technology in your teaching to increase the quality and effectiveness of learning?
   - ☐ No understanding of how to apply technology
   - ☐ Some understanding. For instance, I know how to use skill-and-drill software programs.
   - ☐ Good understanding. For instance, I know how to use a variety of software applications.
   - ☐ Very good understanding. For instance, I know how to use various software, Internet resources, and other high-performance technology.

4. How often do you apply technology in your teaching to increase the quality and effectiveness of learning?
   - ☐ Never or almost never
   - ☐ Infrequently
   - ☐ Frequently
   - ☐ All the time

5. How well do you understand how to design lessons that integrate technology into instruction and learning?
   - ☐ No understanding of this type of lesson-designing process.
   - ☐ Some understanding. For instance, I know how to make sure all my students use technology at some point in a unit.
   - ☐ Good understanding. For instance, I know how to have my students use different types of technology for different learning purposes.
   - ☐ Very good understanding. For instance, I know how to have everyone in my classroom use different types of appropriate technology for learning and instructional purposes and how to evaluate their effectiveness.

6. How often do you use lessons that integrate technology into instruction and learning?
   - ☐ Do not use
   - ☐ Infrequently
   - ☐ Frequently
   - ☐ All the time

7. How well do you understand how to develop a comprehensive planning framework that integrates technology into units and lessons?
    □ No understanding of how to develop a comprehensive planning framework.
    □ Some understanding. For instance, I know how to develop a planning framework that integrates students going to a computer lab once a week.
    □ Good understanding. For instance, I know how to develop a planning framework that plans for students to integrate high-performance technology for special learning projects and some units of study.
    □ Very good understanding. For instance, I know how to develop a planning framework that plans for students to integrate high-performance technology in the majority of the lessons and units.

8. How often do you use a comprehensive planning framework that integrates technology into plan units and lessons?
    □ Do not use
    □ Infrequently
    □ Frequently
    □ All the time

9. To what extent do you have access to sample lessons that demonstrate effective use of technology?
    □ Do not have access
    □ Some access
    □ Good access
    □ Very good access

10. How often do you use sample lessons as a teaching resource that demonstrates effective use of technology in curriculum?
    □ Do not use
    □ Infrequently
    □ Frequently
    □ All the time

11. How often do you have the opportunity to observe and learn from other teachers effectively using technology in their curriculum?
    □ No opportunity
    □ Infrequently
    □ Frequently
    □ All the time

12. From your observations of other teachers, how often do you learn effective ways of using technology in the curriculum?
    □ Do not learn effective ways
    □ Infrequently
    □ Frequently
    □ All the time

13. How familiar are you about what a listserv is and how it works?
    □ Not familiar
    □ Somewhat familiar
    □ Familiar
    □ Very familiar

14. How often do you use listservs to communicate with other educators to improve your teaching?
    □ Never or almost never
    □ Infrequently
    □ Frequently
    □ All the time

B3. OBSERVATION CHILDREN'S ACADEMY NORTH, MINNEAPOLIS PUBLIC SCHOOLS, MINNEAPOLIS, MINNESOTA

Reading Instructional Practices Observation Form

Children's Academy North   Classroom _____   Period _____   Observer initials _____

Reading Instructional Practices Observed	1st 10 min.	2nd 20 min.	3rd 30 min.	4th 40 min.	5th 50 min.
Small Group Instruction (Two to five students of similar reading ability meeting as a group to work with at teacher or E.A.)					
• Teacher working with small reading groups					
• E.A. working with small reading groups					
One-on-One Instruction (Individual students meeting with teacher or E.A. to provide reinforcement for students needing extra help)					
• Teacher working with individual student					
• E.A. working with individual student					
Assessments Help Shape Instruction (Evidence of instruction modified based on determination of student needs)					
• Reteaching or review of concepts					

• Accelerated or enrichment activities						
• Other						
Flexible Group Structure (Evidence of systematically making changes in the makeup of small groups to reflect changing student needs)						
• Group rosters						
• Teacher report						
• Other						
Level of Student Engagement (write a number in the box) 4—Almost all engaged 3—Many engaged (more than half 2—Some engaged 1—Few, if any, engaged						

Source: Minneapolis Public Schools, Children's Academy North, Minneapolis, MN. Used by permission.

B4. ACCELERATED SCHOOLS PROJECT, STORRS, CONNECTICUT

Accelerated Schools Project

School Portfolio

Students' Work Samples—Analysis and Conclusions

The portfolio must include student work that demonstrates Powerful Learning throughout the school. Protocols for analyzing student work are provided and are to be used by cadres, peer support teams, and/or individual teachers when assembling and analyzing the student work samples. After analyzing the student work, cadres, peer support teams, and/or individual teachers should describe what they learned by analyzing the student work. This work and descriptions should then be provided to the steering committee for its study and inclusion in the portfolio.

List the work samples included:

Type of Work	Grade	Subject Area

What does this student work tell you about the implementation of Powerful Learning, classroom inquiry, and its affects on acceleration and achievement at each grade level and throughout the school?

Does this student work give evidence of improved student achievement as the result of classroom-based, cadre, or schoolwide inquiry? Explain.

What solution had been implemented as a result of cadre inquiry and a decision of the school as a whole?

How long has the solution been in place?

What does this collection of student work tell you about how well the solution is working?

Conclusions:

Source: National Center for Accelerated Schools at the University of Connecticut. Reprinted with permission.

B5. COACHING INTERACTION RECORD: NSDC COACHING PROJECT

The NSDC Coaching Project coaching interaction record was developed by Mary Jean Taylor and Joellen Killion to be used as a part of the project's evaluation. The project, funded by Wachovia's Teachers and Teaching Initiative, provided a grant to NSDC to design and deliver the NSDC Coaches Academy to coaches in 11 states between 2004 and 2008. Taylor served as the project evaluator.

Directions:

The interaction records will capture the *nature* of your work with teachers. They are *not* time sheets. A facsimile of the worksheet we show as an example can easily be created as a table in almost any word-processing or spreadsheet program.

1. Customize your record sheet by entering the initials and student grade level for all the teachers you serve in the first column. Devote a separate row to each individual teacher (even if you usually work with them in groups). Once you have created the list, simply copy and paste the name and grade level data for the rest of the months. To assure teacher anonymity, you may want to delete the initials on the file you submit. (Remember to save it under a different name than the original, which you should keep for your records.)

2. Name the file using your last name_state abbreviation_month abbreviation, so the October file from Meghan Smith of New Jersey would be: smith_nj_oct.

3. Enter *one* code (see next page) that best describes the primary nature of your interaction with each teacher in the correct column (in the appropriate cell for the day of the month). Use additional codes sparingly and only if a single code cannot capture the essence of your interaction. Leave spaces blank when you do not have substantive interaction with a teacher on a given day. If you work with a group, enter the same code for every teacher in the group.

4. Use anecdotal notes to keep track of "other" activities, reflect on your work and to record observations, experience, and insights.

5. At the end of each month, send your interaction log as an electronic attachment to _____

Codes

A	Assist with classroom organization and management issues (setting up classroom, establishing routines, managing student behavior, discipline, etc.)
C	Curricular assistance—assisting teachers with selecting content, alignment with standards, pacing, curriculum mapping, selecting instruction appropriate to the content (i.e., the "what" of teaching).
I	Instructional assistance—observe instruction and provide feedback, consult or discuss ideas for effective instructional strategies (i.e., the "how" of teaching).
P	Planning activities related to specific lessons and/or instruction with individual teachers or groups.
R	Resource assistance, help with gathering materials and finding resources.
D	Data-related activities such as assisting teachers with data collection and analysis, examining student work, data-driven decision making, test preparation, etc.
F	Facilitating learning teams, organizing study groups (on general topics such as differentiated instruction, book study, action research, etc.)
T	Teach/model/co-teach—demonstration teaching (model a lesson or strategy) or direct co-teaching of students *with* the classroom teacher.
W	Workshop/training—teacher participated in a professional development activity or workshop conducted or facilitated by you.
O	Other (use anecdotal records to keep track of the nature of the work you do)

Coaching Interaction Record

Coach's Name: _____

School(s): _____

State: _____ Month: _____

List all teachers you work with and enter a code for the primary *nature* of your interaction with each teacher:

Teacher (initials)	Grade level	1	2	3	4	5	6	7	8	9	10	11	12	13	14	15	16	17	18	19	20	21	22	23	24	25	26	27	28	29	30	31
1.																																	
2.																																	
3.																																	
4.																																	
5.																																	
6.																																	
7.																																	
8.																																	
9.																																	
10.																																	
11.																																	
12.																																	
13.																																	
14.																																	
15.																																	
16.																																	
17.																																	
18.																																	
19.																																	

Use anecdotal notes to keep track of "other" activities, to reflect on your work, and to record observations, experiences, and insights.

Sample of Completed Interaction Log for the Month of January

Teacher (initials)	Grade level	1	2	3	4	5	6	7	8	9	10	11	12	13	14	15	16	17	18	19	20	21	22	23	24	25	26	27	28	29	30	31
	K							O														D										
	K							O														D										
	K							O														D										
	K							O														D			O							
	1			O				O											O													
	1							O											I			D										
	1							O														D			O							
	1							O														D							O			
	2	I						O			I											D										
	2							O														D	I									
	2							O														D						I				
	2							O														D										
	3									O												D										
	3								W	O									O			D										
	3							O		O									I			D			O							
	3							O														D										
	4	D							W	F																					D	
	4	D							W	F																					D	
	4	D							W	F																				O	D	
	4	D							W	F																					D	

Source: Reprinted with permission from Killion, J., & Harrison, C. (2006). *Taking the lead: New roles for teachers and school-based coaches.* Oxford, OH: National Staff Development

This is part of a log that was completed by a coach serving 36 staff in one elementary school.

Note that names have been deleted to preserve confidentiality, and assignments are identified for each client.

Once you have listed your clients and their assignments, simply copy and paste columns A and B in all subsequent worksheets.

There are also cases where two codes have been entered in one cell, although a single code is preferable whenever feasible.

B6. INNOVATION CONFIGURATION (IC) MAPS

B6a. Dubuque Community School District

Math Trailblazers

Materials are implemented with fidelity.

3	2	1
Math is taught between 60 and 75 minutes a day.	Math is taught 60 minutes a day.	Math is taught less than 60 minutes a day.
Only Math Trailblazers is taught during math time.	Only Math Trailblazers is taught during math time.	Pacing guidelines are not followed.
In kindergarten, all months are covered as well as the extra units. In 1st, 2nd, and 3rd grade, all 20 units are covered. In 4th grade, 14 units are covered. In 5th grade, more than 12 units are covered.	In kindergarten, all months are covered. In 1st and 2nd grade, all 20 units are covered. In 3rd grade, at least 18 units are covered. In 4th grade, 13 units are covered. In 5th grade, 12 units are covered.	Few of the Adventure Books are read.
All Adventure Books are read.	Most Adventure Books are read.	Few DABs are used in 3rd–5th grade.
Most DABs are used in 3rd–5th grade.	Most DABs are used in 3rd–5th grade.	Few DPPs are completed in Grades 1–5.
All DPPs are completed in Grades 1–5.	Most DPPs are completed in Grades 1–5.	Few LABs are completed in Grades 1–5.
All LABs are completed in Grades 1–5.	Most LABs are completed in Grades 1–5.	

Students are engaged in problem solving.

3	2	1
The teacher is a facilitator, walking around, asking questions, coaching and instructing individuals or groups.	The teacher guides the partners or small groups going through each question one at a time.	The teacher lectures the class.
Partners and small groups are chosen by the teacher before the activity for a specific purpose.	Partners are randomly chosen.	Students work independently.
Students work cooperatively to solve problems.	Students work cooperatively to solve problems.	
Not all students are doing the same assignment.	All students are doing the same assignment.	

Students are encouraged to communicate mathematically.

3	2	1
Students consistently verbalize reasoning using correct mathematical vocabulary.	The teacher asks some higher-level questions.	The teacher asks questions that require a one-word answer or leading questions.
Students are able to represent mathematical ideas in more than one way.	Class discussions are facilitated by the teacher.	The discussion is dominated by the teacher.
Students are expected to use and share several reasoning strategies with the teacher and other students.	Students are encouraged to explain their thinking.	
Students actively listen when other students explain various solution strategies, discuss when a strategy is efficient, and agree when shared strategies are logical and correct by restating or questioning their peers.	Students are able to represent mathematical ideas.	
The teacher asks a majority of higher-level questions.	A variety of students share.	
Class discussions are dominated by a variety of students.		
The teacher identifies particular students to share strategies in order to show a variety of solution methods.		

Interventions are utilized to help students who are struggling.

3	2	1
Deficit areas are identified using assessments like Kathy Richardson or CGI.	Students are identified using classroom data.	An intervention is delivered for students who are struggling.
Interventions are designed around the deficit areas.	An intervention is designed and delivered using appropriate monitoring.	
Appropriate monitoring is in place.		
Interventions are consistently delivered.		

Extensions are utilized for those who need them.

Teachers use assessments to determine students who need enrichment by unit or lesson.	Identified students are given extensions to work on at their own pace when they have free time.	All students or identified students are given extensions to complete.
Students work on extensions as a part of math class in addition to or instead of class work.	Students are consistently given feedback.	Feedback or documentation is inconsistent.
Students are given feedback on their work and are allowed to share with the class consistently.	Performance is consistently documented.	
Performance is consistently documented.		

Source: Copyright © 2007, Dubuque Community School District. Reprinted with permission. Developed by Shirley Horstman and Chris Nugent for the Dubuque Community School District to deepen the implementation of Math Trailblazers, a K–5 math series published by Kendall Hunt Publishing.

B6b. Gadsden Elementary School District #32, San Luis, Arizona

Implementing Change Among School Staff

The principal and other leaders do the following.

Desired outcome	LEVEL I	LEVEL II	LEVEL III	LEVEL IV
Create atmosphere or context for change	Schedule time and place for staff reflection and collaborative work Provide learning environment Develop culture of learning Develop staff's skills of • collaboration • modes of conversation • conflict management • decision-making model Nurture leadership team skills Activate leadership teams for learning Monitor to ensure time is used well	Schedule time and place for staff reflection and collaborative work Provide learning environment Develop culture of learning Develop staff's skills of • collaboration • modes of conversation • conflict management • decision-making model, Activate leadership teams for learning	Schedule time and place for staff reflection and collaborative work Provide learning environment Develop staff's skills of • collaboration • modes of conversation • conflict management • decision-making models	Schedule time and place for staff reflection and collaborative work Provide learning environment
Develop and communicate a shared vision	Identify purpose or school mission Define values and staff beliefs Engage staff in studying data to identify needs for improvement Study and select new programs or practices to address the priority need for improvement Create an innovation configuration that represents and communicates the new practice, the vision of change Keep the vision visible Revisit the vision periodically	Identify purpose or school mission Engage staff in studying data to identify needs for improvement Select new programs or practices to address the priority need for improvement Create an innovation configuration that represents and communicates the new practice, the vision of change	Engage staff in studying data to identify needs for improvement Select new programs and practices to address the priority need for improvement	Engage staff in studying data to identify needs for improvement Adopt new programs and practices to address the need for improvement

(Continued)

(Continued)

Desired outcome	LEVEL I	LEVEL II	LEVEL III	LEVEL IV
Plan and provide resources	Gather staff information (stages of concern, level of understanding, innovation configuration) and relevant data Use six strategies to develop an implementation plan that will achieve the vision Identify resources needed and plan to access them: • currently available • needed as reflected in the vision Establish timelines	Gather staff information (stages of concern, level of understanding, innovation configuration) and relevant data Use six strategies to develop an implementation plan that will achieve the vision Identify resources needed and plan to access them: • currently available • needed as reflected in the vision	Use six strategies to develop an implementation plan that will achieve the vision Identify resources needed and plan to access them: • currently available • needed as reflected in the vision	Identify resources needed and plan to access them: • currently available • needed as reflected in the vision
Invest in professional development	Gather and analyze student data (AIMS, mandated and district assessments) and teacher data (stages of concern, level of understanding, innovation configuration) Use staff and student data to create adult learning activities Create vision-driven action plan for professional development Arrange for, schedule, and deliver adult learning activities Establish timelines	Gather and analyze student data (AIMS, mandated and district assessments) and teacher data (stages of concern, level of understanding, innovation configuration) Use staff and student data to create adult learning activities Create vision-driven professional development plan	Gather and analyze student data (AIMS, mandated and district assessments) and teacher data (stages of concern, level of understanding, innovation configuration) Create professional development plan	Create professional development plan

Check for progress	Gather staff information • stages of concern • level of understanding • innovation configuration Include staff in interpreting data and determining needs Develop a culture of continuous assessment Celebrate small and large successes publicly or privately Establish timelines	Gather staff information • stages of concern • level of understanding • innovation configuration Include staff in interpreting data and determining needs Develop a culture of continuous assessment	Gather staff information • stages of concern • level of understanding • innovation configuration Ask staff what they need for implementation of new practices	Ask staff what they need for implementation of new practices
Provide assistance	Schedule needed professional development • large-group • small-group • individuals Provide coaches or mentors Review time and activities for collaborative work Inventory resources, restock, or share Revisit action plan and revise as needed Celebrate small and large successes publicly or privately	Schedule needed professional development • large-group • small-group • individuals Provide coaches or mentors Review time and activities for collaborative work Inventory resources and restock	Schedule needed professional development • large-group • small-group • individuals Review time and activities for collaborative work Inventory resources and restock	Schedule needed professional development • large-group

Source: Copyright © 2007 Gadsden Elementary School District #32. Reprinted with permission from the leadership team at Gadsden Elementary School District #32, San Luis, AZ; created in collaboration with Wilda Storm and Shirley Hord.

B6c. Gadsden Elementary School District #32, San Luis, Arizona

Writing

The teacher does the following.

Goal: Implements the District-Adopted Writing Program

Component	LEVEL I	LEVEL II	LEVEL III	LEVEL IV
Develops Vocabulary (across the week)	Instructs/models/assigns students on Graphic Organizer strategies three or more times per week. Uses graphic organizer for • friendly definitions • pictograph • synonym/antonym • analogy or extended sentence Keeps graphic organizer for reference Assesses mastery of vocabulary Uses color-coded word wall actively Maintains high expectations for students Directs students to integrate these rich words into their writing Uses the grade-appropriate tier	Instructs/models/assigns students on Four Square strategies three times during the course of the week. Uses graphic organizer for • friendly definitions • pictograph • analogy or extended sentence Keeps graphic organizer for reference Assesses mastery of vocabulary Uses color-coded word wall actively Maintains high expectations for students Directs students to integrate these rich words into their writing	Instructs/models/assigns students on Four Square strategies two times during the course of the week. Uses graphic organizer for • friendly definitions • pictograph • extended sentence Keeps graphic organizer for reference Maintains high expectations for students Directs students to integrate these rich words into their writing	Instructs/models/assigns students on Four Square strategies once during the course of the week. Uses graphic organizer for • pictograph • extended sentence Maintains high expectations for students

| Develops extended sentences (across the week) | Instructs/models/assigns strategies in 80% of writing so students write extended sentences that are linked together on the same topic, that make sense, and that include all these attributes:
• appropriate tier words—one must be an action verb
• correct punctuation
• correct capitalization
• subject-verb agreement
• correct spelling
• use 7 words or more
Instructs/models/assigns the use of self, peer, and teacher editing
Designs tasks that permit students to integrate extended sentences into their compositions
Maintains high expectations | Instructs/models/assigns strategies in 80% of writing so students write extended sentences that are linked together on the same topic, that make sense, and that include all these attributes:
• includes an action verb
• correct punctuation
• correct capitalization
• subject-verb agreement
• correct spelling
• use 7 words or more
Instructs/models/assigns the use of self, peer, and teacher editing
Maintains high expectations | Instructs/assigns strategies in 80% of writing so students write extended sentences that are linked together on the same topic, that make sense, and that include all these attributes:
• includes an action verb
• correct punctuation
• correct capitalization
• correct spelling
• use 7 words or more
Instructs with the use of teacher editing
Maintains high expectations | Assigns strategies in 50% of writing so students write extended sentences that are linked together on the same topic, that make sense, and that include all these attributes:
• correct punctuation
• correct capitalization
• correct spelling
• use 7 words or more
Maintains high expectations |
| **Develops Quick Writes Phase I NOTE: Scaffolds may be removed as students' progress toward proficiency and independence. Teacher uses discretion.** | Instructs/models/assigns as appropriate
• presents prompt
• reads passage (when applicable)
• shares personal experience
• instructs students to think/pair/share their response
• times student writing
• creates word bank
• instructs students to graph number of words written | Instructs/models/assigns as appropriate
• presents prompt
• reads passage (when applicable)
• instructs students to think/pair/share
• times student writing
• instructs students to graph number of words written | Instructs/models/assigns as appropriate
• presents prompt
• reads passage (when applicable)
• times student writing
Takes 1 Quick Write per month to Phase II
Maintains high expectations | Instructs/assigns as appropriate
• presents prompt
• reads passage (when applicable)
• times student writing
Takes no Quick Writes per month to Phase II |

(Continued)

(Continued)

Component	LEVEL I	LEVEL II	LEVEL III	LEVEL IV
	Uses Quick Writes as assessment for automaticity Takes 3 Quick Writes per month to Phase II Maintains high expectations	Takes 2 Quick Writes per month to Phase II Maintains high expectations		
Develops Quick Writes Phase II	Models, instructs, and assigns consistently the revisions to the story frame, which includes introduction, body, and conclusion Uses the story frame for the application of new concepts and literary devices or genres taught throughout the school year Cues the students for editing Maintains high expectations	Models, instructs, and assigns consistently the revisions to the story frame, which includes introduction, body, and conclusion Cues the students for editing Maintains high expectations	Models, instructs, and assigns consistently the revisions to the story frame, which includes introduction, body, and conclusion	Instructs and assigns the revisions to the story frame, which includes introduction, body, and conclusion
Develops Note-taking and Summarizing NOTE: Scaffolds may be removed as students progress toward proficiency and independence. Teacher uses discretion.	Selects appropriate level and length of material Instructs, models, and assigns note-taking and summarizing as follows: • Reads the passage • Assists in choosing pertinent information • Assists students in transferring important details and main ideas of each paragraph into bullets on left margin of paper • Facilitates transferring bullets for each paragraph into summary with well-written sentences using synonyms	Instructs, models, and assigns note-taking and summarizing as follows: • Reads the passage • Assists in choosing pertinent information • Assists students in transferring important details and main ideas of each paragraph into bullets on left margin of paper	Assigns note-taking and summarizing as follows: • Reads the passage • Assists students in transferring important details and main ideas of each paragraph into bullets on left margin of paper • Facilitates transferring bullets for each paragraph into summary with well-written sentences using synonyms	Assigns note-taking and summarizing as follows: • Assists students in transferring important details and main ideas of each paragraph into bullets on left margin of paper Facilitates the gradual release of responsibility

	Directs students to practice every week in content areas excluding English class Facilitates the gradual release of responsibility progressing toward independence Matches this task with skills for research Maintains high expectations Takes summarizing to the next level of creating an end product such as a paragraph summary, one-page essay, or poster	Directs students to practice every week in content areas excluding English class Facilitates the gradual release of responsibility progressing toward independence Maintains high expectations Takes summarizing to the next level of creating an end product such as a paragraph summary, one-page essay, or poster	Facilitates the gradual release of responsibility progressing toward independence Maintains high expectations Takes summarizing to the next level of creating an end product such as a paragraph summary, one-page essay, or poster	progressing toward independence Maintains high expectations
Facilitates Paragraph Development *(Outline)* **or Outline Format: I. II. III. IV. V.**	Guides students consistently in paragraph and essay development: • Teaches components (introduction, body, and conclusion) • Integrates elements such as extended and starter word sentences, and figurative language with the appropriate scaffolding • Directs students through the use of graphic organizer (outline model)	Guides students consistently in paragraph and essay development: • Teaches components (introduction, body, and conclusion) • Emphasizes writing in active voice • Instructs/models/assigns revising editing process	Guides students consistently in paragraph and essay development: • Teaches components (introduction, body, and conclusion) • Emphasizes writing in active voice • Assigns revising editing process	Guides students on occasion in paragraph and essay development: • Suggests to students the use of components (introduction, body, and conclusion)

(Continued)

(Continued)

Component	LEVEL I	LEVEL II	LEVEL III	LEVEL IV
	• Emphasizes writing in active voice • Instructs/models/assigns revising editing process Arranges frequent and authentic opportunities for students to use all elements previously taught Maintains high expectations	Arranges frequent and authentic opportunities for students to use all elements previously taught Maintains high expectations	FArranges random and authentic opportunities for students to use all elements previously taught Maintains high expectations	• Emphasizes writing in active voice • Assigns revising editing process Arranges random opportunities for students to use all elements previously taught Maintains high expectations

Source: Copyright © 2007 Gadsden Elementary School District #32. Reprinted with permission from the leadership team at Gadsden Elementary School District #32, San Luis, AZ; created in collaboration with Wilda Storm and Shirley Hord

Appendix C

Staff Development Planning Guide

PLANNING OVERVIEW

- What are the needed changes for students that various data sources indicate?
- What changes are necessary for others who influence student achievement? Add other stakeholder groups as appropriate. [Use Worksheet 1: KASAB Planning Sheet.]
- What are the goals of your staff development program that are based on needed changes for students, teachers, principals, or other stakeholders? [Use Worksheet 2: Planning Goals and Objectives.]
- Specify the degree of change you desire. This begins to establish the standards and measurable objectives of your staff development program. [Use Worksheet 2: Planning Goals and Objectives.]
- Identify strategies, programs, interventions, or processes that have successfully made these changes in other schools or districts. [Assess them using Worksheet 3: Program Review.]
- From what you have learned about successful programs, what are your assumptions about *how* the change you want will occur? Identifying those assumptions is the beginning of your theory of change for your staff development programs. Identify the actions needed to accomplish the intended results in sequence. [See Worksheet 4 as an example: Sample Theory of Change.]
- Complete your program's logic model by identifying the inputs, the actions (in your theory of change), initial and intermediate outcomes, and the intended results (your program's goal). [Use Worksheet 5: Logic Model.]
- Plan the evaluation of your staff development program. [Use Evaluation Framework Worksheet at the end of Appendix D.]

Worksheet 1: KASAB Planning Sheet					
Desired Changes	*Students*	*Teachers*	*Principals*	*Central Office*	*Organization (policies, practices, structures, systems, etc.)*
KNOWLEDGE					
ATTITUDE					
SKILL					
ASPIRATION					
BEHAVIOR					

Worksheet 2: Planning Goals and Objectives Intended Results (stated in terms of student achievement)					
Measurable Objectives (stated as measurable with standard of success)	Students	Teachers	Principals	Central Office	Organization (Policies, practices, structures, systems, etc.)
KNOWLEDGE					
ATTITUDE					
SKILL					
ASPIRATION					
BEHAVIOR					

Worksheet 3: Staff Development Program Review

Program Title:

Content Area(s):

Grade(s):

Contact Name_____

Address_____

_____

Phone_____

Fax_____

E-mail_____

Web Site_____

Program Goals				
Evidence of Success	**Yes**	**No**	**Measure**	**Notes**
Student achievement				
Student behaviors				
Student attitudes				
Teacher content knowledge				
Teacher behaviors/practices				
Teacher attitudes				

Program Content	Notes
Content	
Pedagogy	

Staff Development Processes					
Models of Staff Development	**Yes**	**No**	**Freq.**	**Length**	**Notes**
Individually guided staff development					
Observation and assessment					
Training					
Development or improvement process					
Inquiry or action research					

(Continued)

(Continued)

Worksheet 3: Staff Development Program Review

Follow-up	Yes	No	Notes
Classroom-based			
Not classroom-based			

Program Context			
Geographic	Yes	No	Notes
Rural			
Urban			
Suburban			
Other			

Student/School Demographics	Notes
Ethnic/racial	
Socioeconomic status	
Size of school/district	
Teaching staff	

Support Needed	Notes
Community	
District	
Building	

Worksheet 3: Staff Development Program Review

Other Features	Notes

Intended Participants	Yes	No	Notes
Individual teachers			
Team			
Grade level			
School			
District			

Cost	Yes	No	Notes
Honorarium			
Travel costs (airfare, lodging, meals, etc.)			
Materials			
Other			

	Site Reference	Site Reference	Notes
School			
Name			
Address			
Phone			
Fax			
E-mail			

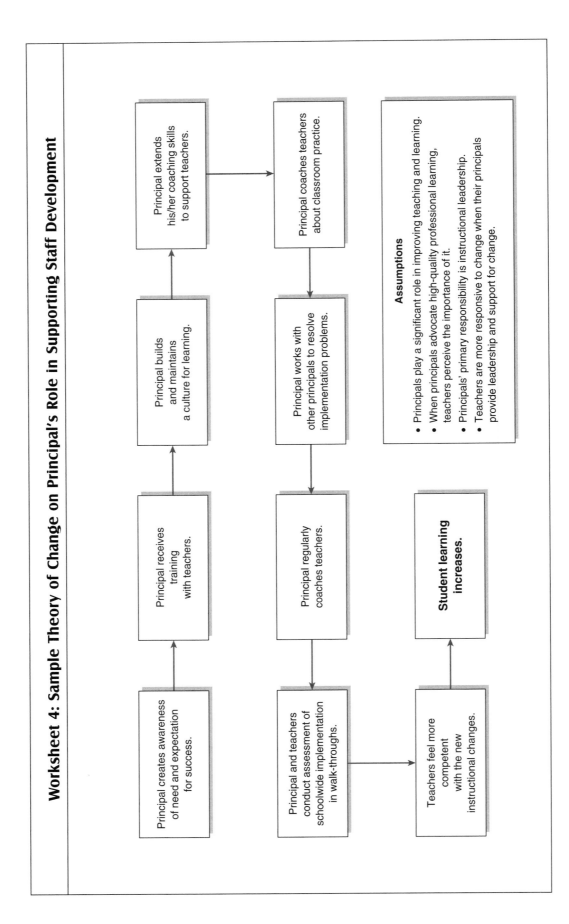

Worksheet 4: Sample Theory of Change on Principal's Role in Supporting Staff Development

Principal creates awareness of need and expectation for success.

Principal receives training with teachers.

Principal builds and maintains a culture for learning.

Principal extends his/her coaching skills to support teachers.

Principal coaches teachers about classroom practice.

Principal works with other principals to resolve implementation problems.

Principal regularly coaches teachers.

Principal and teachers conduct assessment of schoolwide implementation in walk-throughs.

Teachers feel more competent with the new instructional changes.

Student learning increases.

Assumptions

- Principals play a significant role in improving teaching and learning.
- When principals advocate high-quality professional learning, teachers perceive the importance of it.
- Principals' primary responsibility is instructional leadership.
- Teachers are more responsive to change when their principals provide leadership and support for change.

Worksheet 5: Logic Model Planning Guide

Intended Results/Goal (stated in terms of student achievement):

Inputs	Activities	Initial Outcomes	Intermediate Outcomes	Intended Results

Appendix D

Mapping an Evaluation Step by Step

MAPPING AN EVALUATION STEP BY STEP

- What is the purpose of this evaluation?
- Who are the primary users of the evaluation results?
- What is their intended plan for using the results?

Step One: Assess Evaluability

1. What are the program's goals? Are they plausible, student-focused, and results-oriented?

2. What are the program's objectives?
   - Are they measurable?
   - Do they specify the intended change (knowledge, attitude, skill, aspiration, behavior)?

3. Have the standards for acceptable performance been established for all the targeted participants and clients?

4. What are the assumptions upon which the program is based and that make up the program's theory of change? Has the theory of change been created?

5. What is its logic model? In other words, what are the inputs, activities, initial outcomes, intermediate outcomes, and intended results of this program? Has the logic model been created?

6. Do the program's theory of change and logic model make sense?

7. Do key stakeholders understand the program's theory of change?

8. Is this evaluation worth doing?

Step Two: Formulate Evaluation Questions

1. What are the evaluation questions?
   - Program need
   - Program design
   - Program implementation
   - Program impact
   - Multiple use

2. How well do the evaluation questions reflect the interests of the primary users of the evaluation results?

3. How well do the evaluation questions align with the program's goals and purpose of the evaluation?

4. Are the evaluation questions
   - Reasonable?
   - Appropriate?
   - Answerable?
   - Specific about the measurable or observable dimensions of program success or performance?
   - Specific about the measure of program performance?

Step Three: Construct the Evaluation Framework

1. Determine the evaluator.
   - ○ Who will conduct the evaluation?
     - – Internal evaluator
     - – External evaluator
     - – Combination
   - ○ Does the designated evaluator have the knowledge, skills, and resources to conduct the evaluation?

2. Decide how to answer the evaluation question(s).
   - ○ What are the key constructs (terms such as *student achievement, improvement, increase, professional development*) that will be measured? How have they been defined so that they are clear and specific?
   - ○ Does the evaluation question require making a comparison to determine impact? If so, what are possible comparison groups? Which is the most appropriate comparison group for this evaluation?
     - – Cohort
     - – Individual
     - – Group
     - – Panel
     - – Generic

3. Create a data plan.
   - ○ Who or what is expected to change as a result of this staff development program?
   - ○ What types of changes are expected as a result of this staff development program in the identified target audiences or organizational structures?
     - – Knowledge
     - – Attitude
     - – Skill
     - – Aspiration
     - – Behavior
   - ○ What data can provide evidence that the changes intended have occurred?
   - ○ What data-collection methodology is most appropriate for the needed data?
   - ○ From whom or what will the data be collected?
   - ○ What are other possible sources of data to provide evidence of the intended change?
   - ○ How essential is it to have multiple data sources for this evaluation?
   - ○ When will the data be collected?
   - ○ Where will the data be collected?

4. Determine the cost.
   - ○ Are needed resources, including time, fiscal resources, and personnel, available to conduct this evaluation?

○ If resources are not adequate, what aspects of the evaluation plan can be modified without compromising the integrity of the evaluation?

○ If resources are inadequate, how will the evaluation be affected?

○ Is the evaluation worth doing?

Step Four: Collect Data

1. Have the instruments and procedures for data collection been field-tested?

2. What revisions are necessary?

3. How will data collectors be trained?

4. After early data collection, do any data seem redundant? What are the advantages and disadvantages of continuing to collect these data? Is it appropriate to continue or to discontinue collecting these data?

5. After early data collection, what data seem to be missing? Is it essential to collect these missing data? How will a new data-collection methodology be implemented to collect these data?

6. What processes have been established to manage data collection and transfer?

7. What processes are established to ensure safekeeping and integrity of data?

8. If collecting quantitative data, what kinds of scores are needed to accurately reflect the data and to answer the evaluation questions?

Step Five: Organize, Analyze, and Display Data

1. How will data be sorted, grouped, arranged before analysis?

2. What method of data analysis is needed to answer the evaluation question?
   ○ Univariate analysis
   ○ Bivariate analysis
   ○ Multivariate analysis

3. How will data be displayed to facilitate interpretation and understanding?

4. How will stakeholders be involved in the data analysis process?

Step Six: Interpret Data

1. What do these data mean?

2. What findings (interpretations/claims) can be made from these data?

3. How well supported are the findings?
   ○ Major findings
      – Strongly
      – Weakly

      ○ Minor findings
        – Strongly
        – Weakly

4. Does this evaluation support claims of attribution or contribution?

5. Does this program have merit or worth?

6. What recommended actions can help the program stakeholders improve their program and its impact?

Step Seven: Disseminate and Use Findings

1. Will the evaluation reports be interim or final evaluation reports?

2. Who are the primary users of the evaluation report?

3. What components do the primary users want included in the evaluation report?

4. What format for reporting the results are most appropriate for the primary users of the evaluation report?

5. What other audiences are likely to want some version of the evaluation report?

6. What format for reporting the results is appropriate for the other audiences?

Step Eight: Evaluate the Evaluation

1. How will the effectiveness of the evaluation be assessed?

2. What questions will guide the evaluation of the evaluation?
      ○ Resources
      ○ Design
      ○ Findings
      ○ Reporting
      ○ Evaluator

3. What stakeholders will be involved in the evaluation of the evaluation? How will they be involved?

EVALUATION FRAMEWORK WORKSHEET

Program Goals:

Measurable Objectives	*Information/ Data Needed*	*Data Source*	*Data-Collection Method*	*Data Analysis*	*When*	*Where*	*Who*
What do I expect to change?	What will indicate whether there is a change?	Who or what can tell me about the change?	How will I collect the information about the change?	How will I measure or depict change in the information I collect?	When will I collect the data?	Where will the data be collected?	Who will be responsible for the data-collection analysis?
By whom?							
Knowledge							
Attitudes							
Skills							
Aspirations							
Behaviors							
Standard of success							
To what degree?							

Appendix E

Online Resources for Evaluation

———⚬—

Title	URL	Description
Educator's Guide to Evaluating the Use of Technology in Schools and Classrooms	www.ed.gov/pubs/ EdTechGuide/	Evaluating technology use in elementary and secondary schools
Electronic Statistics Textbook (2001)	www.statsoft.com/textbook/ stathome.html	Comprehensive introductory statistics text
The Evaluation Center	www.wmich.edu.evalctr	National center for evaluation resources
Evaluation Cookbook (1998)	www.icbl.hw.ac.uk/ltdi/ cokbook/contents.html	Methodologies for evaluating uses of technology
Evaluation Handbook (1995)	www.ncela.gwu.edu/pubs/ eacwest/evalhbk.htm	General guide to evaluation, primarily educational evaluation
Evaluation Toolkit: Focus Groups & Quasi-Experimental	www11.hrdc-drhc.gc.ca/pls/edd/toolkit.list	This site contains a new series of publications by the government of Canada entitled Evaluation Tool Kit. The objective of the series is to build evaluation capacity and knowledge throughout HRDC and its partner organizations by providing pertinent information about designing, planning and conducting an evaluation.
Foundation Evaluation Handbook	www.wkkf.org/pubs/tools/ evaluation/pub770.pdf	Outlines a blueprint for designing and conducting evaluations, either independently or with the support of an external evaluator/consultant
Introduction to Qualitative Research	www.uea.ac.uk/swk/teaching/ Research%20degrees/MACFR.htm	Basic introduction to qualitative methods is the evaluation focus (despite title)
The National Center for Evaluation, Standards, and Student Testing	www.cse.ucla.edu	Resources on student assessment, evaluation, and standards
Online Evaluation Resource Library	www.oerl.sri.com	OERL contains plans, instruments, and reports used to evaluate projects
Program Managers Guide to Evaluation	www.acf.dhhs.gov/programs/ core/	Novice guide to evaluating programs for children, youth & families
Qualitative Methods Workbook	www.ship.edu/~cgboeree/ qualmeth.html	Broad look at qualitative methods including phenomenology, structural analysis, observation and interviewing
Questionnaire Design and Analysis Workbook	www.tardis.ed.ac.uk/~kate/ qmcweb/qcont.htm	Hands-on with activities approach to learning questionnaire design
Taking Stock: A Practical Guide to Evaluating Your Own Programs	www.horizonresearch.com/ publications/stock.pdf	How to conduct participatory, internal evaluations in community-based organizations
Understanding Evaluation—The Way to Better Prevention Programs (1993)	www.ed.gov/offices/OUS/PES/ primer1.html	Designing and implementing evaluation of drug prevention programs
User-friendly Handbook for Mixed-method Evaluations	www.nsf.gov/pubs/1997/nsf97153/start.htm	Designing, conducting evaluation integrating quantitative and qualitative techniques for outcomes evaluations, "practical rather than technically sophisticated"
User-friendly handbook for Project Evaluation: Science, Mathematics, Engineering and Technology Education	www.her.nsf.gov/HER/Red/EVAL/handbook/handbook.htm	Emphasis on quantitative techniques for outcome evaluations "practical rather than technically sophisticated"

Glossary

Aggregated scores

Scores from individuals collapsed to be viewed as a single group score. For example, the fifth-grade students' individual scores on a state test can be aggregated into a classroom score, school score, district score, and state score.

Artifacts

Data sources that exist within a district or school and that serve as a source of information about a program (e.g., attendance records, course syllabi, descriptions of staff development programs, end-of-course evaluations on file).

Aspiration

Desire or internal motivation to engage in a particular practice; one type of change that can occur as a result of staff development.

Attitude

Beliefs about the value of particular information or strategies; one type of change that can occur as the result of staff development.

Attribution

The claim that a program is solely responsible for the changes that occurred in student achievement and that nothing else could possibly have produced the results.

Backmapping model

Backmapping is a process for planning. This planning model is based on results and begins "with the end in mind."

Behavior

Consistent use of knowledge and skills; regular practices; one type of change that can occur as a result of staff development.

Black-box evaluation

Evaluation conducted without an articulated program theory of change and that does not provide information about what is presumed to be contributing.

Chi-square

A statistical process that is a simple and direct test of significance between groups when the observations can be classified into discrete categories and created as observed frequencies.

Client

In the context of results-based staff development, the clients are the students who are being served by the educators participating in professional learning experiences.

Clustering

A data-analysis method that puts discrete data into classes, categories, or groups on the basis of common features.

Cohort group comparison

Comparing the performance of a group prior to intervention to its performance after the intervention to determine whether change has occurred; it results in a single score for the entire group. For example, change in pre- and posttest scores indicates a change.

Collaborative evaluation

Evaluation in which the evaluator involves key stakeholders in major decisions related to the evaluation and possibly in evaluation activities such as data collection or interpretation.

Comparing

A data-analysis method that examines the similarities and differences in features of individuals or the program before, during, or after the intervention.

Comparison group

A designated group that has not participated in the staff development program against which the outcomes of those who do participate are compared to determine a program's impact.

Comprehensive staff development program

Planned, coherent actions and support systems designed and implemented to develop educators' knowledge, skills, attitudes, aspirations, and behaviors to improve student achievement.

Contribution

The claim that a program contributes to the impact of staff development on student achievement when there is an assumption that other factors are also influencing these results.

Counting

The numerical description of data that allows comparison of the staff development program to another program or to some standard of acceptable performance.

Covariation

A circumstance when changes in a variable always appear in relation to changes in another variable.

Data-collection instrument

An instrument (such as a test or survey) that provides a way for data to be gathered. Both existing and newly developed instruments are an option for evaluators and key stakeholders. Existing instruments are usually field-tested, valid, and reliable. Sometimes they are normed and standardized. Developing an instrument allows for alignment with the constructs of the evaluation and appropriateness to context or population who will complete the instrument.

Decision makers

Individual and groups who have responsibility for the success of a program and typically include administrators, oversight committees, or management teams.

Describing

A data-analysis method based on narrative description of the staff development program often including descriptive statistics such as mean, median, mode, and range.

Disaggregated scores

Scores from a larger group that are broken down into subgroups based on particular characteristics. For example, the entire fifth-grade scores on a standardized achievement test can be broken down into scores for subpopulations such as gender, race, and socioeconomic status.

Distal factors

Factors influencing student achievement that are distant from the teaching and learning process and are often not in the immediate control of the educational system (e.g., socioeconomic status, family support of education).

Documentation

Records, documents, artifacts, and so on that exist within a system that are summarized, rather than analyzed, to explain or judge.

Documents

Artifacts or records within a system that can shed light on a staff development program

Empowerment evaluation

An evaluation in which the evaluator assumes the responsibility of building the capacity of stakeholders to conduct their own evaluations in the future or to use evaluation processes to objectively and rigorously analyze their own work.

Espoused theories

Theories that people claim (and believe) to be their beliefs, values, or theories. People do not always behave congruently with their espoused theories.

Evaluability assessment

The analysis of a staff development program's ability to be evaluated that is based on the design of the program, the utility of the evaluation, and the proposed logic of the program.

Evaluation

Systematic, purposeful process of studying, reviewing, and analyzing data gathered from multiple sources in order to make informed decisions about a program.

Evaluation questions

A set of questions, developed by the evaluators and others, drawn from the program goals and objectives that define the focus of the evaluation.

Evaluation think

How individuals and teams look critically and analytically at their work to discover what is working and what is not, in order to redefine their work and improve results; self-assessing what we learn, do, believe, value, and want; asking for evidence and scrutinizing our practices; generating information to make sound decisions.

Event

An isolated staff development experience that is viewed as an individual occurrence that may or may not be a part of a larger program or the context in which it occurs.

Evidence

Data that serve to answer an evaluation question and to support findings about a program.

Examining outliers

A data-analysis method that looks at situations on the extreme ends of the data set to determine what information, if any, can be learned that does not appear in the data that tend more toward the mean.

Expert judgments

The opinions, observations, or information from a known expert or authority in the field.

Extant data

Records that exist within a system and that might shed light on the staff development program (e.g., performance records, policies, meeting agenda and minutes, annual reports).

External evaluator

Someone hired to conduct an evaluation who is not employed by the school or district where the evaluation is taking place and presumably with no vested interest in the outcome of the evaluation.

Factoring (or factor analysis)

A statistical analysis that breaks down the aggregates into their parts and allows the evaluator to determine how much each contributed to the results.

Finding covariation

A data-analysis method that examines the interaction between two variables to determine whether changes in one relate to changes in another.

Focus group

Small, representative group of individuals who are selected to share their perspectives about a topic of interest. The questions are prepared in advance; the discussion moderated by a facilitator; and responses recorded and analyzed.

Formative evaluation

The analysis of how the staff development program operates, its implementation, and potential barriers; formative evaluation is undertaken to improve the program.

Gain score

Score indicating how much a student improves or progresses.

Generic comparison group

Established measures of progress, such as published test norms, that are used for comparison with the outcomes of interventions. National norms are one example of a generic comparison group.

Glass-box evaluation

An evaluation conducted on a program with a clearly articulated theory of change that provides information on what might contribute to the program's outcome.

Impact

The changes that occur as a result of the staff development program; the impact can be on student achievement, the conditions in a school or district, or educator knowledge, attitudes, skills, aspirations, or behaviors.

Individual comparison

Comparing the performance of individuals after the intervention with their performance before the intervention; results in multiple scores that allow the evaluator to analyze how change affected individuals rather than the whole group.

Innovation Configuration Map

A sophisticated rating scale that delineates the critical components of a program and the continuum of *ideal* to *unacceptable* levels of performance of implementation for each component and that specifies the level of acceptable performance for each component.

Inquiry perspective

A perspective that incorporates an active desire to examine and understand existing phenomena, in this case the impact of professional development on teacher and student learning.

Internal evaluator

Someone who is employed by the school or district where the evaluation is taking place and who agrees to conduct the evaluation with objectivity and rigor.

Intervention

The staff development program designed and implemented to address the identified needs.

Interview

An oral data-collection method in which the evaluator typically uses prepared questions to ask respondents about their knowledge, attitude, skill, aspiration, and behaviors.

Knowledge

Conceptual understanding of information, theories, principles, and research; one type of change that can occur as a result of staff development.

Log

A data-collection method used to document occurrences of particular behaviors, practices, or occurrences.

Logic model

A graphic display that portrays the causal sequence of the critical components of a program, including resources, activities, initial outcomes, intermediate outcomes, and intended results.

Mastery scores

Scores that indicate a level of performance often based on a range of raw scores (e.g., a score of 75 percent indicates that the respondent had 75 percent of the items on the test correct).

Matched-group comparison

Comparison of the performance of a group that received the intervention with the performance of a group that did not receive the intervention or that received a different intervention.

Mean score

The average of a range of scores.

Meta-evaluation

A systematic process of evaluating an evaluation.

Modeling

A data-analysis method that depicts how the program works by creating a graphic display of the program and that depicts the relationship, sequence, and importance among various components of the program.

Multiple interventions evaluation

An evaluation methodology that compares multiple implementations of an intervention as one way to determine impact.

Multivariate analysis

Analysis of multiple variables to determine whether any relationship exists between or among them.

No Child Left Behind Act of 2001

Federal legislation passed by the U.S. Congress in 2001 and signed into law in 2002 to replace the previous Elementary and Secondary School Act; the law has four pillars: stronger accountability for results, more freedom for states and communities, proven education methods, and more choices for parents.

Observation

A data-collection method in which an evaluator directly watches and notes behaviors most often used to measure skill or behavior.

Outliers

An unusual or abnormal case that differs from most other cases in the same situation.

Panel group comparison

Comparison of the performance of one intact group to another group at a later time assumed to be equivalent (e.g., the comparison of seventh-grade scores in one year to seventh-grade scores the next year).

Participants

The adults who are engaged in the staff development program.

Percentile

Scores ranging from 1 to 99 on a test to indicate the percentage of students who achieved a score at or lower than the test score in question; percentiles cannot be averaged, summed, or combined because the intervals between percentile points are not equal.

Planning evaluation

An evaluation conducted before a staff development program that is designed to determine the needs of potential participants or social conditions the staff development program should address.

Policy makers

Individuals or groups who hold decision-making authority over the staff development program and may include funders, administrators, governance committees, and school boards.

Pressure

Specific actions undertaken to counterbalance the status quo and to speed change. When coupled with support, pressure increases the motivation to change.

Process-focused evaluation

An evaluation that seeks to provide critical information to managers about the aspects that are effective, whether there are discrepancies in implementation, how to improve the program, and where problems may interfere with results. The focus of a process-focused evaluation is on how well the program works, whether all components are in place, alignment of implementation with intended plans, and standards of operation. (This evaluation style is sometimes called implementation or formative evaluation.)

Program

A set of related resources and professional learning activities directed toward student achievement (see also comprehensive staff development program).

Program goal

A statement of a desired state toward which a program is directed; the overall purpose of a program.

Program objective

A statement of the specific, measurable, concrete result of the program.

Program's theory of change

The set of assumptions about how a staff development program works to achieve its intended results that is translated into the planned inputs, actions, initial outcomes, intermediate outcomes, and intended results of a staff development program.

Qualitative data

Data that are expressed in descriptions or characteristics. Qualitative research measures results most typically in words rather than numbers and tends to rely on interviews, observations, document analysis, and the like.

Quantitative data

Data that are expressed in numbers and can be analyzed statistically. Quantitative research measures results in numbers and relies on test scores or other events with countable outcomes.

Quasi-experiment

An evaluation methodology in which the comparison group is selected nonrandomly yet which implements some controls to minimize threats to the validity of the conclusions.

Random assignment comparison

Assignment of units of study—such as students, classrooms, or schools—to groups by the laws of chance, one that will receive the intervention (treatment group) and one or more that will not receive the intervention or that will receive an alternative intervention (comparison group).

Rating scale

Data collection method used to measure behavior, performance; rating scales typically specify a continuum of strong to weak practices or list desirable practices.

Raw scores

The number of items answered correctly on a test (assuming there are correct and incorrect responses).

Research

A systematic investigation, including research development, testing, and evaluation, designed to develop or contribute to generalizable knowledge.

Results

The effects of a staff development program. In results-based staff development, results are expressed in terms of student achievement.

Rival explanation

A plausible explanation of the observed changes that differs from the desired explanation. Data-analysis methods work to disprove rival explanations so as to strengthen arguments for the desired explanation.

Role playing

A form of data collection in which subjects demonstrate their knowledge and skills in a simulated experience.

Rubric

A sophisticated form of rating scale that delineates a progression of expected performance and a level of acceptable performance.

Scatterplots

A graph of the relationship between the frequency distributions of two sets of scores (one plotted on the X axis and one plotted on the Y axis) that represents the relationship among the scores.

Scientifically based research

Defined by the U.S. Department of Education as a part of the No Child Left Behind Act of 2001) and includes educational research using experimental and quasi-experimental designs.

Selected group comparison

The determination of a comparison group when units of study cannot be assigned randomly. Matched, generic comparison, cohort, or panel comparisons are examples of selected comparison groups.

Skills

Strategies and processes to apply knowledge; skills are one type of change that can occur as a result of staff development.

Sociogram

An observation record that depicts the patterns of communication among members of a group.

Staff development program

The planned, coherent actions and support systems designed and implemented to develop educators' knowledge, skills, attitudes, aspirations, and behaviors to improve student achievement.

Stakeholders

Individuals or groups with an interest in the staff development program. They might be school or district staff, school board members, community members, or public or private funders.

Standard

The explicit criterion or criteria that define the program's acceptable performance.

Standard score

A recalculation of the raw score that provides equal-interval scales for comparison across students and tests for the purpose of mathematical calculations.

Stanines

Rough approximation of an individual's performance relative to the performance of others in the group; stanine scores range from 1 to 9 with 1 being the lowest.

Summative evaluation

The analysis of a staff development program to determine its impact.

Survey

A systematic collection of information for a defined group or sample usually by means of written questionnaires.

Tests

Data collection method using instruments or tasks to measure knowledge, attitude, aspiration, and, to a limited degree, skill.

Theories in action

The bases on which people act. Theories "in use." What people do, not what they say.

Time series evaluation

An evaluation and analysis method over long time intervals in which repeated measures of a key variable are taken before and after the intervention.

T-tests

A statistical process for testing the significance of the difference between the means of two outcomes.

Univariate analysis

The analysis of single variables.

Use

The intended way in which the users will use the evaluation; it may be used to make decisions about future funding, continuation of the program, staffing, or the like.

User

Stakeholders, policy makers, or decision makers who will use information produced from the evaluation to take further actions related to the staff development program.

Utilization-focused evaluation

An approach to evaluation developed by Michael Quinn Patton (1997) that places significant emphasis on the intended use of the evaluation.

References

Administration of Children, Youth, and Families, U.S. Department of Health and Human Services (n.d.). *A program manager's guide to evaluation.* Retrieved on December 21, 2006, from www.acf.hhs.gov/programs/opre/other_resrch/pm_guide_eval/index.html

American Evaluation Association. (2004). *Guiding principles for evaluators.* Retrieved August 10, 2006, from www.eval.org/Publications/GuidingPrinciplesPrintable.asp

Anderson, A. (2005). *The community builder's approach to theory of change: A practical guide to theory and development.* New York: Aspen Institute Roundtable on Community Change.

Argyris, C. (1982). *Reasoning, learning, and action.* San Francisco: Jossey-Bass.

Argyris, C., & Schön, D. (1978). *Organizational learning.* Reading, MA: Addison-Wesley.

Arter, J., & Blum, R. (1996). *A handbook for student performance assessment in an era of restructuring.* Alexandria, VA: Association of Supervision and Curriculum Development.

Beers, B. (2006). *Learning-driven schools: A practical guide for teachers and principals.* Alexandria, VA: Association for Supervision and Curriculum Development.

Bernhardt, V. (2003). *Using data to improve student learning in elementary schools.* Larchmont, NY: Eye on Education.

Bernhardt, V. (2004). *Data analysis for comprehensive school improvement* (2nd ed.). Larchmont, NY: Eye on Education.

Bernhardt, V. (2005a). *Using data to improve student learning in high schools.* Larchmont, NY: Eye on Education.

Bernhardt, V. (2005b). *Using data to improve student learning in middle schools.* Larchmont, NY: Eye on Education.

Bernhardt, V. (2006). *Using data to improve student learning in school districts.* Larchmont, NY: Eye on Education.

Blalock, H. (1964). *Causal inferences in nonexperimental research.* Chapel Hill, NC: University of North Carolina Press.

Boulmetis, J., & Dutwin, P. (2000). *The ABCs of evaluation: Timeless techniques for program and project managers.* San Francisco: Jossey-Bass.

Brahier, D. (2001). *Assessment in middle and high school mathematics: A teacher's guide.* Larchmont, NY: Eye on Education.

Carnegie Corporation of New York. (2000). *Turning points 2000: Educating adolescents in the 21st century.* A.W. Jackson & G.A. Davis (Eds.). New York: Teachers College Press.

Charles A. Dana Center, University of Texas at Austin. (1999). *Hope for urban education: A study of nine high performing, high poverty urban elementary schools.* Austin, TX: Author.

Charles A. Dana Center, University of Texas at Austin. (2000). *Equity-driven achievement-focused school districts.* Austin, TX: Author.

Chen, H. (1990). *Theory-driven evaluations.* Newbury Park, CA: SAGE.

Connell, J., & Klem, A. (2000). You can get there from here: Using a theory of change approach to plan urban education reform. *Journal of Educational and Psychological Consultation, 11*(1), 93–120.

Connell, J., & Kubisch, A. (1998). Applying a theory of change approach to evaluating comprehensive community initiatives. In K. Fulbright-Anderson, J. Kubisch, & J. Connell (Eds.), *New approaches to evaluating community initiatives* (Vol. 2). Washington, D.C.: Aspen Institute. Retrieved August 14, 2007 from www.aspeninstitute.org/site/c.huLWJeMRKpH/b.613709/k.B547/Applying_a_Theory_of_Change_Approach_to_the_Evaluation_of_Comprehensive_Community_Initiatives_Progress_Prospects_and_Problems.htm

Costa, A., & Kallick, B. (2000). *Assessing and reporting habits of mind.* Alexandria, VA: Association of Supervision and Curriculum Development.

Council of Chief State School Officers. (n.d.). *State Collaborative on Assessment and Student Standards.* Retrieved December 21, 2006, from www.ccsso.org/Projects/scass/1245.cfm

Council on Foundations. (1993). *Evaluation for foundations: Concepts, cases, guidelines, and resources.* San Francisco, CA: Jossey-Bass.

Creighton, T. (2001). *The educator's guide to using data to improve decision making.* Thousand Oaks, CA: Corwin Press.

DuFour, R., & Eaker, R. (1998). *Professional learning communities at work: Best practices for enhancing student achievement.* Bloomington, IN: National Education Service.

Earl, L. (2003). *Assessment as learning: Using classroom assessment to maximize student learning.* Thousand Oaks, CA: Corwin Press.

Fullan, M. (2001). *The new meaning of educational change* (3rd ed.). New York: Teachers College Press.

Garet, M.S., Porter, A.C., Desimone, L., Birman, B.F., & Yoon, K.S. (2001). What makes professional development effective? Results from a national sample of teachers. *American Educational Research Journal, 38*(4), 915–945.

General Accounting Office. (1992). *The evaluation synthesis.* GAO/PEMD-10.1.2. Washington, DC: Author.

General Accounting Office. (1995). *Program evaluation: Improving the flow of information to the Congress.* GAO/PEMD-95–1. Washington, DC: Author.

Glickman, C. (1993.) *Renewing America's schools: A guide for school-based action.* San Francisco: Jossey-Bass.

Gronlund, N. (2005). *Assessment of student achievement* (8th ed.). Boston: Allyn & Bacon.

Guskey, T. (2000). *Evaluating professional development.* Thousand Oaks, CA: Corwin Press.

Guskey, T., & Sparks, D. (1996, Fall). Exploring the relationship between staff development and improvements in student learning. *Journal of Staff Development, 17*(4), 34–38.

Hall, G., & Hord, S. (1987). *Change in schools: Facilitating the process.* Albany, NY: State University of New York Press.

Hall, G., & Hord, S. (2001). *Implementing change: Patterns, principles, and potholes.* Albany, NY: State University of New York Press.

Harkreader, S., & Weathersby, J. (1998). *Staff development and student achievement: Making the connection in Georgia schools.* Atlanta, GA: Council for School Performance.

Hendricks, M. (1994). Making a splash: Reporting evaluation results effectively. In J. Wholey, H. Hatry, & K. Newcomber (Eds.). *Handbook of practical program evaluation* (pp. 549–575). San Francisco: Jossey-Bass.

Holcomb, E. (1999). *Getting excited about data: How to combine people, passion, and proof.* Thousand Oaks, CA: Corwin Press.

Jackson, A., & Davis, G. (2000). *Turning points 2000: Educating adolescents in the 21st century: A report of Carnegie Corporation of New York.* New York: Teachers College Press.

Johnson, R. (1996). *Setting our sights: Measuring equity in school change.* Los Angeles: Achievement Council.

Joint Committee on Standards for Educational Evaluation. (1994). *The program evaluation standards: How to assess evaluations of educational programs* (2nd ed.). Thousand Oaks, CA: SAGE.

Joyce, B., & Showers, B. (1982). The coaching of teaching. *Educational Leadership, 37*(5), 70–78.

Joyce, B., & Showers, B. (1995). *Student achievement through staff development* (2nd ed.). White Plains, NY: Longman.

Joyce, B., & Showers, B. (2002). *Student achievement through staff development* (3rd ed.). White Plains, NY: Longman.

Kaufman, R., Guerra, I., & Platt, W. (2006). *Practical evaluations for educators.* Thousand Oaks, CA: Corwin Press.

Killion, J. (1999a, November). Forge a link between adult learning and student learning. *Results* [NSDC newsletter], p. 3.

Killion, J. (1999b). *What works in the middle: Results-based staff development.* Oxford, OH: National Staff Development Council.

Killion, J. (2001). *E-learning for educators: Implementing the standards for staff development.* Oxford, OH: NSDC & NICI.

Killion, J. (2002a). *Assessing impact: Evaluating staff development.* Oxford, OH: National Staff Development Council.

Killion, J. (2002b). *What works in the elementary school: Results-based staff development.* Oxford, OH: National Staff Development Council.

Killion, J., & Bellamy, G. T. (2000, Winter). On the job: Data analysts focus school improvement efforts. *Journal of Staff Development, 21*(1), 27–31.

Killion, J., & Harrison, C. (2006). *Taking the lead: New roles for teachers and school-based coaches.* Oxford, OH: National Staff Development Council.

Killion, J., & Hirsh, S. (2001, May). Continuous learning: Top-quality professional development is key to teacher effectiveness. *American School Board Journal, 188*(5), 36–38.

Kirkpatrick, D. (1974). *Evaluating training programs: The four levels* San Francisco: Berrett-Kohler.

Kirkpatrick, D. (1998). *Evaluating training programs: The four levels* (2nd ed.). San Francisco: Berrett-Kohler.

Leithwood, K., & Aitken, R. (2001). *Making schools smarter: A system for monitoring school and district progress* (2nd ed.). Thousand Oaks, CA: Corwin Press.

Love, N. (2001). *Using data/getting results: A practical guide for school improvement in mathematics and science.* Norwood, MA: Christopher-Gordon.

Mager, R. (1975). *Preparing instructional objectives* (2nd ed.). Belmont, CA: Fearon-Pitman Publishers.

McLaughlin, J., & Jordan, G. (1999). Logic models: A tool for telling your program's performance story. *Evaluation and Program Planning, 22*(1), 65–72.

Miech, E., Nave, B., & Mosteller, F. (2001, Summer). Large-scale professional development for schoolteachers: Cases from Pittsburgh, New York City, and the National School Reform Faculty. In R. Light (Ed.), *New directions for education: Evaluation findings that surprise* (no. 90, pp. 83–99). San Francisco: Jossey-Bass.

Minnesota Department of Human Services. (1996). *Focus on client outcomes: A guidebook for results-oriented human services.* Minneapolis: Author.

National Staff Development Council. (2001). *NSDC's standards for staff development* (rev.). Oxford, OH: Author.

Office of Evaluation and Inspections. (1990). *Analyzing the information gathered: Technical assistance guide 5.* Washington, D.C.: Office of the Inspector General.

Online Evaluation Resource Library. Retrieved on December 21, 2006, from www.oerl.sri.com

Organizational Research Services. (2004). *Theory of change: A practical tool for action, results, and learning.* Prepared for the Annie E. Casey Foundation. Seattle, WA: Author.

Osborne, D., & Gaebler, T. (1992). *Reinventing government: How the entrepreneurial spirit is transforming the public sector.* Reading, MA: Addison-Wesley.

Parsons, B. (2001). *Evaluative inquiry: Using evaluation to promote student success.* Thousand Oaks, CA: Corwin Press.

Patton, M. (1997). *Utilization-focused evaluation: The new century text* (3rd ed.). Thousand Oaks, CA: SAGE.

Phillips, J. (1997). *Return on investment in training and performance improvement programs.* Houston, TX: Gulf Publishing.

Popham, W. J. (1999). Why standardized tests don't measure educational quality. *Educational Leadership, 56*(6), 8–15.

Popham, W. J. (2001, September 19). Standardized achievement tests: Misnamed and misleading. *Education Week, 21*(3), 46.

Reeves, D. (2000). *Accountability in action: A blueprint for learning organizations.* Denver: Advanced Learning Press.

Rossi, P., & Freeman, H. (1982). *Evaluation: A systematic approach* (2nd ed.). Beverly Hills, CA: SAGE.

Rossi, P., Freeman, H., & Lipsey, M. (2003). *Evaluation: A systematic approach* (7th ed.). Thousand Oaks, CA: SAGE.

Schmoker, M. (2001). *The results fieldbook: Practical strategies from dramatically improved schools.* Alexandria, VA: Association of Supervision and Curriculum Development.

Scriven, M. (1991). *Evaluation thesaurus* (4th ed.). Newbury Park, CA: SAGE.

Senge, P. (1990). *The fifth discipline.* New York: Doubleday/Currency.

Senge, P., Roberts, C., Ross, R., Smith, B., & Kleiner, A. (1994). *The fifth discipline fieldbook: Strategies and tools for building a learning organization.* New York: Currency-Doubleday.

Shapiro, I. (2005). *Theories of change. Beyond intractability: A free knowledge base on more constructive approaches to destructive conflict.* Retrieved January 8, 2006, from www.beyondintractability.org/essay/theories_of_change

Spinelli, C. (2005). *Classroom assessment for students in special and general education.* Englewood Cliffs, NJ: Prentice Hall.

Stiggins, R. (1997). *Student-centered classroom assessment* (2nd ed.). Upper Saddle River, NJ: Prentice Hall.

Stiggins, R. (2000). *Student-involved classroom assessment* (3rd ed.). Upper Saddle River, NJ: Prentice Hall.

Stufflebeam, D. (2001, Spring). *Evaluation models: New directions for evaluation* (No. 89). San Francisco: Jossey-Bass.

Tyler, R. (1950). *Basic principles of curriculum and instruction.* Chicago: University of Chicago Press.

U.S. Department of Education, Office of the Undersecretary, Planning and Evaluation Services. (1999). *The longitudinal evaluation of school change and performance in Title I schools.* Washington, D.C.: Author.

W. K. Kellogg Foundation. *Evaluation handbook.* Retrieved December 21, 2006, from www.wkkf.org/Default.aspx?tabid=90&CID=281&ItemID=2810002&NID=2820002&LanguageID=0

Wahlstrom, D. (1999). *Using data to improve student achievement: A handbook for collecting, organizing, and using data.* Virginia Beach, VA: Successline.

Walker-Wilson, L. (2004). *What every teacher needs to know about assessment.* Larchmont, NY: Eye on Education.

Weiss, C. (1998). *Evaluation* (2nd ed.). Upper Saddle River, NJ: Prentice Hall.

Weiss, C., ed. (1972). *Evaluating action programs.* Boston: Allyn & Bacon.

Wenglinsky, H. (2000). *How teaching matters: Bringing the classroom back into discussions of teacher quality.* Princeton, NJ: Educational Testing Service.

WestEd. (2000). *Teachers who learn: Kids who achieve.* San Francisco: Author.

Wholey, J. (1987). *Organizational excellence: Stimulating quality and communicating value.* Lexington, MA: Lexington.

Wholey, J., Hatry, H., & Newcomer, K. (2004). *Handbook of practical program evaluation* (2nd ed.). San Francisco: Jossey-Bass.

Wiggins, G. (1998). *Educative assessment: Designing assessments to inform and improve student performance.* San Francisco: Jossey-Bass.

Wiggins, G., & McTighe, J. (1998). *Understanding by design.* Alexandria, VA: Association of Supervision and Curriculum Development.

Wilde, J., & Sockey, S. (1995). *Evaluation handbook.* Albuquerque, NM: Evaluation Assistance Center–Western Region.

Zepeda, S. (1999). *Staff development: Practices that promote leadership in learning communities.* Larchmont, NY: Eye on Education.

Index